Table of Contents

Introduction

Back in 2019, our breathing felt different, unfiltered. Whether we were inside or outside, air exiting a stranger's mouth or leaving our close ones' lungs was charged with odours, pathogens, and familiar sounds. We noticed the warm breeze attached to an uttering during an animated conversation. Every morning we smelt the city's pollution as well as the party that occupied the street the night before. We were aware that this all-encompassing substance was anything but empty—it just seemed that we knew how to share it with various miasmas, toxic gases, radio waves and 5G signals.

We started this book then. Air was still a shortcut, a McGuffin, an excuse to continue an investigation into the recently created region of the Indo-Pacific. The region, which encompasses two oceans and spans from the west coast of South America to Africa's east coast, was conceptualised in diplomatic circles in the 1920s. Yet its actualisation came in 2013—years before the nuclear submarines of the AUKUS pact brought the term to virtually every major news outlet worldwide—when Australia became the first country to acknowledge its existence and relocate there.

But what might Santiago de Chile, Delhi and Sydney have in common? What could link Johannesburg and Hong Kong? What did hold the Indo-Pacific region together? Air was part of our answer. New geopolitical regions are complex design projects. Geographical definitions need to be backed up with powerful narratives, stable stories that keep them in place. The EU emerged from WWII, while the USA emerged after the War of Independence and then the Civil War. The birth of the Indo-Pacific region lacked a major traumatic event. The document that placed Australia there, the *2013 Australia Defence White Paper,* mentioned several factors, such as maritime trade, China's growing global influence, and the post-2001 geopolitical order, but failed to provide a unifying origin. The stories that hold the region together were diffuse, and, we imagined, still to be designed.

Air seemed a perfect common denominator, the ultimate vehicle for describing the region. Is there a better substance for discussing the commonalities of distant locations while addressing their idiosyncrasies? Air, one of the commons, connects the region in a continuum. At the same time, it is extremely sensitive to localisms. Pollution, weather, legal definitions, clouds, and cultural readings all change air material conditions, transforming it into a situated substance. The bush fires on the east coast of Australia, the Chilean *Estallido Social,* the Hong Kong 2019 protests, the India Supreme court *suo motu* ruling on Delhi's air quality and Greenpeace's defacement of Johannesburg's statues with respirators proved that air was part of the region's struggles, that breathing in the Indo-Pacific was a highly charged political act.

In our eyes, all these events, and more specifically the masks that emerged from them, became indexes—technologies developed that allowed us to read the air conditions. Architectures for our bodies. Local variations in these micro-architectures rendered the differences between atmospheres visible. Their origins presented a counterproposal to traditional regional narratives, so often set hand in hand with colonial projects. Whether off-the-shelf, DIY or customised, these portable architectures outlined a constellation of forms of dissent —an alternative to the region described in the Department of Defense's strategic documents. We decided to call them folk costumes, assuming that their display of practices of collective care for breathing bodies could resignify nineteenth century traditional garments and their infamous anthropological readings.

To propose narratives for a new region occupying two-thirds of the globe using new formats that discuss localised and global concerns was an ambitious project. And to do so while avoiding the dangers of imperialistic impulses and master narratives even more so. We called on scientific discourses, critical humanities and artistic practices to help in the endeavour. Or, to be more precise and less hyperbolic, we reached out to friends, peers and people we admire and presented our hypothesis. The generosity and support we encountered gave us energy to continue the project. Hashim Sarkis, curator of La Biennale di Venezia's 17th International Architecture Exhibition, 'How will we live together?', extended us an invitation to showcase our research in its main exhibition. The Alastair Swayn Foundation awarded us with a strategic grant. The project seemed on track.

Then, history hit us. COVID-19 went global and masks followed. They continued to be sites of massive controversies. Wearing a mask linked the strength of national health systems to rightwing populism and anti-vax movements' discourses. Access to masks made inequality more visible and the limits of state control more blurry. Masks entered every aspect of our everyday life, from public transportation to TV shows, from family gatherings to online porn. In summary, masks moved from objects of dissent to hegemonic presences.

This book, and the collaborations it includes, are the result of an early impulse as much as the events that followed. While the initial conversations discussed the air of the Indo-Pacific region, when the book went to press two years of COVID had changed our collective perceptions of masks and our own breathing habits. This is the context in which the cover and back cover collages came about. Developed by the paratactical artist Dean Cross, a Worimi man born and raised on Ngunnawal/Ngambri Country, they push us to traverse masks' poetic and political totemic powers in a millenarian region, in the recent pandemic. Our initial argument follows, transformed into an archeology of our current masked state. Outlined in five case studies —Sydney, Hong Kong, Santiago, Delhi, and Johannesburg—it takes the form of five socio-technical cautionary tales of the regions' political communities.

The rest of the chapters are organized in twos, forming duos that resonate, and are in conversation or expand each other's arguments. Each pair casts light on the topic from angles our tales did not reach, such as histories and stories of other masks; the science behind mask design, aerial truth and post-truth; air's impending past and imminent future. Visual pieces link each pair of essays to the next. Developed by photographers or visual artists operating locally, they document one of the five sites we studied.

The Sydney based photographer Hamish McIntosh opens the visual pieces by capturing the city's landscapes and peoples under bushfire smoke. The two essays that follow include one by the visual culture and fashion historian Peter McNeil, who presents a personal collection of uses and misuses of masks at the core of political protests, and the architectural theorist and philosopher Hélène Frichot, who imagines a scenario where we might not want to breathe anymore.

The second visual intermission is called *El Manifesto Capucha*, which was penned by La Escuela Nunca y Otros Futuros at one of its appearances in Santiago de Chile during *el Estallido Social*. The authors translated it into English specially for this volume, and made their awareness of the colonial impulse behind such an action explicit. This contribution precedes physicist Lidia Morawska's account of how science makes masks that perform technically and culturally, and the architect Juan Elvira's recent history of mask design as the ultimate design exercise of micro-architecture, one that unpacks bodies, nature, and politics.

The photographer Matthew Connors authors the next image-based break, a series of portraits of Hong Kong protesters' faces protected from tear gas and facial recognition technologies. Next, the designer, educator and researcher of critical fashion, Ricarda Bigolin, describes a post-truth dystopia we may already be living in, while Peter Irga and Fraser Torpy, from the UTS Plants and Environmental Quality Research Group', explain the impacts of air pollution on our bodies in Australia and China.

In the fourth interlude the work of the Delhi based photographer Sharbendu De portrays post-climate-crisis domestic spaces we may be headed towards, and how these might already exist in the city. The Supreme Court of India's Suo Moto ruling on Delhi Air Pollution from 13 November 2019 follows. The last pair of essays brings together the writing of the artist and curator Enoch Cheng on the precarious futurity of the future itself, and Forensic Architecture's Senior Researcher Samaneh Moafi research on the relation between tear gas and architecture's role in Santiago de Chile's Plaza Dignidad. The series closes with the South Africa based architect Sumayya Vally's representations of Johannesburg's air.

By a way of conclusion, the photographer Matteo Dal Vera snaps our very own hybrid aerial creatures—or five well-dressed friends—in familiar environments like lobbies, streets, and kitchens with objects, plants and other humans. Developed in collaboration with the copy nature office, with Umi Graham, Ellie Skinner and Harrison Stockdale, these Folk Costumes for the Indo-Pacific Air were exhibited at the Venice Biennale, but seem far more comfortable in domestic spaces with other beings. Fearing an excess of reflectiveness but not enough vision, a brief postscriptum seemed necessary. Achille Mbembe's manifesto, translated by Carolyn Shread, on the universal right to breathe, packs a huge lyrical and political punch, and reminds us that our present, which is increasingly breathless, still leaves space for the reader's hope.

Please take a breath, if only for a moment, using your mask. Do not take it off to read this book. Accept the hesitance of our words and the book's proposed fragmentation by embodying its mediation. It is now part of your respiratory system. While you read, please re-imagine the Indo-Pacific region's air, and its wearable architecture, with all of us. You are already breathing it.

...

10

Urtzi Grau & Guillermo Fernández-Abascal

Sydney, Santiago, Hong Kong, Delhi, Johannesburg: The Unbreathable Architecture of the Indo-Pacific

In the months that preceded the global spread of COVID-19, a series of events transformed the atmosphere of the Indo-Pacific region: bushfire smoke on the East Coast of Australia, the tear gas used in the Santiago de Chile and Hong Kong protests, the Supreme Court of India's ruling on Delhi's pollution failures, and activists covering iconic statues with respirators across Johannesburg and Pretoria. They all mapped political struggles taking place in relation to the region's air. They all triggered a pre-pandemic proliferation of masked faces.

The events in Santiago, Hong Kong, Johannesburg, Delhi, and Sydney form a story. In each city, the atmospheric composition led to the development of protective respiratory devices, particular to each urban centre's local particles and gasses. These protective architectures illustrate how, before our global pandemic, masks and respirators were already part of the Indo-Pacific imaginary. Together, they form a partial map of that amorphous substance that connects the Indo-Pacific—its air.

Unlike air purifiers, humidifiers, or AC filters—appliances traditionally used at the building scale—masks control the air that an individual breathes. By complementing the respiratory system, they establish an intimate relationship with the body. Yet this is not without consequences. Although they allow us to safely breathe harmful air, masks and respirators also deface us. They obscure a set of physical features and present another. Hiding behind a mask, becoming *other*, has a long tradition. From superheroes to protests, from heists to carnivals, a new visage constructs a new identity—whether it's individual like plastic surgery, or collective like the Zapatista ski mask. The explosion of new faces across the Indo-Pacific region was not a decision but rather a side effect, an unintended collective face triggered by environmental conditions. The resulting new faces, however, engendered new political communities, through which the citizens of the Indo-Pacific started taking ownership of the recently created region.

Sydney's P2 masks

The demand for commercially available P2 masks[*1] dramatically increased in the cities across the East Coast of Australia in the last months of 2019. The reason for this sudden popularity was the 2019-2020 bushfire season. In three months, the fires burned an estimated 18.6 million hectares, destroying close to 6000 buildings, killing over 30 people and more than one billion animals, and releasing 306 million tons of CO_2 into the atmosphere, close to 60 per cent of Australia's CO_2 total yearly emissions.[*2] Ninety per cent of the total particle mass emitted were fine particles under 2.5 microns ($PM_{2.5}$). The dimensions of $PM_{2.5}$ particles allow them to reach the pulmonary alveoli and jump straight to the bloodstream. The health impacts of extended exposure to $PM_{2.5}$ particles range from respiratory tract irritation to asthma, reduced lung function, heart failure, and premature death. Through December and January, the $PM_{2.5}$ levels reached 400 $\mu g/m^3$ in Sydney Central Business District and went over 200 $\mu g/m^3$ in most Sydney suburbs (for reference, the worst Air Quality Index or AQI for Beijing in the infamously polluted 2017 had a $PM_{2.5}$ reading of 121 $\mu g/m^3$). As the overall AQI reached 600, the means of measuring became meaningless. This reading was literally off the scale, as the value for the worst atmospheric condition, named 'hazardous' and represented with a deep red, was 200.[*3]

At that concentration level, online AQI maps are unnecessary. Suspended $PM_{2.5}$ particles scatter the sun's shorter wavelength light (blue colours) and skip longer wavelengths (red colours). As the material qualities of ashes tinted the atmosphere, the resulting orange sky became a substitute for the colour coding provided by the New South Wales government daily reports on air quality. Around the world, images of burned koalas, exhausted firefighters refusing to shake Australian Prime Minister Scott Morrison's hand, masks shortages in Aboriginal communities, and vacationers trapped by the fire at the beaches all shared the same coloured sky. Orange air became a symbol of public outrage.

On 11 December, with Sydney's AQI over the 'hazardous' mark, a first public protest, the Climate Emergency Rally, gathered 20,000 people in Sydney's CBD. It was followed on 10 January, under similar atmospheric conditions, when 30,000 people gathered in the same location under the rallying cry 'Sack SCOMO!' (a reference to Australia's Prime Minister Scott Morrison). Organized by Extinction Rebellion and University Students for Climate Justice, both protests demanded national resources to fight the ongoing bushfires and changes to Australia's climate change policies.

The P2 masks were an essential feature during the protests. Their non-woven polypropylene fabric filters at least 94 per cent of airborne particles under 0.5 microns, making them especially effective in dealing with $PM_{2.5}$ particles and reducing the toxic air's effects on the human. But the nonwoven layers not only allowed protesters to breathe, they also provided demonstrators with a distinctive feature. Covering one's own face with a garment traditionally reserved for construction sites defined the demonstrators' collective identity.[*4] The mask also became a literal demonstration of the reasons to protest. They evidenced the increase of $PM_{2.5}$ particles in the air caused by a bushfire, which was rooted in climate change-related drought, and intensified by the national government's support of 'clean coal'.[*5] The mask showed how coal dust was literally and metaphorically making Sydney's air unbreathable. In summary, the fabric's materiality mirrored the stratification of political practice, agency, and performance—these all collapsed into the form of the garments.

Santiago's bandana-wrapped collection of ashes soaked in soda lime

In January 2020, NASA released images of Australian bushfire ash crossing the Pacific Ocean and arriving in Chile. However, since October 2019, charcoal dust of a different origin had been soaking face bandanas in Santiago, Valparaíso, Concepción, Arica, Iquique, Antofagasta, La Serena, Rancagua, Chillán, Valdivia, Osorno, Puerto Montt and Punta Arenas in response to a different kind of airborne health risk.

Between October 2019 and January 2020, these sites witnessed the largest civil unrest in Chile since the end of Augusto Pinochet's dictatorship. Initially triggered by the increase of public transportation fares in Santiago, the protests encapsulated social discontent with years of economic, racial, and gender inequality. The scale and repercussions of the events were unprecedented. The largest march gathered more than a million people; eight ministers resigned and, eventually, the government agreed to hold a referendum to rewrite the 1980 constitution.

The initial reaction of the Chilean government was more familiar. On 19 October, the declaration of the state of emergency transferred the control of the affected areas to the army, which, subsequently, imposed a curfew citing civil unrest for the first time since the end of the dictatorship. Thirty-two people were killed and 2000 police were injured.

The number of injured demonstrators remains unknown, but the National Institute of Human Rights (Instituto Nacional de Derechos Humanos, INDH), reported more than 11,180 hospitalized and over 8800 detained, documenting cases of torture, sexual abuse, and sexual assault.[*6] The police made extensive use of truck-mounted water cannons, pellets, rubber bullets, and tear gas canisters.[*7]

The gas canisters contained 2-chlorobenzalmalononitrile ($C_{10}H_5C_1N_2$) commonly known as CS gas (the initials of Ben Corson and Roger Stoughton, the two scientists who first synthesized it in 1928). CS gas is one of around fifteen different types used regularly as tear gas and the one preferred by most police forces, including the Chilean, for riot control due to its powerful effects, which include tears, profuse coughing, burning sensations in the eyes and throat, disorientation, dizziness, and breathing difficulties. Although CS is routinely used on civilians worldwide, it is deemed unacceptable for war. Like any lachrymatory agent, its use in warfare has been internationally prohibited since the end of World War I.[*8]

Widely distributed digital instruction manuals recommend that demonstrators use vinegar or lime juice to counter the effects of the gas. An alternative method involves smashing up charcoal as the ashes might filter CS gas out. Both methods involve soaking a bandana and tightly tying it around the face. Yet these methods are as popular as they are discouraged, as charcoal and acidic liquids close to the eyes and mucous membranes not only won't protect them from CS gas, but might actually be the source of irritation.[*9]

The effectiveness of the bandanas needs to be accounted for in the realm of political agency and performance. Although its ability to filter CS gas is limited, its role in protests is essential. During the Pinochet regime, anonymity was crucial for avoiding repression. Its use as a disguise persisted in the 2019-2020 protests, yet partially covering one's face with fabric also indicated other political practices.

The widespread eye injuries, including globe ruptures during the protests,*10 made covering one's eye a symbol of the fight against police brutality. In parallel, LASTESIS's performance 'Un violador en

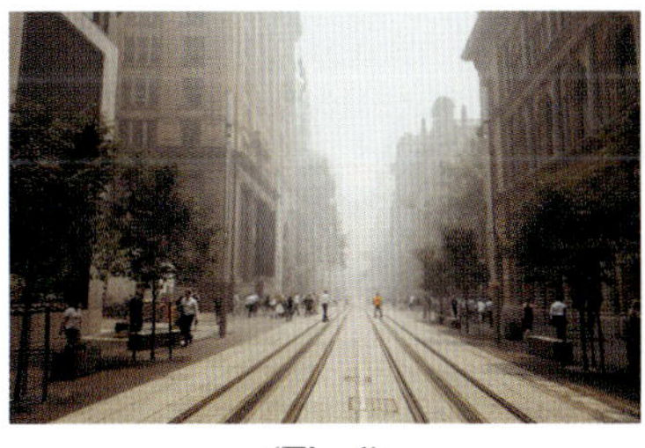
(Fig. 1)

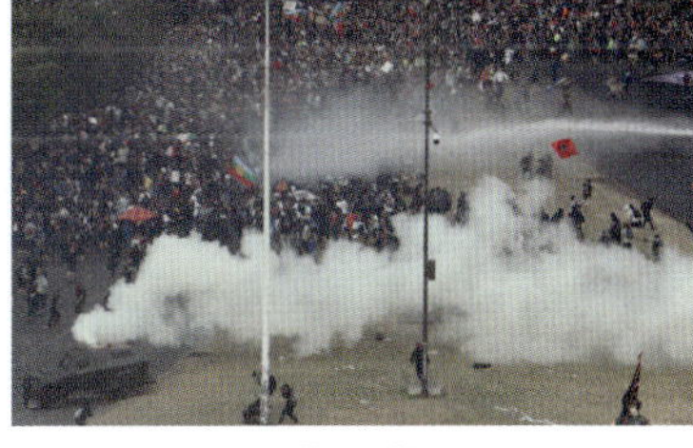
(Fig. 2)

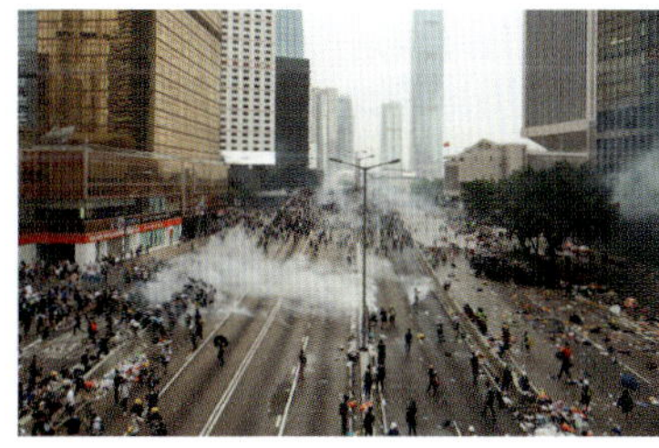
(Fig. 3)

tu camino' (A rapist in your path), became a global icon of the fight against violence against women. Initially staged in Valparaiso on 18 November by four members of the collective—blindfolded with black fabric and wearing a green bandana around the neck to support abortion rights—the performance was reproduced in Chile's protests and eventually all over the world. Worth mentioning is La Escuela Nunca's 'Manifiesto Capucha,'*11 presented near Plaza de la Dignidad on 1 February 2020. Its claim, '[r]enunciamos al nombre propio, llamamos a perder la identidad, a perder la cara, el género, la nación, a devenir capucha, carne, sangre, organismo vivo y múltiple',*12 is perhaps the most self-aware example of how their masks combine practice, agency and performance. The manifesto presents them as an essential tool for the political imagination required for the coming constituent process. On the other hand, the Chilean government indicated the inherent danger that they believed these garments posed to traditional architecture when it sponsored the 'anti-mask and anti-looting laws.'*13 The regulation, approved 27 November by the House and on 4 December by the Chilean Senate, linked masks to building destruction, thus suggesting that these garments were capable of reducing architecture to nothing.

Fig. 1. Sydney bushfire smoke on George Street. Photograph by VirtualWolf, December 10, 2019.

Fig. 2. Tear Gas in Concepción during the Estallido Social (Chilean protests). Photograph by Alvaro Navarro, 21 October, 2019.

Fig. 3. Tear Gas in Harcourt Road during the 2019 Hong Kong protests. Photograph by Wpcpey, June 12, 2019.

Hong Kong's combination of respirator, goggles, makeup and laser pointers

Two months before the Chilean ban on masks another government implemented a similar ban. On 4 October 2019, the executive authorities of Hong Kong invoked a colonial-era law, the Emergency Regulations Ordinance, that conferred exceptional powers of legislation to Carrie Lam, the Chief Executive-in-Council, bypassing the city's parliament. The following day, Lam implemented the Prohibition on Face Covering Regulation (PFCR),*14 an anti-mask law to prevent protestors from 'destroying the city'.*15

The PFCR appeared in the context of the Hong Kong 2019-2020 protests, the longest and most extensive in the city-state history. The protests started with limited demonstrations as early as March 2019, triggered by the introduction of the Fugitive Offenders amendment bill, which weakened the separation of Hong Kong's jurisdiction from Mainland China's legal system. By June, the demonstrations hit record-breaking numbers—more than a million on 9 June, according to the organizers.

Protesters stormed the city's Legislative Council and managed to close the Hong Kong International Airport intermittently over the course of several months. By November, demonstrators occupied several universities that the police subsequently sieged and stormed. Police and demonstrators—and also demonstrators and pro-Beijing groups—clashed through the city. More than 9000 people were arrested and at least 2000 have been prosecuted.[*16]

The protests also affected the city's air, which raised concerns about its effects on Hong Kong's population. Through 2019 the police fired more than 10,000 tear gas canisters, releasing an unprecedented amount of CS gas in a densely populated urban environment.[*17] The connections between the city's atmosphere and the demonstrations were not new. The name of the 2014 Umbrella Revolution had originated in the instruments used for defence against police tear gas canisters.[*18] Umbrellas still played a role in 2019, however, the large amounts of gas and its indiscriminate use in enclosed interiors rendered them less effective. Covering the face became essential—not only as a means of protection against the gas, but also to prevent identification. As the development of facial recognition technologies turned faces into weapons to be used against the face's owner, masks became the image equated with the movement.

As choking demonstrators proved less effective than being able to capture their biometric data, the PFCR expanded the definition of mask to include paint or any form of face-covering. Nevertheless, masks of painted faces proliferated in the Hong Kong protests, specifically that of Guy Fawkes, popularized in the 2005 film *V for Vendetta* that then went on to symbolize the Occupy movement in 2011 and 2012, and the Joker from the eponymous movie from 2019. Together with the Dali-inspired mask from the Netflix series *Money Heist*, popular in the Chilean protests, they illustrate how popular insurrection icons are well-marketed cultural products.[*19] The demonstrators' ability to appropriate film characters also indulged in gender stereotypes. As female demonstrators reported, preconceptions about makeup became an effective form of camouflage, since women going to protest were not expected to wear it.[*20] Other countermeasures against facial recognition focused on the technology. Disabling cellphones' Face ID capabilities[*21] and directing hand-held laser pointers to blind surveillance cameras complemented the masks' camouflage capabilities.[*22]

Umbrellas, protective goggles, makeup, Hollywood stereotypes, phone apps, construction helmets, respirators—the list of ad-hoc technologies, cultural identities and digital camouflage that shaped Hong Kong's masks goes on and on, well beyond the demonstrators' faces. Masks merged with the city through lasers and phone networks and even set in motion the legal case that came to define the city's fate. On 18 November, the Hong Kong High Court declared several sections of the PFCR unconstitutional. Subsequently, the Legislative Affairs Commission—China's top legislative body—claimed that the sole authority to rule on constitutional matters in the city was the Standing Committee of the National People's Congress (NPCSC).[*23] At stake was the 'one country, two systems' approach, a constitutional principle of the People's Republic of China describing the economic and administrative autonomy of Hong Kong. The legal standoff between Beijing and Hong Kong over who had the right to legislate on covered faces lasted for more than a year. On 20 December, 2020, the Hong Kong High Court declared that the PFCR was constitutional and affirmed that it could legislate over the constitutionality of Hong Kong's laws without diminishing the authority of the NPCSC.[*24] This exercise of legal contortionism showed how Hong Kong's masks not only allowed people to protest or breathe while escaping facial recognition systems, but also that they were the object of the dispute—the dispute over the separation of judicial systems.

Delhi's asthmatic-Swedish-émigrée-designed luxury mask

Meanwhile, on 1 November 2019, the government of the National Capital Territory of Delhi (NCT) distributed five million masks throughout Delhi's schools, triggering the opposite reaction from the Supreme Court of India: masks were not enough. After a week of severe air pollution, the court ordered the government to find an immediate solution, imposed restrictions on the use of firecrackers during the five-day celebrations of Diwali, the Hindu festival of light, and directed the NCT and adjacent regions to enforce previous rulings regarding pollution effectively.[*25] Air quality was not a new issue in India, yet, over November 2019, Delhi endured one of the worst periods of pollution on record, forcing the authorities to declare a public health emergency. The AQI reached 450 (India's hazardous threshold is anything between 300 and 500), and the concentration of $PM_{2.5}$ particles hit levels twenty times higher than WHO health standards. Pedestrians struggled to breathe. The thick smog limited visibility and caused burning eyes. The end of the year added the seasonal stubble burning to the city's constant car emissions, burning of waste, and construction dust. More than two million farmers burn 23 million tons of crop residue on some 80,000 square km of farmland in northern India every winter. The city's land-locked geography, the low-speed winter winds filled with dust from the Gulf and cold-air inversion kept pollution close to the ground. Combined, they produced a lethal cocktail of particulate matter, carbon dioxide, nitrogen dioxide and sulphur dioxide.

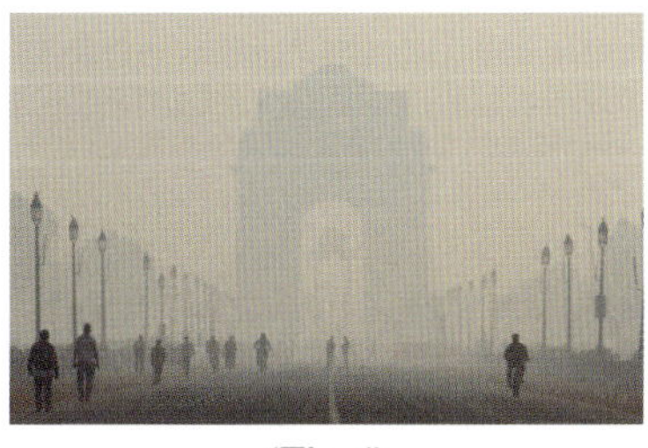
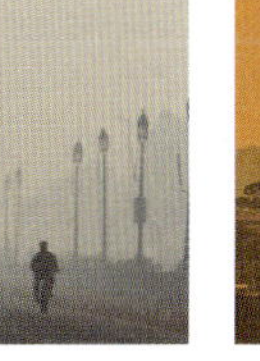

(Fig. 4)

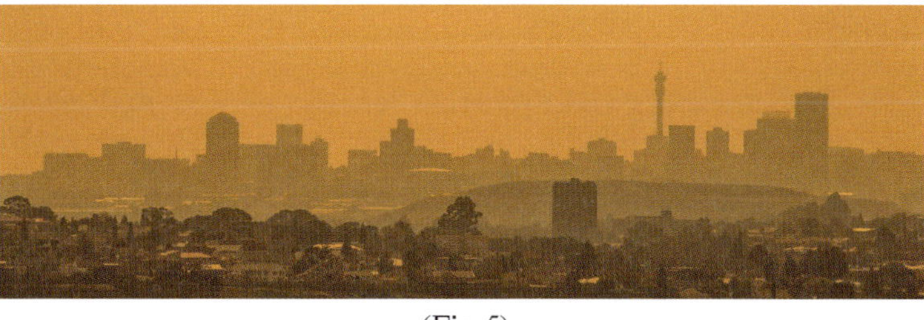

(Fig. 5)

Following the free distribution of masks, the city introduced a scheme to cut traffic pollution—only cars with odd or even-numbered license plates could drive on given days. Construction stopped. The Supreme Court considered these measures insufficient and demanded action in a series of rulings on cases brought by the legal activist M.C. Mehta. On 4 November, the Supreme Court issued an order accusing the NCT Government and the state governments of Punjab, Haryana, and Uttar Pradesh of not performing their duties in relation to stubble burning.[*26] On 6 November, it issued a second order directing the state governments to urgently put in place a subsidized scheme towards zero stubble burning.[*27] On 13 November, acting *suo motto*—of its own accord, without a prior motion or request from any parties—the court ordered the closure of Delhi-NCR schools and advised residents to avoid outdoor exposure and to work from home wherever feasible.[*28] On 13 November and 15 November, two new rulings on M.C. Mehta's cases called on Delhi's government to install air-purifying towers across the city within ten days.[*29]

Fig. 4. Air pollution surrounding New Delhi's India Gate monument on Rajpath. Photograph by Bloomberg, November 6, 2019.

Fig. 5. Air pollution on the Johannesburg skyline. August 8, 2019.

This requirement for public air filtration infrastructure continued the court's history of environmental jurisprudence grounded in Article 21 of the Constitution of India: 'No person shall be deprived of his life or personal liberty except according to a procedure established by law.'[*30] Since the 1980s the court has consistently interpreted the word 'life' to include the right to a healthy environment. The court's push for public and collective solutions also explains its attitude towards individual masks. The constitution implies that the state must protect their citizens' wellbeing. Equal access to breathable air is a collective right. It cannot be addressed individually, especially when the difference in life expectancy of middle-class children living in Delhi with access to filtered air is five years higher than lower-class infants.[*31] As the cleanliness of the air one breathes dictates how many years Indian citizens have left to live, access to masks becomes an index of the privilege, of the right to stay alive.

This is the context in which Alexander Hjertstrom, a Swedish asthmatic emigrant living in India, conceived Airinum, the fashion utility that would allow him to breathe in Delhi. His reusable and adjustable award-winning Scandinavian design was made in China from a KN95 certified air mask that filters out PM2.5 particles. Padded around the nose, it prevents glasses from fogging and unfiltered air leaks. Its replaceable filters last for 100 hours, and its expulsion valves hinder CO_2 build-up. With its online US$75 price tag—US$100 for the limited editions developed with global brands such as Bally, Woolrich, Alan Walker, Nemen, Marine Serre, and MoMA—Airinum masks capture the gentrification of clean air, after all, India's average monthly wage is US$437. But beyond extracting value from Delhi's polluted atmosphere for European profit, Airinum masks join a global trend where masks have become luxury items and their filtration function is a secondary concern.[*32]

Johannesburg and Pretoria's locally crafted and globally constructed sculpture-sized masks

Months before, masks had travelled in the opposite direction—from Europe to another former colony, South Africa—to protest Johannesburg and Pretoria's atmospheric conditions. On 14 March 2019, as part of the global campaign 'Clean Air Now!', Greenpeace activists climbed the statues of Mother with Child at Bree Taxi Rank, Brenda Fassie in Newtown, the Miner outside the Chamber of Mines, and Chief Tshwane outside Pretoria City Hall, to fit them with giant handmade respirators to protest the NO_2 contamination caused by coal-fired power stations.[*33]

The protest was directed to Mpumalanga, a neighbouring region that has the highest levels of NO_2 globally. The small province accounts for 83 per cent of South Africa's coal production and produces 75.2 per cent of Southern Africa's energy in twelve coal-fired power stations.[*34] Due to the region's nocturnal temperature inversions, the pollution fails to disperse, exceeding WHO standards by 6 to 7 times during winter months.[*35] The prevailing east winds expose the Johannesburg-Pretoria conurbation, with a population of approximately 10 million people, to the effects of NO_2—including wheezing, flu, bronchitis, asthma, and increasing rates of heart disease and lung cancer—a key factor in the estimated 20,000 South African casualties from air pollution-related causes every year.[*36]

The masked statues were not only part of the local protest, but also a global effort. On 18 April 2016, in London, activists climbed the 52-metre column of the Admiral Lord Nelson monument in Trafalgar Square and fit a gas mask to the statue. The flag officer of the Royal Navy was not alone.[*37] On 18 May 2018, the statue of Diana Cazadora in Mexico City was also fitted with a respirator in protest of the city's air. Dates and places show the masks' route towards Johannesburg, implying that pollution transcends cultural contexts to affect colonial admirals, post-colonial heroes and goods equally.

The NO_2 pollution data backing up this hypothesis also arrived from Europe. In October 2017, the European Space Agency launched the satellite Copernicus Sentinel-5P dedicated to monitoring air pollution. Developed by a Dutch government-funded consortium,[*38] the satellite's Tropomi spectrometer over-performed current instruments in space, taking measurements every second to cover an area of 2600 km wide and 7 km long at a resolution of 7 × 7 km. Greenpeace, whose coordinating body is based in the Netherlands, cited the Sentinel-5P-generated NO_2 maps showing a red cloud over the Johannesburg-Pretoria conurbation as the evidence behind the protest.[*39] These representations of the South African atmosphere, albeit publicly available, are still constructed in and controlled by Europe,[*40] just as the masked statues reinforce colonial histories and resonate with the reanimation of political agency. The Black Live Matters movement brought global attention to public monuments of confederate figures, colonizers, conquistadors or slaveholders. As the open letter demanding the relocation of the Captain Cook statue explained, monuments' public presence makes them bearers of—often traumatic—collective histories in the present. Their power to actualize the past is the reason why these infamous monuments belong in the museum. There, they can be treated as historical artefacts, re-evaluated, and contextualized properly.[*41] If public monuments are sites that are meant to address common values, what better place is there to discuss one of the few commons left, our air? Indeed, the masks in Johannesburg and Pretoria actively enrolled these powerful inanimate beings in the disputes over the air we breathe.

Indo-Pacific Air

The link between these events is, of course, a construction. In 2013, the Australian Defence White Paper[*42] formally shifted the country from the Pacific to the Indo-Pacific region. Thus, Australia officially moved to a region created *ex proposito,* expanding from the west coast of South America to the Gulf, from South East Asia to Africa's east coast. The new region had been theorized in diplomatic circles since the 1920s.[*43] Yet, it was not until increase of maritime trade in the 2000s, the emergence of the BRICS' economies, China's regional hegemony, and the post-2001 geopolitical reorganization that Australia became the first country to recognize the proposition and relocate there.

Since this shift, the existence of the Indo-Pacific region has been treated as a de facto reality in trade agreements, cultural exchanges and development grants, while its actual characterization varies according to the agencies, parties or policies involved. It is not a strange condition—a cacophony of legal definitions also delineates well-established regions such as Europe.[*44] In fact, its blurry contour is not the Indo-Pacific's most distinctive feature. Instead, its distinction would be the instantaneous nature in which it came about. The Indo-Pacific region's sudden invention was a twofold operation: both an act of naming and of storytelling. And while the region's geographical limits were stated in its name, the narratives that hold its geography together are barely in place. They conflate, for example, deep-time histories tracing back its origin to Gondwanaland, the ruins of colonizing empires, First Nations People's struggles, and the commonalities of recent but geographically distant political upheaval.

Like any other section of the earth's atmosphere, the Indo-Pacific air's central components are nitrogen, oxygen, argon, and carbon dioxide. Its changing levels of humidity are linked to the amount of water vapour it contains. Its composition is also defined by increases and decreases in temperature and speed flow, gasses such as nitrogen dioxide, sulphur dioxide, ozone and other pollutants, dust particles, and ashes, each one with its own chemical and physical qualities. Air is both universal and local, a continuum that does not respect political boundaries and is anything but homogeneous. Local regulations, aggregations of vegetation, industrial emissions, discharges of tear gas, weather conditions, or volcanic eruptions are all localized. As such, their effects are never contained and always geographically situated. Paradoxically, while the air's heterogeneity is not limited by nation-state or regional borders, its representations are. Atmospheric descriptions vary according to the agency in charge. For example, the AQI is globally used to describe the air quality and its associated health risks. There are as many AQIs as there are different national air quality standards, each with its own units, colour codes, and alerts.[*45] In turn, the meaning of 'air quality' differs according to location.

Local definitions respond to local controversies and often have global consequences. For example, in later years, coinciding with the rise of climate change denial, the US has loosened the limits on acceptable levels of pollutants.[*46] The EU has tightened its standards since the European Commission approved the New Air Quality Directive in 2008.[*47] China has used its newly released AQI to address the critical levels of pollution in major cities.[*48] These differences further complicate the description of air, linking its representations with the region's local politics, and establishing different standards for what is acceptable for their citizens' health.

Folk Costumes

As the line that makes air unbreathable is constantly shifting, masks function as markers of this position. They do not exist in a void, but are tied to concrete locations through the AQI, legal definition and chemical compositions they respond to. They imply specific users, who have knowledge of air quality and an awareness of our right to breathe, and are invested in the commons and its values. They construct a shared, heterogenous face. In summary, these masks build political communities that provide collective representation and temporary common values, performed through dissent.

Can we call them folk costumes? Nineteenth-century romantic nationalism infamously constructed folk costumes as a tool to ascertain the essential link between national identity and land. In Europe, their materiality and design became the vehicle to connect local cultural traditions endangered by modernization with idealized accounts of peasant life firmly rooted in weather, agricultural labour and the countryside. Meanwhile, anthropology flagrantly used these robes as symbolic, structural, or semiotic explanations to cement cultural superiority theories supporting colonial empires and the existing social order back at home. Read as indexes of development, World Fairs profusely displayed non-western garments—often worn by members of the ethnic group which the costume attempted to represent—reinforcing the exoticizing gaze of the western visitors. In short, folk costumes go hand-in-hand with the exercise of power.[*49]

Describing the 2019 masks as folk costumes might draw parallels. Similar to those invented in the nineteenth century, these folk costumes are also socio-technological constructions. Their descriptions also combine responses to environmental conditions, cultural and political concerns, and available techniques and technologies. Yet, they neither illustrate an essential link between national identity and land nor imply symbolic, structural, or semiotic explanations to validate neocolonialism or inequalities. Instead, these garments exemplify culture as a process emerging through agency, practice, and performance. Like air itself, they navigate—and often challenge—the relationships between local conditions and global networks. They are masks, wearable architecture that renders the air of the region visible.

Urtzi Grau & Guillermo Fernández-Abascal
Sydney, Santiago, Hong Kong, Delhi, Johannesburg: The Unbreathable Architecture of the Indo-Pacific
* **footnotes & references**

---

*1 P2 is a mask classification under the Regulation of Personal Protective Equipment defined by the Australian Government Therapeutic Goods Administration. Similar masks are also known as EN 149 FFP2 under the standards of European Committee for Standardization (CEN), N95 respirators when certificated by the U.S. National Institute for Occupational Safety and Health, or KN95 masks when they comply with the national standard GB 2626-2019 Respiratory Protection by the Standardization Administration of China.

*2 There has not been an official report on the consequences of the bushfires but various news organizations have reported similar numbers. See Graham Readfern,"Australia's Bushfires Have Emitted 250m Tonnes of CO2, Almost Half of Country's Annual Emmissions," *The Guardian*, December 13, 2019, https://www.theguardian.com/environment/2019/dec/13/australias-bushfires-have-emitted-250m-tonnes-of-co2-almost-half-of-countrys-annual-emissions; "The Numbers Behind Australia's Catastrophic Bushfire Season," *SBS News*, January 3, 2020, https://www.sbs.com.au/news/the-numbers-behind-australia-s-catastrophic-bushfire-season/eff3fd3b-1bc5-40b2-a434-f86bbfdf8c85.

*3 The historical air quality data, including the 2019 – 2020 bushfire season for Sydney and New South Wales is publicly available at https://www.dpie.nsw.gov.au/air-quality/air-quality-concentration-data-updated-hourly/daily-air-quality-data.

*4 Before becoming a basic product at pharmacies due to COVID-19, P2 masks were available in hardware stores like Bunnings and Sydney Tools. That connection was soon to be undermined. Twelve days after the first event the Australian Government announced the purchase of one million masks to address the shortage in the face of the growing numbers of COVID-19 cases in China. See Dana McCaulay & Rachel Clun, "One Million P2 Masks Ordered as Authorities Respond to Coronavirus," *Sydney Morning Herald* January 22, 2020, https://www.smh.com.au/politics/federal/one-million-p2-masks-ordered-as-authorities-respond-to-coronavirus-20200122-p53tqv.html.

*5 The protests specifically asked to stop support of 'clean coal', a euphemism used to validate Australia's preference for fossil fuels over sources of actual clean energy. Coal and its dust have played a key role in climate-change policies in Australia. In February 2017 the treasurer of the Australian Government, soon to be prime minister, Scott Morrison, smuggled a piece of coal and scorned the commitment of the Labor and Green opposition towards renewable energy. His words, 'Don't be afraid, don't be scared, it won't hurt you. It's coal', accompanied an image that became an infamous icon of global warming negationists. The piece of coal, held by the pristine hand of the treasurer and leaving no residue, became literal evidence of 'clean coal'.

*6 INDH, *Informe Anual Sobre la Stuación de los Derechos Humanos en Chile en el Contexto de la Crisis Social* (INDH: 2019), accessed October 20, 2021, https://bibliotecadigital.indh.cl/bitstream/handle/123456789/1701/Informe%20Final-2019.pdf.

*7 According to Forensic Architecture the police shot up to 596 tear gas canisters in one single location, la plaza de la Dignidad, in one single day: 20 October. "Investigation: Tear Gas in the Plaza de la Dignidad," Forensic Architecture, accessed October 20, 2021, https://forensic-architecture.org/investigation/tear-gas-in-plaza-de-la-dignidad.

*8 The full text of the Post-WWI 'Protocol for the Prohibition of the Use in War of Asphyxiating, Poisonous or Other Gases, and of Bacteriological Methods of Warfare' treaty at the UN: http://disarmament.un.org/treaties/t/1925. The current version of the ban is included in the Chemical Weapons Convention from 1993: https://www.opcw.org/chemical-weapons-convention.

*9 The International News Safety Institute "Protecting yourself from tear gas," News Safety, accessed October 20, 2021, https://newssafety.org/safety/advisories/protecting-yourself-from-tear-gas/.

*10 According to the INDH 427 persons received eye injuries at the hands of the police during the protests.

*11 La Escuela Nunca is a para-institutional school—personal, open and free—organized by the Grupo Toma through short lived 'appearences'. Their *Manifesto Capucha* can be found at https://laescuelanunca.org/Ap-1-manifiesto-colectivo.

*12 La Escuela Nunca, *Manifiesto Capucha*, last accessed January 10, 2022. https://laescuelanunca.org/Ap-1-manifiesto-colectivo. The Manifesto is re-published in this publication.

*13 The Anti-Mask law is the popular name of the law approved by the Chilean Senate on 28 November, 2019.

*14 The full text of the Prohibition on Face Covering Regulation can be found at https://www.elegislation.gov.hk/hk/cap241K.

*15 Carrie Lam cited in "Hong Kong: Anger as Face Masks Banned After Months of Protests," BBC NEWS, October 4, 2019, https://www.bbc.com/news/world-asia-china-49931598.

*16 Hong Kong Watch gives daily reports of arrests and prosecutions in its protest prosecution database: https://www.hongkongwatch.org/protest-prosecution.

*17 Associated Press has reported on the long term effects of CS gas in the Hong Kong protests: Eileen Ng, "Hong Kong Residents Living With Tear Gas Worry of Effects," AP News, December 5, 2019, https://apnews.com/article/0467edbcbc544878bd5f3c520c6a735f. Propublica has raised similar concerns in the context of the COVID pandemic: Lisa Song, "Tear Gas Is Way More Dangerous than the Police Let On—Especially During the COVID Pandemic," ProPublica, June 4, 2020, https://www.propublica.org/article/tear-gas-is-way-more-dangerous-than-police-let-on-especially-during-the-coronavirus-pandemic.

*18 On 26 September 2014 the term 'Umbrella Revolution' appeared for the first time on Twitter. By 29 September *The Independent* was using the name to describe the protest: https://www.independent.co.uk/news/world/asia/hong-kong-protests-pictures-umbrella-revolution-9761617.html.

*19 The proliferation of these masks in global protests as anti-establishment icons is well documented.

*20 *This American Life* 'Umbrellas Up' highlighted the use of makeup in the protest in its October 18, 2019 episode: https://www.thisamericanlife.org/686/umbrellas-up.

*21 Paul Mozur, "In Hong Kong Protests, Faces Become Weapons," The New York Times, July 26, 2019, https://www.nytimes.com/2019/07/26/technology/hong-kong-protests-facial-recognition-surveillance.html.

*22 August 10, 2019, Hong Kong Police used the expression 'offensive weapons' to refer to the laser pointers after arresting a university student for purchasing ten of them. That night protesters responded by staging a collective light-show on building facades. See Adam Jacobsen, "Hong Kong Protesters Use Laser Pointers to Deter Police, Scramble Facial Recognition," CBC News, August 11, 2019, https://www.cbc.ca/news/world/hong-kong-protest-lasers-facial-recognition-technology-1.5240651.

*23 Verna Yu, "Hong Kong Courts Have no Power to Rule on Face Mask Ban, Says China," *The Guardian*, November 19, 2019, https://www.theguardian.com/world/2019/nov/19/hong-kong-courts-cant-rule-on-face-masks-says-china-constitution-basic-law.

*24 Helen Davidson, "Hong Kong Court Reinstates Mask Ban at Public Gatherings," *The Guardian*, December 21, 2020, https://www.theguardian.com/world/2020/dec/21/hong-kong-court-reinstates-mask-ban-public-gatherings-protest.

*25 On October 15, 2019, a special report on pollution hot spots in NCR with requests for urgent directions to improve enforcement and pollution control was launched. This report was set up to inform the Supreme Court about the toxic air in the adverse weather conditions of Delhi's winter.

*26 The complete Order of the Supreme Court of India in the matter of M. C. Mehta Vs Union of India & Others dated 04/11/2019 regarding pollution in Delhi and the NCR region being particularly compounded by stubble burning can be found at http://www.indiaenvironmentportal.org.in/files/file/Delhi_pollution-SC_Order_04-Nov-2019.pdf.

*27 The complete Order of the Supreme Court of India in the matter of M. C. Mehta Vs Union of India & Others dated 06/11/2019 regarding air pollution in Delhi aggravated by stubble burning can be found at http://www.indiaenvironmentportal.org.in/files/file/stubble-burning-SC_Order_06-Nov-2019.pdf.

*28 The complete *suo motu* Order of the Supreme Court of India in the matter of 'Severe problem being faced by the citizens in Delhi and adjoining areas due to acute air pollution' can be found at http://www.indiaenvironmentportal.org.in/files/file/air-pollution-north-India-SC_Order_13-Nov-2019.pdf. The order is re-published in this publication.

*29 The complete Order of the Supreme Court of India in the matter of M. C. Mehta Vs Union of India dated 13/11/2019 regarding air pollution in NCT of Delhi can be found at http://www.indiaenvironmentportal.org.in/files/file/smog-towers-SC_Order_13-Nov-2019.pdf, and the complete Order of the Supreme Court in the matter of M. C. Mehta Vs Union of India & Others dated 15/11/2019 regarding air pollution control in Delhi NCR can be found at http://www.indiaenvironmentportal.org.in/files/file/airpollution-Delhi-SC_Order_15-Nov-2019.pdf.

*30 Article 21, "Protection of Life and Personal Liberty," *Constitution of India*, 1950, https://www.constitutionofindia.net/constitution_of_india/fundamental_rights/articles/Article%2021.

*31 *The New York Times*, "Who Gets to Breathe Clean Air in New Delhi?" *The New York Times*, December 17, 2020, https://www.nytimes.com/interactive/2020/12/17/world/asia/india-pollution-inequality.html.

*32 The list of brands producing fashionable masks proliferates around the world and includes O2Today, MetaMask, Cambridge Mask and Respro. All of their masks are both preventive care products and lifestyle accessories.

*33 Greenpeace press release announcing the action can be found at https://www.greenpeace.org/africa/en/press/6543/activists-scale-statues-to-draw-attention-to-deaths-caused-by-eskoms-air-pollution/.

*34 The protests were also directed to the South African governments as all twelve power stations in Mpumalanga are owned and operated by the national electricity public company Eskom.

*35 The effects on air pollution of Mpumalanga's cluster of coal-fired power stations in combination with its climate pattern were acknowledged by the South African Government in its Initial National Communication under the United Nations Framework Convention on Climate Change in 2000—see https://unfccc.int/resource/docs/natc/zafnc01.pdf.

*36 The World Bank, *The Cost of Air Pollution: Strengthening the Economic Case for Action*, http://documents1.worldbank.org/curated/en/781521473177013155/pdf/108141-REVISED-Cost-of-PollutionWebCORRECTED file.pdf.

*37 The city-wide protest over air pollution included other statues such as Oliver Cromwell in the grounds of the Houses of Parliament, Winston Churchill in Parliament Square, Queen Victoria opposite Buckingham Palace, Thierry Henry at Arsenal's stadium and Eros's plinth at Piccadilly Circus.

*38 The Dutch government invested €78 million in the consortium to build the Tropomi that included the Netherlands Space Office, Royal Netherlands Meteorological Institute, Netherlands Institute for Space Research, Netherlands Organisation for Applied Scientific Research and Airbus Defence and Space Netherlands.

*39 Greenpeace Africa, *New Satellite Data Reveals that Mpumalanga is the World's Largest Nitrogen Dioxide (NO_2) Air Pollution Hotspot* (Johannesburg: Greenpeace, n.d.), https://www.greenpeace.org/static/planet4-africa-stateless/2018/10/3ce9a5c3-sa-briefing_-global-air-pollution-map-no2-5-1.pdf.

*40 Copernicus Sentinel 5P Data and a 14-day moving average of nitrogen dioxide concentrations across the globe are publicly available at the ESA online portal: https://maps.s5p-pal.com/no2/.

*41 Published in the aftermath of Black Lives Matter, Tristen Harwood and Nicholas Tammens' open letter asks for the relocation of the Captain Cook statue (1878) by Thomas Woolner (1825–1892), currently sited in Sydney's Hyde Park, to a public museum. Tristen Harwood and Nicholas Tammens, "Open Letter: Relocation of Cook Statue," *The Saturday Paper*, July 4-10, 2020, https://www.thesaturdaypaper.com.au/opinion/topic/2020/07/04/relocate-the-captain-cook-statue/159378480010061#hrd.

*42 Government of Australia, Department of Defence, *Defence White Paper 2013*, retrieved December 26, 2020, https://www.defence.gov.au/whitepaper/2013/docs/WP_2013_web.pdf.

*43 The Indo-Pacific region was first theorized by the General Karl Ernst Haushofer in his analysis of the geopolitics of the Pacific Ocean, translated in Lewis A Tambs & Ernt J Brehm, *An English Translation and Analysis of Major General Karl Ernst Haushofer's Geopolitics of the Pacific Ocean: Studies on the Relationship Between Geography and History* (Lewiston, N.Y: Edwin Mellen Press, 2002).

*44 OMA/AMO has been tracing some of the maps that define Europe via their research *The Image of Europe* and *Europe Iconography* among others.

*45 The US started its AQI in 1968, which is publicly available at https://www.airnow.gov/. Since then, countries and regions have developed their own indexes. Canada started reporting its own Air Quality Health Index (AQHI) in 2005: https://www.canada.ca/en/environment-climate-change/services/air-quality-health-index.html. Hong Kong released its own AQHI in 2013: https://www.aqhi.gov.hk/en.html. Mainland China's Ministry of Environmental Protection (MEP) announced its own AQI in 2012 and implemented a unified colour coding for the entire country in 2014, the same year that India launched its own AQI: https://cpcb.nic.in/naqi/. The European Union launched its Common Air Quality Index (CAQI) in 2006, now rebranded European Air Quality Index (EAQI): https://airindex.eea.europa.eu/Map/AQI/Viewer/.

*46 Juliet Elperin & Brady Dennis, "Trump Administration Rejects Tougher Standards on Soot, a Deadly Air Pollutant," *The Washing Post*, December 7, 2020, https://www.washingtonpost.com/climate-environment/2020/12/07/trump-air-pollution/.

*47 See the European Commission's New Air Quality Directive here: https://ec.europa.eu/environment/air/quality/directive.htm.

*48 Angel Hsu, "China's New Air Quality Index: How Does it Measure Up?" Data Driven Environ Lab, March 28, 2012, https://datadrivenlab.org/air-quality-2/chinas-new-air-quality-index-how-does-it-measure-up/.

*49 Since the late 1980s, the arrival of cultural criticism to fashion studies has dismantled these readings, while anthropology has pursued new research agendas on clothing, placing the body surface at center stage. Elizabeth Wilson sets the foundations of the critique in *Adorned in Dreams: Fashion and Modernity* (London: Bloomsbury, 1984), and the shift has been well documented in Jennifer Craik's *The Face of Fashion* (London: Routledge, 1993).

Hamish McIntosh

Bushfire Smoke, Sydney, 2019

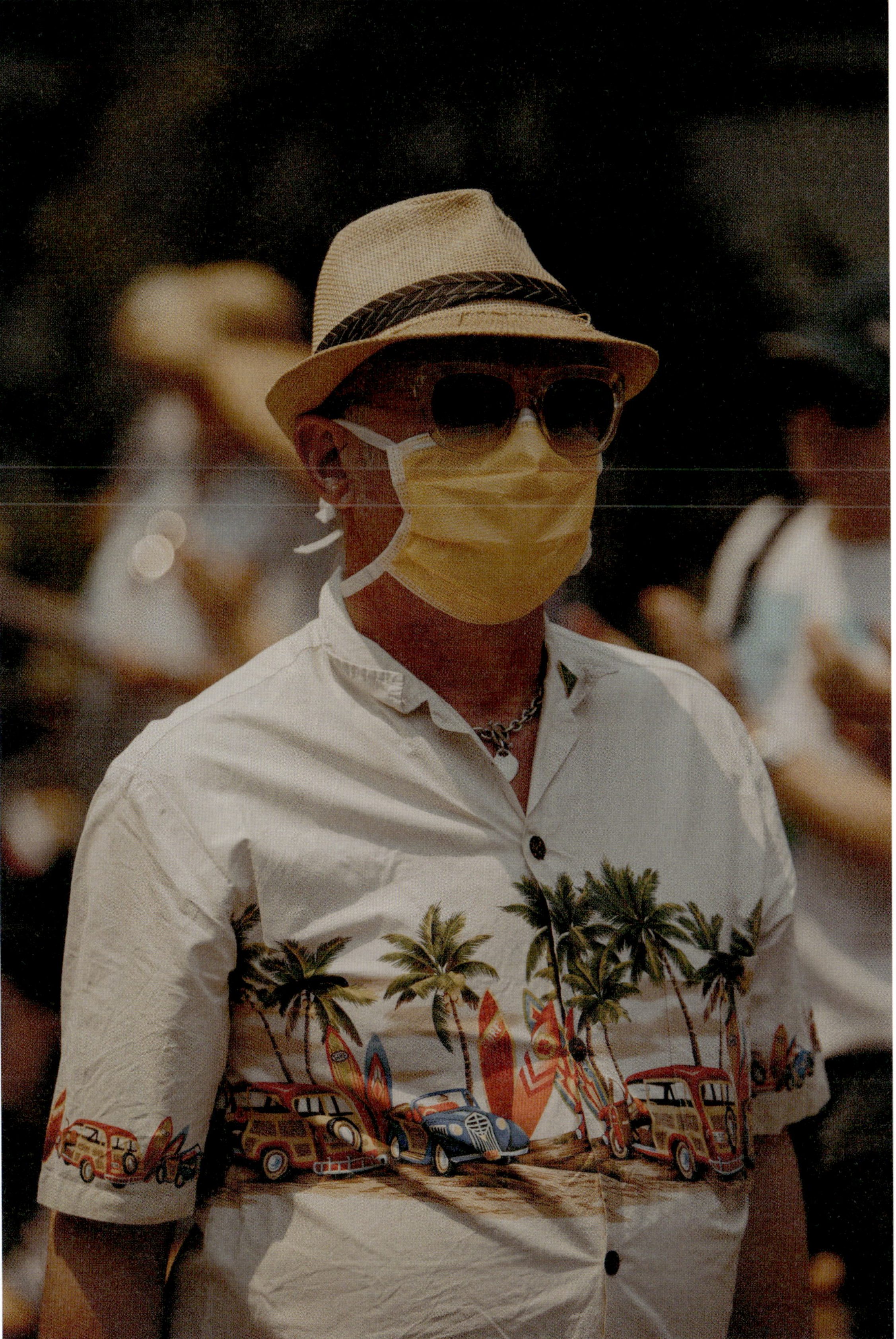

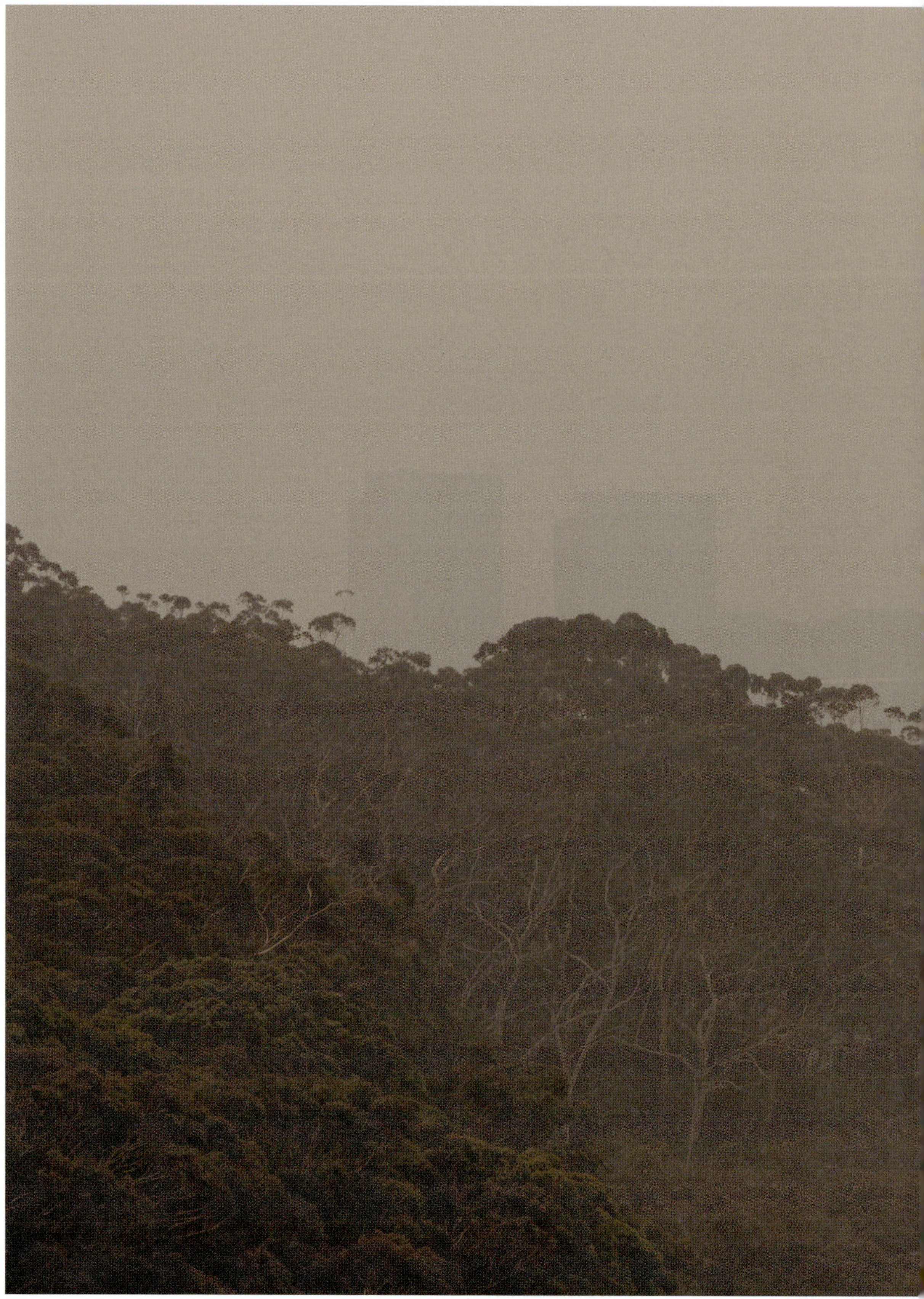

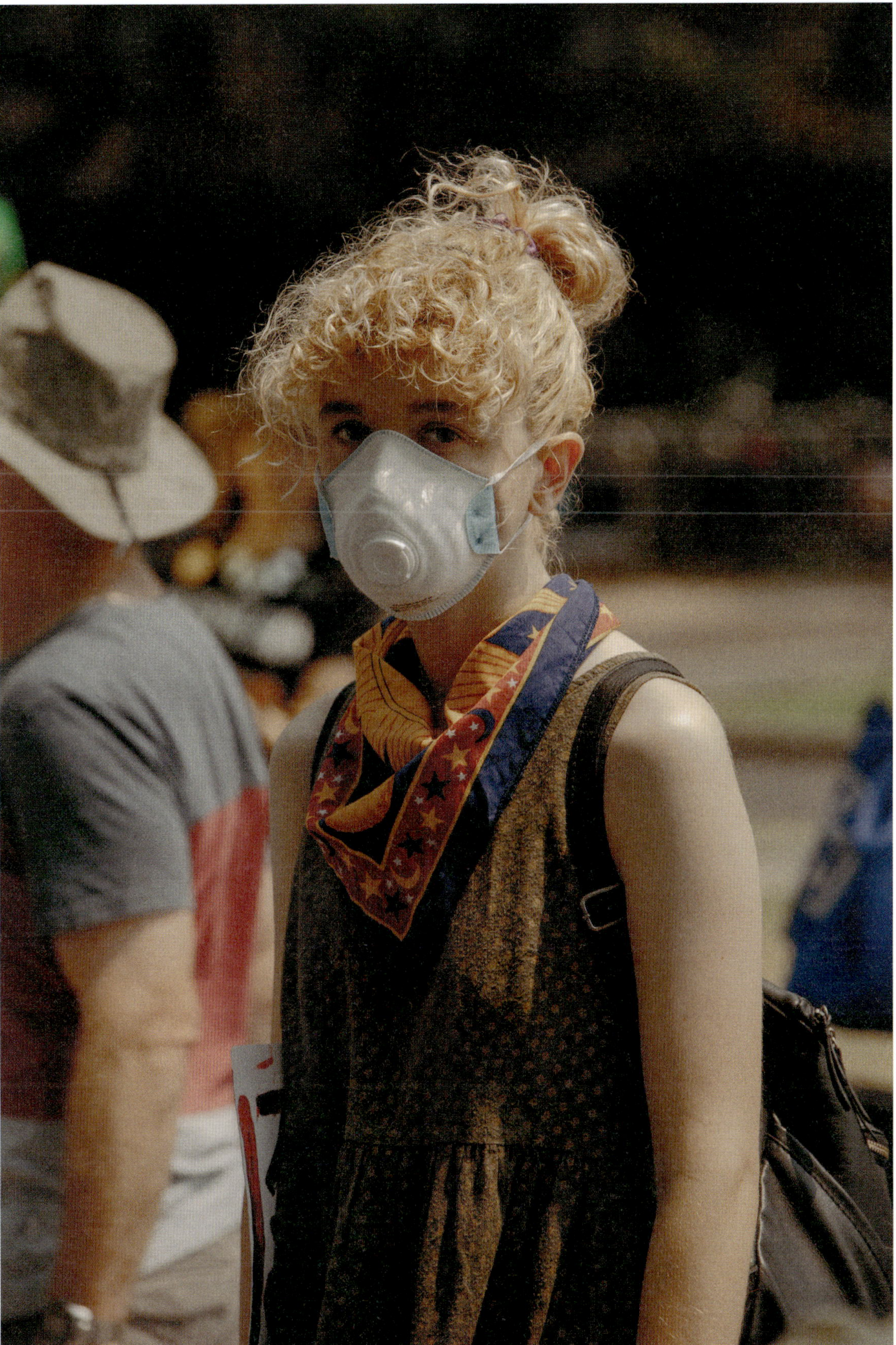

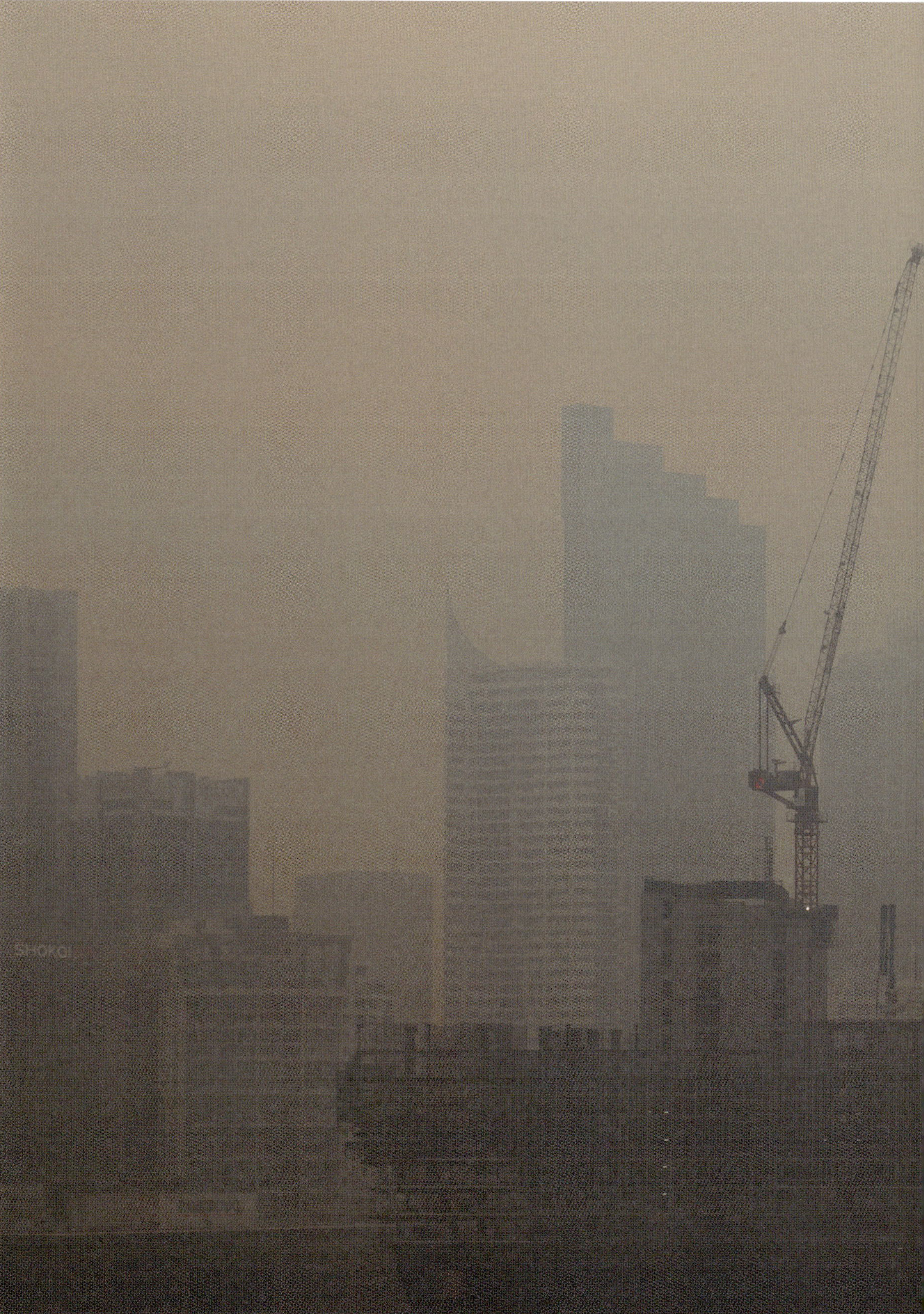

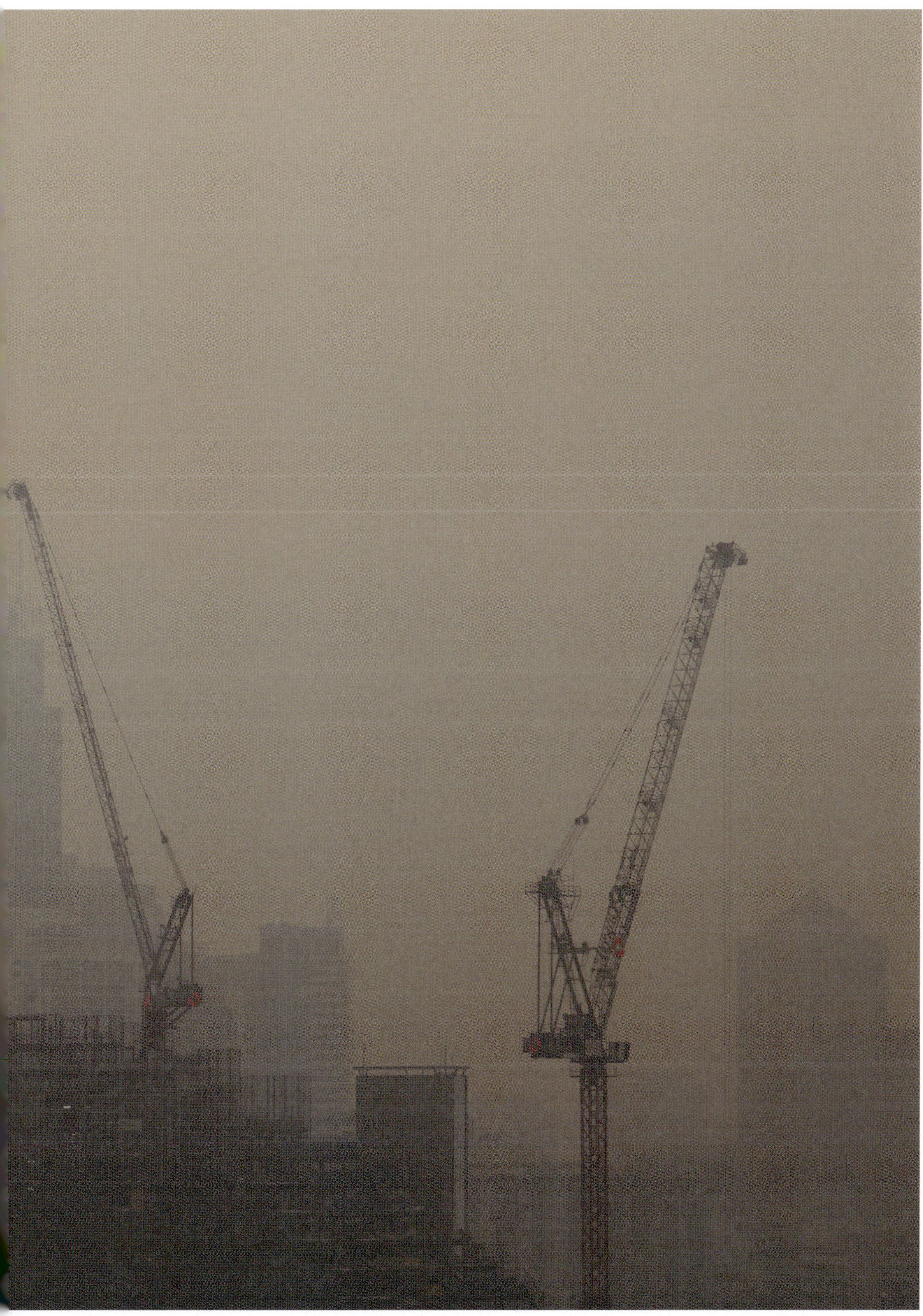

Peter McNeil

30

The 'laughing skull': Masks and political protest

The neutral mask helps them to find a stable position where they can breathe freely...
— Jacques Lecoq*1

Safety and protest masks were already omnipresent in the southern hemisphere before surgical mask-wearing was mandated by governments in response to COVID-19 in 2020 – 2021. Massive bush fires raged across eastern Australia in 2019 – 2020, burned 19 million hectares and poured toxins into the environment, causing urban as well as country residents to stay indoors or wear masks. At the same time, the former British colony of Hong Kong, returned to China in 1997, erupted into protest against the plan to allow extraditions to mainland China. Protestors attempted to evade identification and the effects of tear gas by wearing both improvised and shop-bought masks, as well as surgical masks. The wearing of all face coverings, including scarves and paint, was banned in Hong Kong in October 2019 under the 'Prohibition on Face Covering Regulation'. Around the same time, the 'masked feminists' of Chile co-opted the ski masks worn by protesters in the 70s and 80s, held mask-making 'workshops' and proposed sequinned, crocheted and embellished masks as feminine push-back against anti-mask laws. Many included safety glasses to protect the eyes from rubber bullets and tear gas. Such masks amplified the surprising effect of deliberate nudity. Protesters exposed their breasts, an assertion of the 'right to anonymity' and a push back against patriarchal rape culture. Such costumes relate to the concept of 'artivism' or 'costume as conflict'.*2

The compulsory wearing of surgical masks in many nations during the COVID pandemic is not without irony, as countries including France, Belgium, the Netherlands, Bulgaria, Austria and Denmark have in the past decade banned face coverings—such as the wearing of Muslim veils in public and in government—funded spaces like public schools. The issue is generally framed in Europe as an affront to gender equality and secular post-Enlightenment constitutions. Denmark's restrictions comprise 'any garment that hides the face in public'. As such laws were debated, many women who did not ordinarily wear veils began to wear them in protest. In Austria, where the law states that no full-face covering may be worn at any time, men have been arrested for wearing shark and rabbit costumes and foreign tourists cautioned for wearing medical masks, a common hygiene practice in many Asian countries pre-COVID.*3

Regulations concerning the covering of part or all of the face find echoes in other clothing prohibitions. Patrons are often asked to remove their caps and hats in North American restaurants, even when they are part of contemporary fashion culture. Caps are banned from being worn in Singapore banks; wearing a motorbike helmet will raise similar alarm in Australia. The reason is that the face is obscured for purposes of security. The regulation of clothing in our contemporary societies is more extensive than many people imagine, and operates without the so-called 'sumptuary laws' of the past that defined what a person could or could not wear. Sumptuary laws were legal edicts common across Eurasia that regulated the types, materials and amounts of cloth, colours, jewellery and accessories permitted to various social groups. They were little used after the seventeenth century in England and were only repealed in France following the Revolution. It was a feature of North American democracy that clothing would not be prescribed in the new republic and that the formal clothing codes of the old regime might be actively resisted: George Washington was sculpted by Houdon in 1785 – 1791/2 with the buckle missing from his waistcoat and wore plain brown, home-spun American cloth instead of the silk or velvet that might have been expected for his inauguration. The modern American ideal of clothing functioned more around notions of place-specific respectability, as it did in most settler societies.

Despite the lack of sumptuary laws in our times, clothing is more and more regulated in the west, often by stealth. In the past two decades, many POPS ('privately owned public spaces', managed by landlords and developers) have proliferated. These vary from North American gated communities to enormous shopping centres such as the 42 acres of the UK's 'Liverpool One'. Their rise is linked to increasingly draconian policing of dress. Items of clothing, particularly that worn by youth, is often connected to purported criminality and deviance by security firms, and simply banned. Prohibitions against the 'hoodie' were famously imposed at the Bluewater Shopping Centre, Kent (UK) in 2005 and became even more strongly associated with youth criminality during the UK urban rioting of 2011.[*4] Authorities saw the wearing of such clothes as a mechanism to evade identification or detection. The hoodie, often worn over a baseball cap (another prosthetic frame), not only shrouds the face of the wearer but also obscures the modern conception of dress as expressing individual identity. The word 'hoodie' now means both a garment and a wearer.

The hood has traditionally functioned as a source of protection from the weather and the elements, and it makes sense that poorer working-class youth might manage their thermo-regulation in that way. The Georgia Supreme Court ignored such clothing functions in 1990, citing a 1949 decision thus:

> public disguise is a particularly effective means of committing crimes... From the beginning of time the mask or hood has been the criminal's dress. It conceals evidence, hinders apprehension and calms the criminal's inward cowardly fear.[*5]

Masking Up

For centuries, masks have been associated with a range of actions from entertainment and leisure to protest, urban terror and lawlessness. Masked balls, relatively democratic events in which anyone might craft a costume at any price point, were one of the preferred entertainments of the nineteenth century. Also called 'fancy dress balls', they derive from the commercialised leisure of early eighteenth-century London and Paris. Revellers attended either masked in fancy dress or in a body-obscuring 'domino' cape derived from Venetian carnival. In eighteenth-century English a 'mask' might mean an artefact (covering the face), a space (the venue) or a person (those at the masquerade).

Eighteenth-century masquerades were associated with licentious behaviour, social mixing, same-sex mingling and prostitution. The author of a 1724 *Essay on Plays and Masquerades* described masquerading as 'entering into a League with the World, the Flesh, and the Devil, Nature, Passion, and Art, against Reason and Religion'.[*6] Such behaviour took place in managed spaces such as Vauxhall and Ranelagh Gardens, and therefore held a liminal charge due to the temporary suspensions of societal norms. Macaroni or ultra-fashionable men of the 1760s-80s (so just before the French Revolution) were often associated with masquerade and night-time activity.

The mask worn at masquerades indicated moral and physical detachment. Within eighteenth-century visual traditions, masks also indicated duplicity. Many masqueraders wore the dress of characters from plays and novels, emphasising the interplay between the 'real' and the fictive self. The history of cosmetics has a role to play here. Worn by women and men over the course of history, they came to be associated with Catholic and continental European courts by the eighteenth century. The effect of makeup, like court dress and the powdered wig, was to create elite human subjects with a particular approach to hygiene and means of managing the body that conformed to courtly values of deference and display.[*7] When worn by men in non-court, non-Continental settings, cosmetics took on a variety of other meanings. The primary one was

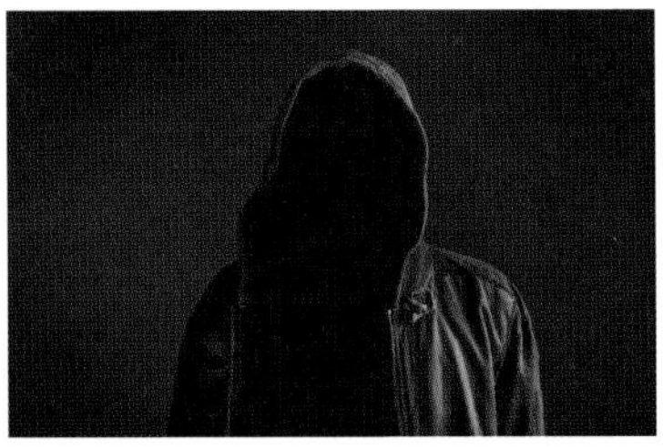

(Fig. 1)

Fig. 1. Hoodies have become the object of legislation due to their disguise potential. Getty Images, stock image.

vanity, but cosmetics also might connote fashionability, effeminacy, homosexuality, debauchery or deceit. Caricaturists often emphasised the relationship between heavy makeup that obscured the face, rendering it opaque and un-natural, and the mask, which also performed the 'work' of obscuring the 'natural' face. Thus, a made-up face became a type of mask, over which a second cloth or paper mask was commonly worn at commercial masked balls in cities such as London or Paris. Surviving costumes from the period blur the boundary between theatrical and masquerade modes. Furthermore, masks began to be painted to simulate stage make up, such as appear in the porcelain modeller Kändler's harlequin figures.[*8] Images such as *The Pantheon Macaroni* depicted proto-queer men who have turned their back on any semblance of conventional masculinity. Wrinkles around the lips indicate the attempt to mask or disguise age and the cat's head on a chair inferred the catimate or *catimatus* (kept boy or minion).

Sometimes the mask could be literally 'deadly'. Gustav III (King of Sweden 1771–1792) was shot in an assassination attempt by a masked attacker at the Royal Opera House Stockholm, midnight, on 16 March 1792, dying from his wounds nearly a fortnight later. The king was likely murdered by assassins opposed to the war with Russia and the Union of Security Act of 1789. The idea was used by Verdi in the opera *A Masked Ball* (1859). As Gustav was maligned as a 'queer' ruler at the time who liked masking and diamonds too much, the surviving relics of the assassination such as the mask worn by his assassin and the leather chair in which he was lain, heavily bleeding, take on the aura of gay relics.[*9]

Cross-dressing was common at masquerades and often connected with survival via sex-work in this period. Occupational and pleasurable cross-dressing continued across the nineteenth-century: consider the infamous London case of Stella and Fanny, as well as draggers in Melbourne, Australia. Such figures often frequented the artificial light connected with the world of theatre-going. When such men cross-dressed at fancy dress balls and masked themselves as was customary, it became difficult for authorities to pin down their purported deviance.

This rich iconography of travesty and risk travelled forward into a range of counter cultures, including the queer dress worn at clandestine, underground and later licensed entertainments and at events that began as protests or riots, such as the Sydney Gay and Lesbian Mardi Gras. Revellers at dance parties in the 1980s and 1990s borrowed from older conventions of the masque, the fancy-dress ball, and the carnival, and mirrored the carnivalesque interest in perversity and fantasy. Venetian dress was a popular mode of dress in the mid-1980s, relating to both carnival and London 'Blitz' culture at night-clubs, which was associated with Steve Strange and the New Romantics' flirtation with the dissolution of gendered sartorial codes.

Australian Brenton Heath-Kerr made a specialty of ironic, masked costumes that he wore at both the Gay Mardi Gras and to exhibition openings such as a Christian Dior show at the Powerhouse Museum. His 1992 "Tom' or Tom of Finland character was made from a photographic bromide print on flat plastic of an articulated male body in leather, which was worn over a black body stocking, with 3-dimensional knee boots and gloves, as well as a photographic penis which could be raised, and with alternative 'Tom' faces. Heath Kerr partly adopted such costumes as he was HIV positive, was aware of his thinness, and critical of the compensatory body building culture typical of many gay men in that period. His Tom figure has a relationship to the gay American Arthur Tress's *Superman Fantasy* (1977), in which the naked artist cradles a flat effigy and mask-like face of the comic character Superman, his own penis poking out from superman's underwear. I danced next to Tom in 1992 and witnessed the uncanny effect of the costume. When seen from the side it merged with the dark void of the dance floor. Heath Kerr literally 'disappeared'. Like many of his contemporaries, he died from AIDS.

The mask and the costume, therefore, takes on multifarious meanings which range from the ludic to the sinister. The relatively innocent ski mask is another garment that has taken on entirely new connotations. Since 1972, when armed Palestinians wearing balaclavas killed Israeli athletes at the Munich Olympics, it has become synonymous with global terrorism, violent robbery and assault. Rosemarie Trockel scrambled the logic of this once handknitted garment in her work *Balaclava* (1986), in which she created boxed sets of masks decorated with woven cyphers including the 'Playboy Bunny' and the Soviet hammer and sickle.*10

The mask also plays an essential social role as a cypher of uncovering distress, disenfranchisement, hypocrisy or greed. In the hands of a photographer such as Diane Arbus, wearing a mask highlights the artifice of appearances commonly explored in her work. Her masked and disabled series underscore the double invisibility of Down's-syndrome peoples locked away in a rural location, the horror of urban childhood poverty, or the dislocated emptiness of modern existence. Arbus' subjects polarise opinion: Susan Sontag famously read them as exploitative in her 1973 essay 'Freak Show'. Others argue Arbus' affinity with the contemporary social science of Erving Goffman, who argued that 'normal appearances' (the name of one of his essays published in 1971) were part of social control, both contrived and normative: 'the individual is regarded as a "set of performance masks hiding a manipulative and cynical self"'.*11 A more recent reading of Arbus' freaks note that they depict subjects 'liberated from the repressive constraints of liberal capitalism'.*12 Arbus' photography is the heir to James Ensor's *Entry of Christ into Brussels in 1889* in which Ensor based several of the people in the mainly masked crowd on those of the court of Belgian King Leopold II. He based this on a photograph of an 1886 socialist demonstration and the work has been interpreted as a work of personal bitterness towards the art world and the bankrupt hypocrisy of his contemporary society.

Masked figures stream in to Ensor's dysfunctional city 'entry', as depicted in the painting. Their sense of chaotic and violent anonymity is reminiscent of the function of the novelty fun masks used in both 1960s protest and more recent cinema concerning bank robberies. In the movie *Point Break* (1991), a group of robbers known as the 'Ex-Presidents' wear rubberised caricature masks to become Ronald Reagan, Richard Nixon, Jimmy Carter and Lyndon B. Johnson. The over-scale features underscore the treachery of their co-option from Halloween parade to bank robbery. A Nixon mask as disguise was famously worn by psychiatrist and gay rights activist John E. Fryer to make a speech at the American Psychological Association in 1972. Plaster Nixon masks were sometimes hand-made by 60s' & 70s' protesters. The 'Nixon mask' is one of the best-selling shop-bought masks today (manufactured by Cesar, France) and is generally purchased to wear at protests where the aim is to signal disaffection.

Hyper-realistic, hand-painted silicon masks created by experts in the makeup industry are now retailed for upwards of $US1000. Such masks mould realistically to the neck and face and can obscure even race. The use of one such mask in Ohio in 2010 saw people of colour arrested instead of the white male bank robber who disguised himself as a person of colour.*13 A young man disguised himself as the 'Geezer' bandit for a series of robberies, and a 20-year-old Chinese man seeking asylum at an airport slipped past security disguised as an elderly white man.*14

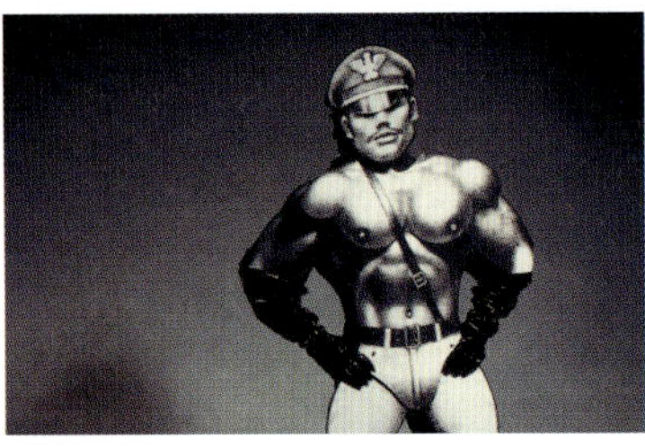

(Fig. 2)

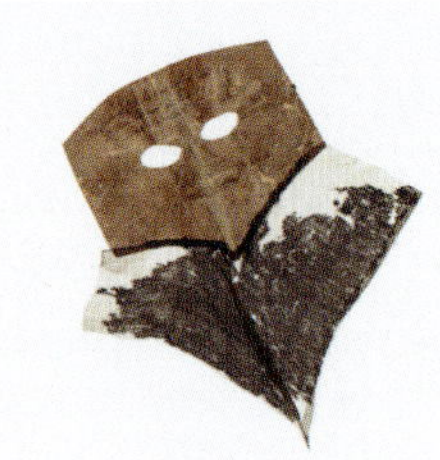

(Fig. 3)

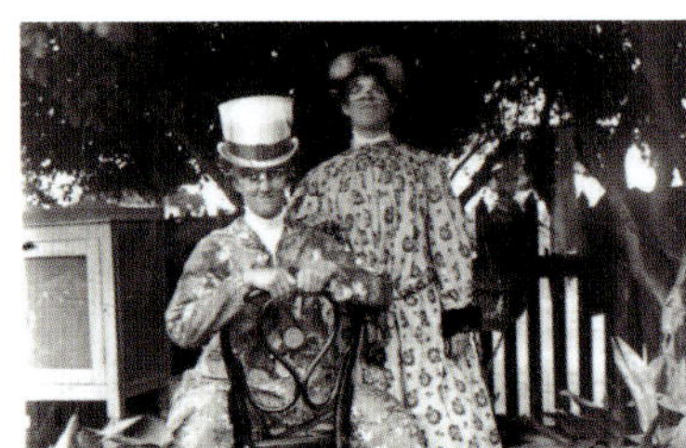

(Fig. 4)

Fig. 2. *Tom*, photo by Brenton Heath-Kerr, from the MAAS Collection (Sydney, 1992).

Fig. 3. Face mask of pressed and pleated waxed linen; lower section black Japanese silk to resemble a black beard, purchased from a Stockholm hatmaker. Used by J. J. Ankarström during the assassination of Gustav III at midnight 16-17 March 1792. Photo by Helena Bonnevier, Royal Armoury Stockholm/ Livrustkammaren/SHM (CC BY).

Fig. 4. Unidentified Australian people (men or women?), wearing masks and possibly Indian cloth in a garden setting, likely attending a fancy dress ball (figure with the top hat and trousers, possibly a cross dressed woman although both figures are ambiguous), late nineteenth century.

The wearing of the same mask by many amplifies the ludic structuring of an event: I remember the power of wearing the 'Rev. Fred Nile horror mask' on 2 October 1989. Along with hundreds of others I protested against this politician's 'Cleansing March', which comprised a group of moral conservatives who marched the streets of the gay district of Darlinghurst (Sydney) to protest purported queer sinfulness. The Christian crusaders were met at a prominent crossroads (Taylor Square) by masked gay and lesbian protesters. Public protest was aided by deliberate strategies of dress in which the disparate bodies of protesters, male, female and trans, young or old, were unified by a sea of masks. This tactic was possibly derived from the strategies of ACT UP's (AIDS crisis activists) New York chapter. ACT UP's membership included skilled figures from advertising and design who transferred their approach to create unified and stylish T shirts, posters and banners. The effect of their design was to create optimum impact for ACT UP's protests in the news media and had the secondary impact of creating new gay identities 'and a new aesthetic as a mode of identification'.*15 The Nile masks came in several colours such as green or pink and we were dispatched to different parts of the street to greet Nile in unison. The Christians chanted 'What's so gay about AIDS?' to which the counter-demonstrators responded with 'Repent, Relent, Re-decorate!'.*16

The 'Guy Fawkes' (a figure who planned to blow up English parliament in the seventeenth century) mask was created by illustrator David Floyd in the early 1980s. It has been popularised within popular culture via the 2005 film *V for Vendetta* and internet memes, and much adopted by anti-establishment groups of various stripes—from vegans through to protestors against the Church of Scientology and the 'Free Julian Assange' movement (Assange wore such a mask himself). Notably used by Bahrainis during the Arab Spring (2013), the mask was subsequently banned by the United Arabs Emirates. The mask has also been deployed in protests in settings as different as Thailand, Turkey, Brazil, Egypt and France. The Fawkes mask was much used during the 6 January 2020 storming of the US Capitol. Ironically, something often deployed by the Left supports capitalism: the mask is copyrighted to conglomerate Time Warner, which earns profits from the tens of thousands sold on Amazon each year.

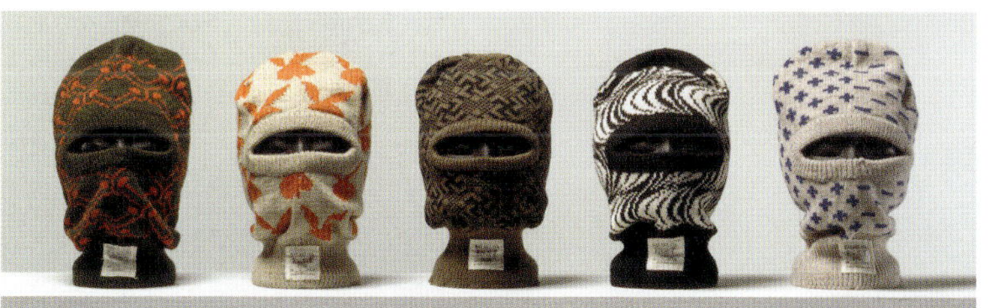

(Fig. 5)

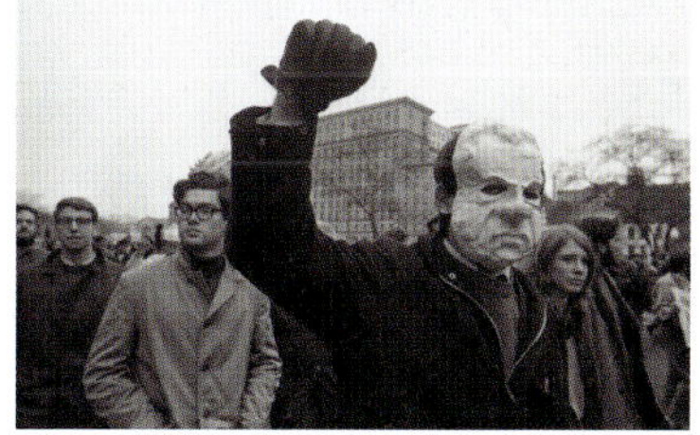

(Fig. 6)

Fig. 5. *Balaklava*, by, Rosemarie Trockel, 1986. Image courtesy of bpk Berlin / Hamburger Kunsthalle / Christoph Irrgang.

Fig. 6. Anti-Vietnam War protester in a papier mâché Nixon mask, raising his fist, during the counter-inaugural demonstrations opposing the war in Vietnam and inauguration of Richard Nixon as President, organized primarily by the National Mobilization Committee to End the War in Vietnam. Photo by Rowland Scherman, U Mass Amherst Collection (1969).

Debating the mask

The United States of America has a mosaic of state based anti-mask laws which legal experts believe all violate the United States Constitution. Therefore anti-mask laws are much debated in the USA. Such laws are generally proposed under the general premise of crime prevention, but their effects are much wider. This is because they likely breach the First Amendment and the right to 'expressive conduct'. It can easily be argued that mask wearing serves an 'expressive function' as they enable speakers who might require anonymity in order to speak openly and to avoid subsequent discrimination.*17

The banning of masks in the USA has a long back story. Masks were banned in connection with mid-nineteenth century east coast farmer/tenant landlord disputes (when leather masks were worn by farmers), and in some jurisdictions to address the masks and hoods of the Klu Klux Klan. Some parts of the USA have prohibitions against the wearing of women's clothes and wigs by men as pertaining to deception; in New South Wales arrest for cross-dressing was related to the charge of 'public nuisance'. The city of Pineville (USA) argued for the upholding of anti-mask laws in 1927 thus:

> If every one [sic] is permitted to go disguised up in the streets of a city or town, the innocent and unwary may fall easy victims to the criminal and vicious, and peace officers be powerless to afford protection ...*18

Similar arguments were made for the compulsory use of number plates on cars: 'fear or discovery and punishment will lead the ... driver to observe the requirements ...'*19 This sounds very much like the world described in Batman's Gotham, which I will expand on later.

Challenges to anti-mask laws in the USA revolve around direct violation or inhibition of the First Amendment in terms of the ability to convey a message through expressive conduct, as anonymity reduces the 'risk of physical, economic and social reprisals' when a person delivers a speech or message that might render them unsafe or lose their job.*20 The act of mask wearing finds a theoretical frame in some of this legal argument: a 1969 case argued that mask wearing was not 'expressive conduct' but akin to 'pure speech', the latter term applying to arm-bands.*21 Both sides of the abortion debate have worn masks—surgical in the case of pro-choice, and others, such as skeleton ones in the case of pro life. Several state laws that prohibit masks exempt parades, but only where they satisfy educational, religious or historical tests. The complexity of these legal arguments includes jurisdictions that uphold the wearing of masks to make a political point when it is clear the wearer is not attempting to conceal their identity. Exemptions are also often made for sporting masks such as hockey, football or snorkelling.

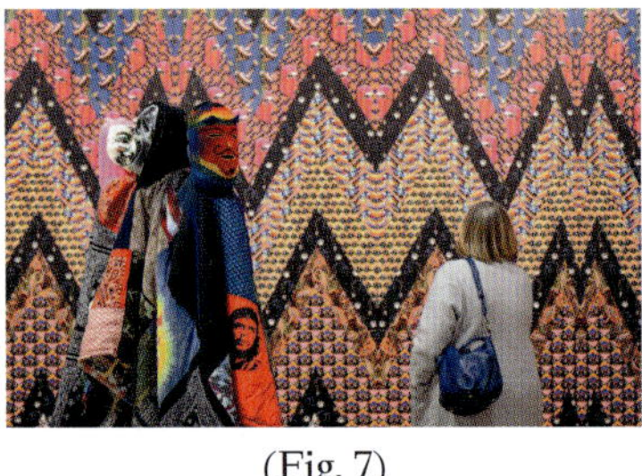
(Fig. 7)

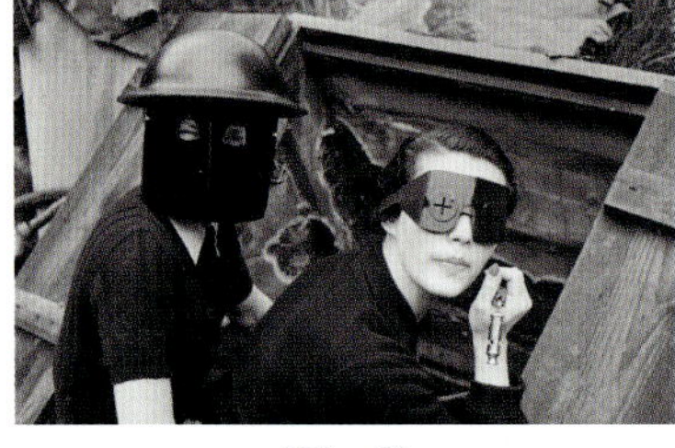
(Fig. 8)

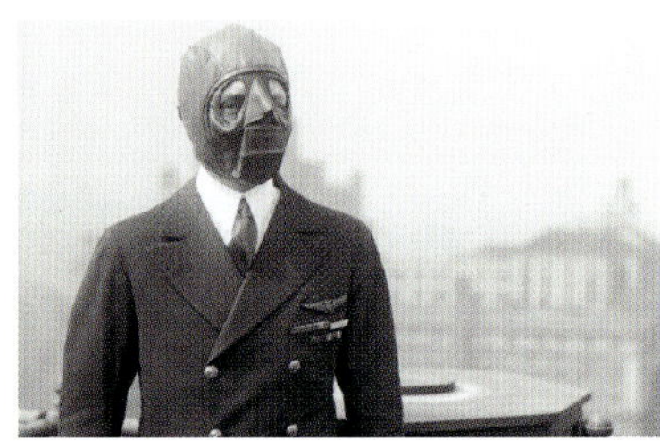
(Fig. 9)

Fig. 7. *Iconography of Revolt*, exhibition 28 July to 18 Nov 2018 at City Gallery Wellington, New Zealand. Piece pictured by Jemima Wyman.

Fig. 8. *Fire Masks, Downshire Hill, London, England, 1941* by Lee Miller © Lee Miller Archives

Fig. 9. Commander Richard Byrd, wearing a specially designed leather helmet and mask, used during his flight from Spitzbergen over the North Pole and back. Commander Byrd and Pilot Floyd Bennett used a Fokker Plane, making the trip of 1360 miles in little more than 15 hours, May 10, 1926. Getty Images (1926).

Masks also provide occupational protections. War-time Britain saw the welding masks worn by women new to the factories turned into stylish quasi-surrealist gestures by photographer Lee Miller. Miller's photography was coincidental with the surrealist practice of women artists such as Leonor Fini and Eileen Agar, who often made use of the mask and the proto-concept of the 'female masquerade' (Joan Riviere) in their visual practice.

'Disguise with intent'

Many European countries have laws against any mask or clothing that obstructs identification: these include Italy, Norway, Spain, many cantons of Switzerland, Ukraine and Sweden. In the United Kingdom, the 'Black Act' banned covering or blacking the face, with a possible penalty of death, until it its repeal in 1823. The wearing of masks during a riot or unlawful assembly has been banned in Canada since the G20 protests of 2011 and carries a maximum five-year sentence.*22 Australia is one of the few advanced economies that does not ban the wearing of masks, although in New South Wales a woman cannot give evidence in a niqab.

Mask, body & gesture as protest

The USA constitutional framing of the 'expressive' gesture connected to Free Speech finds an adjacent corollary in post-war acting technique. Jacques Lecoq was a French stage actor and acting movement coach best known for his work with physical movement and mime. He taught at his own theatre school from 1956 to his death in 1999. Lecoq brought together strands of performative thinking from domains including sport and the *commedia dell'arte*. His work popularised the idea of the 'neutral mask' within acting pedagogy. The first neutral masks were based on medieval and Renaissance Italian theatre and made of leather by Amleto Sartori. Originally Caucasian-centric in their design, they now have corollaries in 'Afro-neutral' masks and are frequently crafted by actors themselves in a range of materials. Lecoq intended the neutral mask to perform particular resting-state work for the actor and, as the opening epigram here notes, 'to find a stable position where they can breathe freely'. By this Lecoq meant a position of expressive neutrality prior to the work of acting. This desire finds an unexpected corollary in the contemporary function of masks to protect against pollution or toxins in the atmosphere, as well as to disguise, which ensures a degree of safety.

Lecoq had made careful studies of a range of theatrical traditions including the *Bouffons* (theatre steeped in the non-classical effects of the grotesque and parody). During the 1968 Paris student riots, Lecoq's school was one of the only to stay open: 'while the student movement exploded onto the streets, we were exploding the traditions of gesture and text in search of a new language and new meanings'. Lecoq was subsequently invited to join the École nationale supérieure des Beaux-Arts where he taught a form of somatic architecture. 'I began my research into built environments and adapted my movement teaching for the training of architects.'[*23]

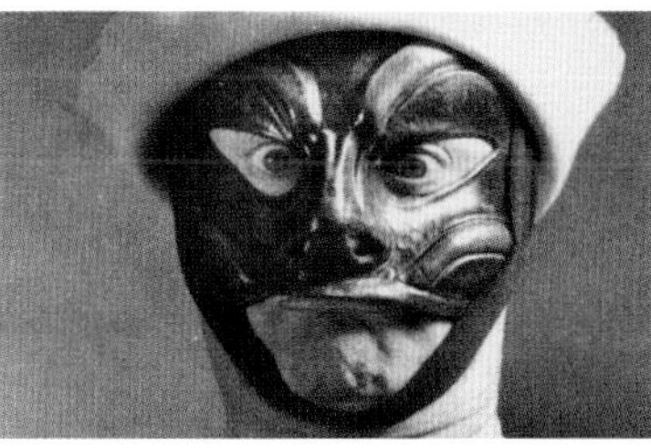

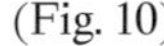

(Fig. 10)

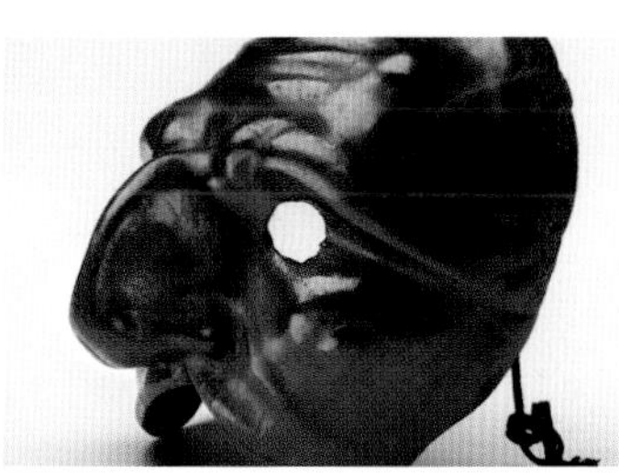

(Fig. 11)

Fig. 10. Leather Harlequin Mask by Amleto Sartori from Wikipedia commons (Commedia dell'arte; Italy, 1915).

Fig. 11. Commedia Dell' Arte Mask: Arlecchino or Harlequin (currently catalogued as Pulcinella), moulded leather, Italy, 1700–25. Museum no. W.60-1929 © Victoria and Albert Museum, London. Donatella Barbieri notes the importance of its form during performance: being 'angled in different directions', the mask is explicitly designed to drive 'the movement of the character through the performance space'.

Lecoq sees the mask as an active agent rather than passive receptacle. In this regard, his thinking is Althusserian and prefigures Actor-network theory and the speculations of Bruno Latour concerning objecthood. The neutral mask is the primary mask or inner experience from which all other masks can then be activated: 'This object, when placed on the face, should enable one to experience the state of neutrality prior to action'.[*24] These include counter-masks (in which the opposite is inferred), expressive masks (tending to have stylised features to indicate a particular character), larval masks (featureless masks used in Basel carnival), *noh* masks (Japanese masks in which the slightest tilt can change the appearance of the actor) and utilitarian masks (sport, occupations). To Lecoq a mask is not simply any covering: his neutral mask must be slightly larger than the face and there must be space between the face and the device.[*25] The neutral mask, he remarked, is not the same as the white mask commonly used in carnival, which often represents death. Actor's masks must be larger than life and therefore are not concerned with verisimilitude.*26

The 'laughing skull'

Audiences, many of whom grew up with Cesar Romero's chilling version of the Joker in the TV series *Batman* (1966), have been transfixed in recent years by the new cinema renderings of the character. Yet the Joker, a sadistic robber who used laughing gas on his victims, was almost written out of the Marvel comic at one time. The Joker was created in 1940 by Bob Kane, Bill Finger and artist Jerry Robinson. The character was a psychopathic murderer in early iterations; later a violent thief. His biography asserted that a chemical accident had burned his face, leaving a permanent scarred smile, white face and green hair. His look was based on a study of playing card and knowledge of the 1928 silent film *The Man Who Laughs*, which in turn was based on a Victor Hugo novel of that name *(L'Homme qui rit*, 1888). The Victor Hugo novel was much more horrific than the early film version, as the character Gwynplaine had been a victim of botched surgery and therefore carried a carved, permanent grin:

> It was by laughing that Gwynplaine provoked laughter. And yet, he did not laugh. His face laughed, not his thought. [...] It was an automatic laugh, and all the more irresistible because it was petrified. No one could withstand that gaping. Two convulsions of the mouth are infectious, a laugh and a yawn.*27

Jürgens argues that the iconography of the Joker also stems from a nineteenth century French tradition of the violent pantomime clown, a 'neo-modern circus creature'. He also has roots also in Baudelaire's *comique absolu*, Bergsonian laughter, and Charcot's concepts of hysteria. Charcot called the 'deuxième période de l'hystéro-épilepsie' [second period of the hystero-epilepsy] with its convulsions 'clownisme'. Hugo's Gwynplaine therefore resembled both a human clown and a death mask:

> He is 'plutôt une création de l'art qu'une œuvre de la nature' ['rather a creation of art than a work of nature'] and a kind of **laughing skull** [my emphasis] at the same time.*28

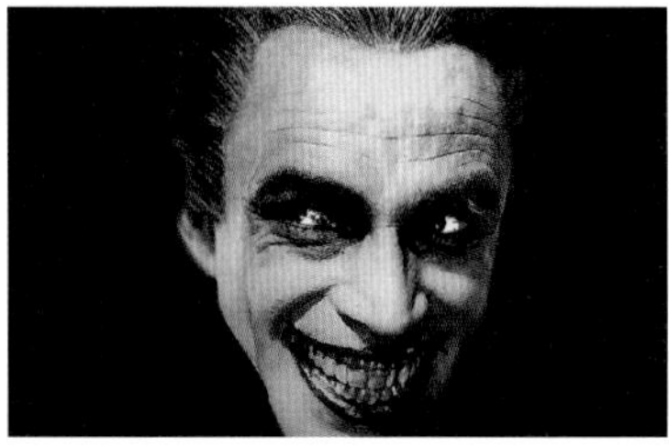

(Fig. 12)

Fig. 12. Conrad Veidt As Gwynplaine in The Man Who Laughs #3, Fine Art America (1928). Image by David Lee Guss.

These literary references informed the subsequent iconography of Batman's Joker, as seen in Paul Leni's 1928 film starring Conrad Veidt. The gaping mouth and glowing eyes underlined with broad-stroke makeup have a strong relationship to the contemporary Guy Fawkes mask.*29

Making Up

Much of the power of the horror in the cinematic renderings of the Joker in recent years is generated by the slippage between the makeup which disguises his horrific face and a mask he sometimes dons for a second layer of disguise. *The Dark Knight* (2008) clown robbery scene includes one such horrific example of the Joker's clown mask over an already grotesque, painted face.*30 Here the Joker undoes the assertion by Le Coq, who called the clown's red nose the smallest mask in history: 'It inspires no fear, which is why children like it'.*31 Much of the power of the recent Jokers therefore concerns going far beyond the expectations of *The Comics Code* (USA, 1954), which was designed to address the claim that comics glorify crime. The code commenced with 'Crimes shall never be presented in such a way as to create sympathy for the criminal' and included the statement 'All characters shall be depicted in dress reasonably acceptable to society'.*32 The appearance of the Joker in the most recent iteration of Batman is all about how his unacceptable face, body, dress, subjectivity and conduct place him outside hope of rehabilitation or social contract.

Here I return to the topic of this essay, the mask. The word 'mask' comes from the Arabic, *maskharat*, meaning 'clown'. Masks and makeup have been associated with deception in many cultures, from Bali to Japan. The clown's 'archaic-mythical origins issue from Indian cultures, antique gods and the *Commedia dell'Arte'* and occur in most cultures.*33 The specific violence of the clown type evoked here derives from a Pierrot mimed by Gaspard Debureau in the Théâtre des Funambules between 1819 and 1846. This in turn recalls imagery by the artist Daumier in which King Louis Philippe, dressed as a grotesque clown, stands in a box above his errant parliamentarians, and calls out in reference to Rabelais, 'Draw the curtain, the farce is ended'.

In our own time clown imagery and the grotesque have been deployed in organised protest that aims to call out the 'farce' of the G8 and other heavily politicised events. CIRCA (Clandestine Rebel Insurgent Clown Army) have declared 'The War on Error' and formed a Rebel clown army: 'we are an army because we live on a planet in permanent war ... we are an army because a war that gorges itself on death and blood and shits money and toxins, deserves an obscene body of deviant soldiers'.*34

Conclusion
Costume into Fashion

In recent years a blurring between the categories of dress, costume for performance and fashion is much in evidence. The wearing of surgical facemasks has been normalised in fashion practice with examples ranging from pop-art inspired Japanese mouth coverings to indigenous Australian motifs launched at fashion weeks. The makeup artist Hungry blurs the distinction between facial skin and mask via makeup and prosthetics.*35 Bjork wears a series of digital masks by James Merry in Losss.*36

'Dazzle' makeup to deter facial recognition systems has been developed, although it is generally recognised that 'scraping' images will likely reveal the identity: 'You can just wear a mask now, it's much easier' remarks a protagonist.*37 A Chinese facial recognition vendor states that their technology can now identify people in masks or bandanas.

The mask, then, might be object, action or person. It might deform the human form while at the same time exposing truths. It refers to nature but is at the same time profoundly anti-natural. The mask is a paradox: it both amplifies and conceals. In obscuring the premise of the face, it is widely understood as deviant. We cannot read the lips or understand the emotions. The eyes must do that work, and sometimes they, too, are obscured. In the era of COVID-19 we have normalised mask wearing as social good rather than social dread, state directive rather than summary offence. As more nation states deploy facial

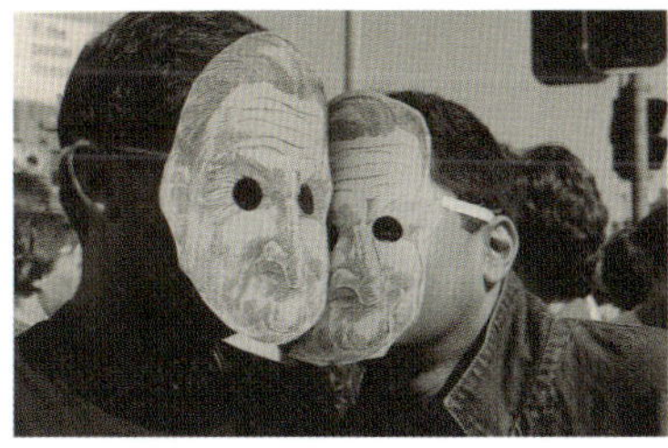

(Fig. 13)

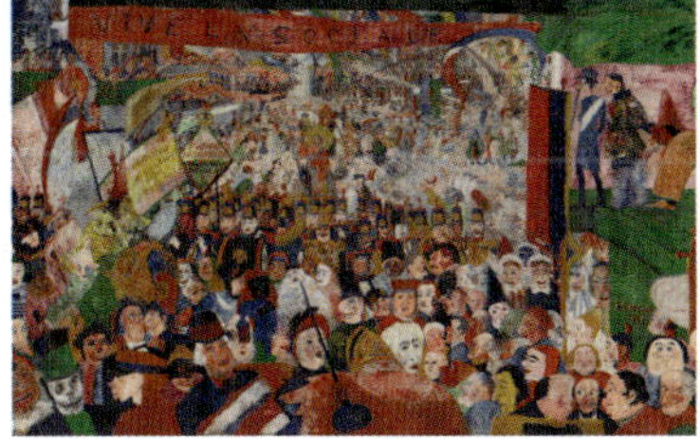

(Fig. 14)

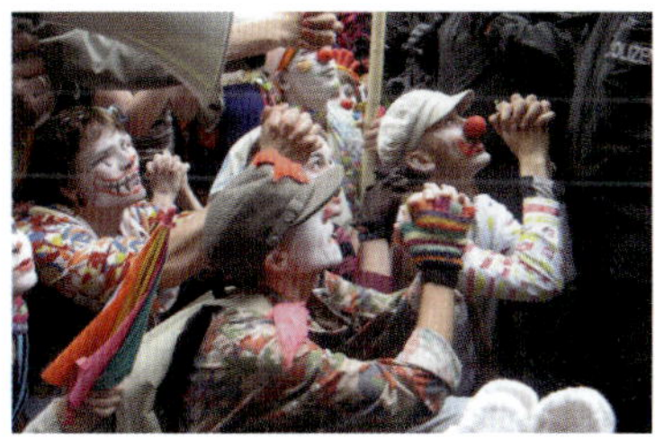

(Fig. 15)

Fig. 13. *Rev. Fred Nile horror mask* (Sydney, 1989). Photograph courtesy of Australian Queer Archives (AQuA).

Fig. 14. *Christ's Entry into Brussels in 1889.* Image by James Ensor (1888, o/c, 252.7 × 430.5 cm, Getty Museum).

Fig. 15. *CIRCA (Clandestine Rebel Insurgent Clown Army).* Photographer unknown (London, 2003).

recognition technologies, ban face coverings in order to tame citizens, and yet insist on surgical coverings during the pandemic, we see the ongoing transformation around masking played out across social, cultural and political registers.

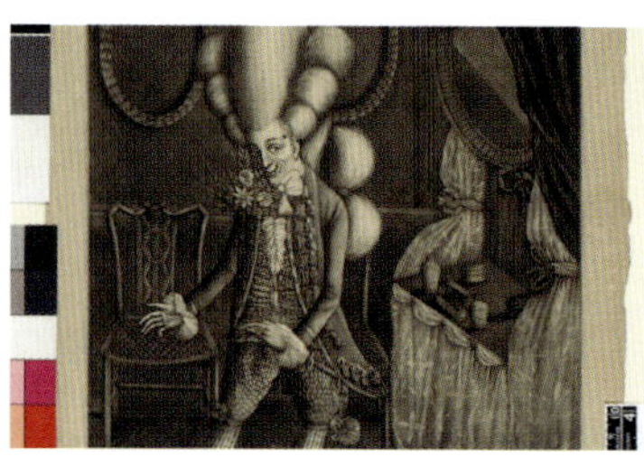

(Fig. 16)

Fig. 16. Philip Dawe (printmaker), *Pantheon Macaroni*, a differently titled version of *The Macaroni. A real character at the late Masquerade / Philip Dawe fecit.* [London:] Printed for John Bowles, at No. 13 in Cornhill, published as the Act directs July 3d 1773. Mezzotint, 351 × 250 mm.

Peter McNeil
The 'laughing skull':
Masks and political protest
* **footnotes & references**

*1 Peter Lecoq, *The Moving Body (Le Corps Poétique): Teaching Creative Theatre* (London: Bloomsbury, 2020): 39.

*2 *Artivism* is the concept of Slovenian theatre theoretician Aldo Milohnić. See Mateja Fajt, "Costume of Conflict," in Sofia Pantouvaki and Peter McNeil (eds), *Performance Costume: New Perspectives and Methods* (London: Bloomsbury, 2021), 361-376.

*3 Sigal Samuel, "Banning Muslim Veils Tends to Backfire—Why Do Countries Keep Doing It?" *The Atlantic*, August 4, 2018, https://www.theatlantic.com/international/archive/2018/08/denmark-burqa-veil-ban/566630/.

*4 Jo Turney (ed.), *Fashion Crimes: Dressing for Deviance* (London: Bloomsbury, 2019).

*5 Stephen J. Simoni. "Who Goes There—Proposing A Model Anti-Mask Act," *Fordham Law Review* 61 (1992): 254.

*6 Terry Castle, *Masquerade and Civilization: The Carnivalesque in Eighteenth-Century English Culture and Fiction* (Stanford University Press, 1986); Peter McNeil, *Fashion Victims: Macaroni Men and the Eighteenth-Century Fashion World* (New Haven: Yale University Press, 2018).

*7 This concept derives from the writings of the French cultural historian Georges Vigarello.

*8 Meredith Chilton, *Harlequin Unmasked: The Commedia dell'Arte and Porcelain Sculpture* (George R. Gardiner Museum of Ceramic Art and Yale University Press, 2001), 43.

*9 Peter McNeil, "Crafting Queer Spaces: privacy and posturing" in A. Myzelev, & J. Potvin (eds.), *Fashion, Interior Design and the Contours of Modern Identity* (Hampshire: Ashgate, 2010), 19-41.

*10 I saw these displayed at the exhibition *Iconography of Revolt*, curated by Robert Leonard, Wellington City Gallery, 2018. Leonard argued persuasively that the theatre and garments of protest and terrorism had become part of the wider visual and contemporary fashion system.

*11 Eamonn Carrabbine, "Unsettling Appearances: Diane Arbus, Erving Goffman and the Sociological Eye," *Current Sociology* 67, no. 5 (2019) —online, unpaginated version.

*12 Robin Blyn, *The Freak-Garde: Extraordinary Bodies and Revolutionary Art in America* (Minneapolis: University of Minnesota Press, 2013), 166.

*13 Sharon Bernstein, "Masks so Realistic They're Arresting the Wrong Guy," *Los Angeles Times,* December 8, 2010, https://www.latimes.com/archives/la-xpm-2010-dec-08-la-fi-mask-20101209-story.html.

*14 See note 12.

*15 Sarah Schulman, *Let the Record Show: A Political History of ACT UP New York, 1987-1993* (New York: Farrer, Straus and Giroux, 2021), 318.

*16 Colin Clews, "1989. Politics: Evangelist attempts 'Cleansing March' on Sydney's Queer Heartland," Gay in the 80s, December 22, 2014, http://www.gayinthe80s.com/2014/12/1989-politics-evangelist-attempts-cleansing-march-on-sydneys-queer-heartland/.

*17 Simoni, "Who Goes There—Proposing A Model Anti-Mask Act," *Fordham Law Review* 61 (1992): 273.

*18 Stephen J. Simoni. "Who Goes There," 249.

*19 *Ibid.*

*20 Simoni, "Who Goes There," 245.

*21 *Ibid.*

*22 Bill C-309, Concealment of Identity Act, 2013, Canada, https://www.parl.ca/LegisInfo/BillDetails.aspx?Language=e&Mode=1&billId=5136691.

*23 Jacques Lecoq, Simon McBurney, and David Bradby, *The Moving Body (le Corps Poétique): Teaching Creative Theatre* (London: Bloomsbury, 2020), 11.

*24 Ibid.

*25 Lecoq, *The Moving Body,* 38.

*26 Lecoq, *The Moving Body,* 38.

*27 Victor Hugo, *L'Homme qui rit,* cited in *Batman's Joker,* n.p.

*28 A-S. Jürgens, "Batman's Joker, a Neo-Modern Clown of Violence," *Journal of Graphic Novels and Comics* 5, no. 4 (2014): 441-454.

*29 The Joker had no understandable motives for his crimes in earlier iterations of the character and was therefore the index of evil compared to other Batman characters. The recent film *Joker* (2019) starring Joaquin Phoenix as the Joker explained a motive for the first time.

*30 Christopher Nolan et al., *The Dark Knight* (United States: Warner Bros, 2008).

*31 Jacques Lecoq, *Theatre of movement and gesture* (Routledge, 2006).

*32 The Comics Code of 1954, adopted 26 October 1954, Code of The Comics Magazine Association Of America, http://cbldf.org/the-comics-code-of-1954/.

*33 Lars van Amerongen-Kruisselbrink, 'The Psychological Complexity of Batman,' (unpublished Masters dissertation, University of Agder, 2020).

*34 Paul Routledge, 'Reflections on the G8 Protests: An Interview with the General Unrest of the Clandestine Insurgent Rebel Clown Army,'ACME: *An International Journal for Critical Geographies* 3, no. 2 (2004): 113.

*35 Vogue, "Inside Hungry's Extreme Beauty Routine," YouTube, February 25, 2020, https://www.youtube.com/watch?v=x4F_7SjE7Gc.

*36 Martin Guttridge-Hewitt, "Björk Shares New Video For 'Losss': Watch," DJ Magazine, August 7, 2019, https://djmag.com/news/björk-shares-new-video-losss-watch.

*37 Amrita Khalid, "'Dazzle' Makeup Won't Trick Facial Recognition. Here's What Experts Say Will," Digital Trends, June 5, 2020, https://www.digitaltrends.com/news/cv-dazzle-makeup-facial-recognition-protests/.

Hélène Frichot

An Airborne Toxic Event (Mask Wearing Recommended)

When I opened my eyes yesterday,
I saw the sky in total revulsion.
— Frantz Fanon [*1]

Humming like TV static, emulating cathode-tube-projections as though on a phosphorescent screen, an airborne toxic event blossoms over the skies of the College-on-the-Hill. [*2] The environmental event emits a dull, sickly pulse, producing its own atmospheric affects as it contaminates the local townspeople. Likely symptoms include nausea, skin irritation, sweaty palms. But are the symptoms real, or do the symptoms emerge following the power of suggestion? The public no longer trusts experts the way they once did; the media proves to be increasingly unreliable. Does the event take place, or is it a figment of a town's collective imagining? It really depends on your news source. Is the toxic cloud a kind of hysterical object projected across the skies? Could this be the expression of an atmospheric simulacrum, where all essences and appearances are collapsed into one miasmic surface of swarming sense? Are you, too, spending too much time plugged into your online TV streaming service?

Don DeLillo's novel *White Noise*, an exemplary piece of postmodern literature, is famous for its depiction of an 'airborne toxic event' spreading across the skies of an American mid-western university town, home to the College-on-the-Hill. The acrid cloud, a hybrid form, is said to be the result of an industrial accident mixed with local weather conditions. Overwhelmed by this life-threatening poisoning of the local air, the townspeople form, albeit briefly, an unintentional community. For a time, they share the same specific concerns, and much the same symptoms, as they are all facing the intrusion of a nature-culture disruption to their normal state of affairs—what Isabelle Stengers calls the intrusion of Gaia, and what Bruno Latour describes as a stand-off, a confrontation, whereby humans find themselves facing off with Gaia. [*3]

The main protagonist is a professor and the Chair of Hitler Studies, a knowledge domain he has himself invented, and in which the university Chancellor has recognised strategic value. The Chair of Hitler Studies hides behind a mask that performs the authority of his expertise: 'I am a false character that follows the name around.' It becomes clear that the production of an academic persona is a marketing exercise. The professor is taking German lessons on the sly, anxiously awaiting the arrival of a German delegation impressed by his research, which may or may not be based on reliable methods. A fascination with Hitler is equally a fascination with National Socialism and its mesmerising propaganda effects, which create their own intoxicating political atmosphere. What is of interest to us here and will be explored in this essay is how environmental and political atmospheres are combined, creating toxic admixtures as well as forming communities of survival that perform with the benefit of different identitarian masks

Reading DeLillo soon after the publication of *White Noise*, Jayne Ann Philips suggests that 'Group identity is a "white noise" in itself, the white noise of history'. [*4] She goes on to explain that 'DeLillo has dealt not so much with character as with culture, survival and the subtle, ever-increasing interdependence between the self and the national and world community'. [*5] Atmospheres and their 'affects' combine both environmental conditions as well as political ones, drawing attention to the sway of emotions and to mood swings which 'affect' a body politic in so far as they are enabled or incapacitated. [*6] Environmental and political challenges unsettle psychic life and disrupt the social habits and performances of everyday life, creating tensions and even contradictions, and producing what can be called a cognitive dissonance. These days the kind of cognitive dissonance suffered by DeLillo's professor and his blended family, inside the comfortable surrounds of their white middle class bubble, has become even more acute in the face of environmental collapse mixed with the fervent rise of populism and the far right, and the accompanying divisions that have torn societies apart.

We see this cognitive dissonance, this combination of environmental and political upheaval impacting our lives, in the rise of Trump and his enduring hold over an American voter base who could be led to believe in anything, who would happily argue for a political state of affairs likely to result, paradoxically, in their own lives becoming less liveable. These are the avid followers of a political cause, who stridently insist on not wearing a mask when faced with a pandemic, despite the recommendations of medical experts.

This essay reflects on the relationship between masks and the political communities the mask connects us to, sometimes helping us to 'pass' for the purposes of survival. 'Passing' is a queer and performative concept describing how we perform an identity to 'pass' as white, as male, as an identity not ascribed to us at birth. This passing might be undertaken for critical and polemical purposes or to survive within oppressive socio-political circumstances. The mask can help us to pass and functions in diverse ways: to save you from possible death; to release you from conventional behaviours at Carnevale; to designate religious observance; to celebrate at a children's party; to disguise a masked bandit; to express dissent as a member of the Extinction Rebellion.

There is the question of the mask in its relation to community itself, and what void or emptiness community circulates around when it has no shared project nor any transcendent goal, except perhaps, for the basics of planetary survival. Today, as Leslie Hill remarks, raising the concept of community raises more questions than answers. It is a formulation that stands too readily as an 'all purpose vehicle for the thwarted yearnings and seductive compensations of its own history'.[*7] Community values turn out to be more contradictory than ever, swaying between a fascist expression of communion and the radical impossibility of working together, even for the benefit of our own survival. Hill issues an injunction to 'think again, think anew, think otherwise'[*8] or as Stengers and Despret put it, 'think we must!'[*9] because the challenges of living together have become even more acute. Our lives do depend on it, irrespective of what mask you choose to don.

In what follows, one mask after the other will be removed, or else secured in place to maintain a disguise or protect a life. Each mask will point toward a socio-political context increasingly entangled with environmental concerns. At the conjunction of mask, community, and environmental atmospheres might we find liberation from prescribed subjective identity, or even an invitation for the construction of new relations and affects? Could the construction of new relations enable the creation of a greater composition, a social construct with a revived politics of the multitude? Or are we going to end up with, as in the case of the Chair of Hitler studies, another marketing campaign?

...

If the professor's mask is denominated Mask One and speaks to the professional disguises we use to put on a good performance, Mask Two, presented in what follows, applies to those that protect us from deleterious environmental conditions. The mask —a gas mask, a medical mask, a deep-sea diver's bell, an astronaut's outfit (though perhaps these last two would be better defined as full-body protective gear)—is used to save us from imminent environmental harm, speaking directly to the mortal need to defend ourselves from life-impairing circumstances.

The polemical cultural theorist Peter Sloterdijk dates the emergence of the concept of the environment as 22 April 1915 when a German gas regiment launched an operation in the trenches of Ypres Salient.[*10] Concomitant with this event, he argues, a novel theory of the environment abruptly presented itself. Chlorine gas was discharged into the air, the result of which was a profound shift in the conceptualisation of what counted as a target for attack. Sloterdijk explains that a cloud 6 kilometres wide and 600 to 900 metres deep billowed across the French positions following favourable winds. Presumably, the French had no protective gas masks at the ready. In his inimitably imperious manner, Sloterdijk announces: 'The 20th century will be remembered as the age whose essential thought consisted in targeting no longer the body, but the enemy's environment'.[*11] This, Sloterdijk adds, is the basic idea of terrorism: attack the environment and the vulnerable subject will succumb. The role of the mask here, when it is available, is to protect the 'basic pre-requisites of life',[*12] filtering air and modulating atmospheric conditions. Mask and environment are figured as co-constitutive correspondents. Furthermore, the individual who wears the mask does not stand alone; they belong to a socio-political collective sheltering under shared skies.

One mask suggests the proliferation of other masks, because we all wear a variety of masks, getting by with our daily performances. Not one mask then, but a multitude, 'a network of adjacent islands constituting mid-sized or larger structures—a national assembly, a "Love Parade," a club, a Freemason lodge, a work force, a shareholder meeting, a concert hall audience, a suburban neighborhood, a school class, a religious community, drivers stuck in a traffic jam, a convened federation of taxpayers'.[*13] These are confederations of life, as Sloterdijk explains, yet he places an emphasis on their co-isolation, calling them an 'insulated multiplicity', describing them as foams wherein the shared cell walls of each singular bubble operate according to an 'interautistic minimum'.[*14] Sloterdijk allows for little communication, little sign of closeness and connection in the cellular worlds he characterises, which cluster as (anti)social foams. He presents the limit case of being clustered together but remaining incapable of forming communities that might act together, even if only to share their vulnerabilities and frustrations. What is surely more interesting in the examples he gives is that they do form communities, even if only transitory ones, even if unintentional. The event of their gathering manifests as an embodied potential to act, to make a difference.

All the while, and as I write, a contagion takes hold, making people feel like they are all in it together, whether in a traffic jam, in a classroom, in an assembly hall, in a queue, or under the conditions of a pandemic. In each case the collective circulation of affect must be acknowledged; both political and viral affects can be contagious. Admittedly, what results can speed off in many unexpected directions, from the storming of the Capitol to a series of carefully secured decisions that shift policy and enable greater equity and access to basic rights for a population. Even if it has become increasingly difficult to believe in democratic process today.

...

Let us return to *White Noise*. The professor is a fake. He knows you have to fake it till you make it. The chancellor recommends that he gains some weight and grow a beard to better project gravitas. On campus the professor always wears his academic gown and dark glasses. His mask hides anxieties about the quality of his research on Hitler and National Socialism, a period whose fascistic excesses seem so relevant today as an analytical lens. Today, the faces of fascism loom large, and too often political lies are enunciated with presumed impunity. I follow this political thread back in time to the Weimar Republic, which anticipated the violent upheavals of National Socialism.

The third mask I examine is one composed by German Dadaist Hannah Höch, celebrated for her critical collages, especially her series *From an Ethnographic Museum* (1924–1930). The study of ethnography and access to ethnographical museums were novelties at the beginning of the twentieth century, and were bound up with colonial presumptions about the civilised investigation of the 'uncivilised' and their primitive accoutrements. As Irene Chang, Charles L. Davis II, and Mabel O. Wilson explain in their work on race and modern architecture, the intensification of colonial expansion populated the European imagination with an expanding array of languages, peoples, and artefacts.[*15] Hannah Höch captures this zeitgeist. *Her Half Caste* (1924) depicts an African woman's dark-skinned face at a three-quarter angle, with her original lips cut out and collaged with a pale skin swatch showing a neatly lipsticked bow shaped mouth. *Sadness* (1925) part of the series from *From an Ethnographic Museum*, shows a figure with hanging pale breasts and six arms waving up and down, and reaching out, topped by an African mask, and steadied by two slender dark legs. A dark frame encircles the collage and is held up by two of the arms. *The Sweet One* (1926) shows an ethnographic figurine with lips, one open eye, one cut and paste hand, and elegant legs concluding in delicate Mary-Jane slippers. The deployment of the ethnographic mask as marker of the Other across all these instances is an uneasy one, and as Maud Lavin suggests, Höch never explicitly challenged the racist and colonialist ideas of her time.[*16]

Nevertheless, in Höch's collages her redeployment of ethnographic fragments is a vitriolic critique of the ways in which women are oppressed by their sex and their demarcated roles, as seen in the logic of *Kinder, Küche, Kirche* (Children, Kitchen, Church), which subsequently came to dominate in Nazi Germany. Höch's collages, with their primitive masks appended to women's bodies, speak of the role of performance and seek lines of escape from oppressive gender norms. The Dadaist challenges the assumption of women's role in society. She undoes presumptions around domesticity, she challenges ideals of beauty, and she explores androgyny, or what today we would call gender non-binary performances. The mask here becomes one that unsettles the status quo and calls into question what a woman can do. Lavin explains that Höch's collaged juxtapositions offer a means of constructing and reconstructing subjectivity during a period of rapid rationalisation and modernism, including the emergence of 'new mass media consumers'.*17

Advertising images and an image-saturated world has by now made us immune to what would have been received as violent image juxtapositions at the time, arousing what Rachel Withers calls 'Perception in the form of shocks'.*18 Today we might read Höch's collages retrospectively as orientalist in their orientation of othering a non-western expression and fetishizing a primitive Other as a means of accessing an unconscious mind. Lavin suggests two readings: on the one hand, an ironic critique of the commodification of both the New Woman and so called primitive culture' and, on the other hand, a reading alert to 'a disturbance about the public display of self, and a tension between ego and anonymity'.*19 Reading these collage experiments from the present provokes both critique of a racialized unconscious bias as well as intersectional questions pertaining to the complex construction of identity according to gender, sexual orientation, class, race, and bodily ability and how associated concerns might be performed and collectivised.

Subjectivity is constructed, and genderis real only to the extent that it is performed, feminist philosopher Judith Butler has famously argued.*20 Performances, such as those associated with drag for instance, give rise to a pleasure and giddiness exactly in that they reveal gender identity to be radically contingent in its relation to sex. The concept of the performative 'suggests a dramatic and contingent construction of meaning'.*21 Gender performance, as Höch reveals with her collages, is neither natural nor necessary. What Butler demonstrates is that performances, when mobilised, can become a line of escape from patriarchal norms. In her later work Butler extends this radical possibility of performance to public assembly, thereby expanding her philosophy of gender performance on the part of the individual to a consideration of how a collective might perform toward ideals of justice, equality, and democracy itself.*22 Furthermore, this becomes an architectural problem. Butler writes, 'if politics is oriented toward the making and preserving of the conditions that allow for liveability, then it seems that the space of appearance is not ever fully separable from questions of infrastructure and architecture.'*23

...

If Mask Three challenges gender norms that extend to the collective performance of a body politic, when we lift that mask, a fourth mask directs us toward decolonial struggles. Mask Four returns to Frantz Fanon's astonishing collection of essays *Black Skins, White Masks.**24 Fanon attacks those colonised subjects who perform according to the white man's norms, who remain, nonetheless, captured by an oppressive 'epidermal racial schema'.*25 Fanon argues passionately about how the colonised are trapped inside these performances, in the pernicious devaluation and obliteration of what he calls black man's lived experience. As a retort Fanon demands the restructuring of the world, the rethinking of the relation between the individual and the environment, for, as he adds, a mere 'change of air' will not suffice; more profound environmental and socio-political transformation is what is required.

The question is whose identity is being imposed on whom? As Édouard Glissant remarks in a footnote in *Poetics of Relation*, 'When one says civilisation, the immediate implication is the will to civilise. This idea is linked to the passion to impose civilisation on the Other'.*26 That is, to impose a mask fashioned by the colonizer, the invader, on the Other. The mask in this instance is to be ripped off so that adequate performances can be reclaimed, and political identities collectively forged. In the process, new masks are constructed with reclaimed collective subjective performances to go with them. Achille Mbembe talks of Fanon's struggle with 'the case of Africa and its mask, the Negro'. He asks, is the mask here the catchall that becomes an empty category, or can it exert its own force, 'reach its own concept and write itself into this new planetary age?'*27 Here, then, the mask becomes that which might be refashioned for an emancipatory project.

Some reservations must be expressed. In her essay collection *Teaching to Transgress*, bell hooks reflects on Fanon's contributions to what has subsequently come to be called Critical Race Theory, or Critical Race Studies, and discusses her concern with the enduring sexism embedded in his language, as he constructs a patriarchal mask. She writes of her concern for the 'phallocentric paradigm of liberation —wherein freedom and the experience of patriarchal manhood are always linked as though they are one and the same'.*28 Instead hooks forwards a pedagogy of hope as the way to freedom. In *Teaching Community*, for instance,*29 she speaks of resisting the institutionalisation of feminist theories and practices and describes the urgent need to extend such praxis to ordinary folks, to work on building community together. We need to foster connection and closeness in the community beyond the academy, she passionately argues. This might be another way of arguing for shared socio-political infrastructures.

...

A mask to hide behind to shield the fake; a mask to protect from life-threatening environmental conditions; a mask to perform a new identity as an escape from the norm; a mask to rip off and reveal oppression; a refashioned mask to highlight a denigrated political identity. All are manifest as constructions and reconstructions of identity in relation to community and milieu. Here it may be worth listening to Glissant again, who argues for working through a relational logic: 'We are not prompted solely by the defining of our identities but by their relation to everything possible as well the mutual mutations generated by this interplay of relations'.*30 This might constitute the practice hooks speaks of toward fostering connection and closeness. The challenge here is to achieve this by making the perceived boundaries between communities and institutions of higher education more porous. In the Australian context, a growing enmity between these domains has produced great infrastructural damage, assuming we take infrastructure in Butler's sense of opening up the ground for shared vulnerabilities and differences. Butler powerfully argues that the spaces in which we publicly gather, to share stories, to agree and disagree, depend on the facilitative milieu that is underwritten by adequate infrastructural conditions and 'when infrastructural conditions for politics are themselves decimated, so too are the assemblies that depend upon them'.*31 Education, for instance, is a fundamental infrastructure that should be rendered publicly available so as to support informed public discourse.

Recently, in the Australian parliament, the right-wing coalition of the Liberal Party and the National Party brought about a motion to remove Critical Race Studies from the Australian high-school curriculum. The Senate voted in support of the motion. The irony is that Critical Race Studies was not in the curriculum in the first place, at least not formally. In *The Conversation*, Mick Tsikas explains that 'Critical Race Theory, or CRT, is an academic theory developed primarily by Black scholars and activists to highlight the systemic and institutional nature of racism'.*32 Chang, Davis, and Wilson speak of the emergence of Critical Race Studies in the American context as a critical analytical method that exposes 'the structural role whiteness' plays in shaping institutions. It joins the myriad studies that collectively compose the ways in which the diverse research projects of the humanities organise themselves, from cultural studies (which historically takes the lead) through to communication studies, literary studies, women's studies, critical studies in architecture, and so on. Nevertheless, as Stuart Hall argued over thirty years ago now, the relationship between these different studies or sub-groups and the larger domain of the humanities has always been marked by controversy.*33 With respect to the formulation of various studies and how far they provide new techniques and critical weapons, he warns that 'It is perfectly possible to write elegant treatises on the "other" without ever having encountered what "otherness" is really like for some people actually to live'.*34 The formation of studies is inherently precarious, and their critical attacks on the institutional castle are always at risk of being co-opted or else obliterated, especially when funding cuts are afoot.

If you care to look over the shoulder of your teenagers' required reading material, you can see why Pauline Hanson, a key populist political figure in the debate concerning Critical Race Studies in the Australian context, might have become concerned. Tony Birch's *White Girl*, Robert Newton's *Mr Romanov's Garden in the Sky* and Zana Fraillon's *The Bone Sparrow*[*35] are young-adult novels that speak powerfully in terms of the historic and enduring violence inflicted on First Nations peoples including the dilemma of 'passing' for white when you are not; the violence that infiltrates Housing Commission high-rise flats struggling with diverse identities; the violence of Australia's approach to refugees, who are strategically reclassified as asylum seekers in order to remove their rights as refugees under the UNHCR convention. Each of these narratives challenge historic yet persistent origin stories of a singular Anglo-European white Australian identity. The concept of national identity is challenged because it cannot reside comfortably under one unified mask. This disturbs the imaginaries of right-wing populists, like Pauline Hanson, who would be keen to eradicate all difference, all dissenting and critical thought. Why not get to the core of the issue, and attack the humanities *tout court?* This is exactly what the residing Australian right wing coalition government did on 19 June 2020 when it announced a price hike of 113 per cent on the cost of completing a humanities degree. The Higher Education Bill was passed late afternoon on 9 October 2020.[*36] The message is clear: if you want to waste your time learning the skills of critical thinking and equipping yourself with adequate weapons to speak truth to power then you will have to pay for it. The same government is happy to disregard scientifically formulated warnings of a warming planet and the subsequent concatenating ecological devastation. A toxic mix of political and environmental atmospherics ensues.

Let's return, in conclusion, to the College-on-the-Hill and to the innovative creation of Hitler Studies, which was, as the professor and chair himself explains 'an immediate and electrifying success'. DeLillo is writing his parody of academia in the mid 1980s from the midst of a postmodernist quagmire. By the mid 1990s, a crisis in the humanities has already been identified, the Science Wars are in full swing, and the physicist Alan Sokal's hoax article has been published in *Social Text* with the aim of discrediting postmodern critiques of scientific epistemology and method.[*37] Meanwhile, much disparaged, various studies of the humanities become the sacrificial domains of knowledge production. They are the dangerous places that provoke us to ask questions and claim minoritarian positions, in the process trying on too many masks, queering the norms of social convention and disrupting the status quo. As for community formations, these would appear to be based on contagion. A cause takes off and takes hold, infecting the imagination of a body politic. Discovering the environmental conditions ripe, the atmospherics just so, a populist imagination all too readily erupts, but in which direction will it swerve? The outcome is uncertain, will the body politic survive the fevered crisis, or succumb?

An Airborne Toxic Event
(Mask Wearing Recommended)

Hélène Frichot
An Airborne Toxic Event (Mask Wearing Recommended)
* **footnotes & references**

*1 Frantz Fanon, *Black Skins, White Masks* (New York: Grove Press, 2008), 119.

*2 Don DeLillo, *White Noise* (New York: Viking Press, 1985), 17.

*3 Isabelle Stengers, *In Catastrophic Times: The Coming Barbarism* (Ann Arbor, MI: Open Humanities Press and Meson Press, 2015); Bruno Latour, *Facing Gaia: Eight Lectures on the New Climatic Regime* (Cambridge: Polity, 2017).

*4 Jayne Ann Philips, "'White Noise' by Don DeLillo," *New York Times*, January 13, 1985, accessed 1 August 2021, https://www.nytimes.com/1985/01/13/books/white-noise-by-don-DeLillo.html.

*5 Jayne Ann Philips, "'White Noise' by Don DeLillo".

*6 See Ben Anderson, "Affective Atmospheres," *Emotion, Space, Society* 2 (2009): 77-81.

*7 Leslie Hill, *Nancy, Blanchot: A Serious Controversy* (London and New York: Rowman & Littlefield Publishers, 2018), 2. See Jean-Luc Nancy, *The Inoperative Community* (Minneapolis: University of Minnesota Press, 1991); Maurice Blanchot, *The Unavowable Community* (New York: Station Hill, 1988). Blanchot's discussion of community was made as a response to Nancy's. The original publications in French as follows: Jean-Luc Nancy, "La Communauté Désoeuvrée," *Aléa* 4 (February 1983) and Maurice Blanchot, *La Communauté Inavouable* (Paris: Minuit, 1983).

*8 Hill, *Nancy, Blanchot*, 2.

*9 Isabelle Stengers and Vinciane Despret, *Women Who Make a Fuss: The Unfaithful Daughters of Virginia Woolf* (Minneapolis: University of Minnesota Press, 2014).

*10 Peter Sloterdijk, *Terror from the Air* (New York: Semiotext(e), 2009), 10.

*11 Sloterdijk, *Terror from the Air*, 14.

*12 Sloterdijk, *Terror from the Air*, 15.

*13 Peter Sloterdijk, *Foams: Spheres 3* (New York: Semiotext(e), 2016), 564.

*14 Sloterdijk, *Foams*, 565.

*15 Irene Cheng, Charles L. Davis II, Mabel O. Wilson, "Introduction," in *Race and Modern Architecture: A Critical History from the Enlightenment to the Present*, eds Irene Cheng, Charles L. Davis II, Mabel O. Wilson (University of Pittsburgh Press, 2020), 5.

*16 Lavin, *Cut with a Kitchen Knife*, 160.

*17 Lavin, *Cut with a Kitchen Knife*, 1.

*18 Rachel Withers, "Hannah Höch," *Artforum* (Summer 2014): 376, http://www.rachelwithers.com/hannah-hoch/.

*19 Maud Lavin and Hannah Höch, "From an Ethnographic Museum," Grand Street, no. 58, (Autumn 1996): 120-128; Maud Lavin, *Cut with a Kitchen Knife: The Weimar Photomontages of Hannah Höch* (New Haven and London: Yale University Press, 1993).

*20 Judith Butler, *Notes Toward a Performative Theory of Assembly* (Cambridge, MA: Harvard University Press, 2015); Judith Butler, *Gender Trouble: Feminist Theory and the Subversion of Identity* (New York and London: Routledge, 1990); Judith Butler, "Performative Acts and Gender Constitution: An Essay in Phenomenology and Feminist Theory," *Theatre Journal* 40, no. 4 (1988): 519—I'd like to thank Helen Stratford for alerting me to this specific Butler reference.

*21 Butler, *Gender Trouble*, 139.

*22 Butler, *Notes Toward a Performative Theory of Assembly*, 124.

*23 Butler, *Notes Toward a Performative Theory of Assembly*, 127.

*24 Frantz Fanon, *Black Skins, White Masks* (New York: Grove Press, 2008).

*25 Fanon, *Black Skins, White Masks*, 92.

*26 Édouard Glissant, *Poetics of Relation* (Ann Arbor: University of Michigan Press, 1997), 13.

*27 Achille Mbembe, *Necropolitics* (Durham and London: Duke University Press, 2019), 7.

*28 bell hooks, *Teaching to Transgress: Education as a Practice of Freedom* (New York and London: Routledge, 1994), 49.

*29 bell hooks, *Teaching Community: A Pedagogy of Hope* (New York and London; Routledge, 2003).

*30 Glissant, *Poetics of Relation*, 89.

*31 Judith Butler, *Notes Toward a Performative Theory of Assembly* (Cambridge MA: Harvard University Press, 2015), 126-127.

*32 Mick Tsikas, "The Senate Has Voted to Reject Critical Race Theory from the National Curriculum: What Is It, and Why Does It Matter?" *The Conversation*, June 22, 2021, https://theconversation.com/the-senate-has-voted-to-reject-critical-race-theory-from-the-national-curriculum-what-is-it-and-why-does-it-matter-163102.

*33 Stuart Hall, "The Emergence of Cultural Studies and the Crisis of the Humanities," *October* 53 (Summer 1990): 11-23.

*34 Hall, "The Emergence of Cultural Studies and the Crisis of the Humanities," 28.

*35 Tony Birch, *White Girl* (Brisbane: University of Queensland Press, 2019); Robert Newton, *Mr Romanov's Garden in the Sky* (Australia: Penguin, 2017); Zana Fraillon, *The Bone Sparrow* (Melbourne: Lothian Children's Books, 2016).

*36 See https://ministers.dese.gov.au/tehan/minister-education-dan-tehan-national-press-club-address; see https://www.abc.net.au/news/2020-10-06/minority-support-for-higher-education-bill/12734980; https://campusmorningmail.com.au/news/tehan-funding-package-passes-senate/.

*37 Alan Sokal, "Transgressing the Boundaries: Toward a Transformative Hermeneutics of Quantum Gravity," *Social Text*, no. 46/47 (Spring-Summer 1996): 217-252.

La Escuela Nunca y los Otros Futuros
El Manifiesto Capucha

Plaza Dignidad and the air

Plaza Dignidad[*1] is an off-centred centre around which Santiago de Chile, a metropolis of 7 million inhabitants is organised. It is a strange space that interweaves multiple urban communication systems. Spatially, it is governed by a roundabout and a monument. The centrality of the space, both metropolitan and spatial, has operated as a centre of attraction for multiple social events, incidents and protests.[*2] Self-convened crowds time and again put the efficient circulation of urban capital into crisis.

During the massive social demonstrations that began in October 2019, and that still keep the Chilean political scene in tension today, the square was transformed into a multidimensional space where millions of people converged political claims and historical demands with street parties and artistic performances. Among many other things, this square was also a battleground. The repression by the police and military forces was fierce. The dead, wounded and tortured were counted in numbers reminiscent of the worst moments in the country's history.[*3]

Since those days, the air in the square has changed. It has become thick. Columns of smoke, fires, bonfires and barricades, hundreds of green laser beams, fireworks, light projections with political slogans, drones from various media, video cameras on the neighbouring towers, among others, combine with the police helicopters that fly over the city and with the repressive bullets and gases that make life in the place dangerous.

Plaza Dignidad is constantly on air.[*4]

The school, the appearance, the performance, the masks

In January 2020, in Santiago, Chile, in a house near the city centre, *La Escuela Nunca y los otros Futuros* (The Never School and Other Futures)[*5] had its first appearance. About fifteen people shaped seven consecutive days and nights of meeting, conversation and work. The appearance was called: *La calle en disputa: monumento, infraestructura y multitud* (The street in dispute: monument, infrastructure and multitude).

The group worked on the construction of a political fiction that took the name *Territorio Autónomo de la Dignidad* (Autonomous Territory of Dignity). Maps, plans and collages gave shape to a territorial imagination that combined facts of the burning reality with political and social utopias. On the last day, masks were made by combining scraps of clothing and fabric with materials brought from Buenos Aires.[*6] On the final night, a performance was held and a text was written collectively: El Manifiesto Capucha (The Hooded[*7] Manifesto).

The text was read as part of the closing performance; a strange mix between a Zapatista press conference and an erotic orgy in a peripheral brothel. That is the text we have tried to translate below.

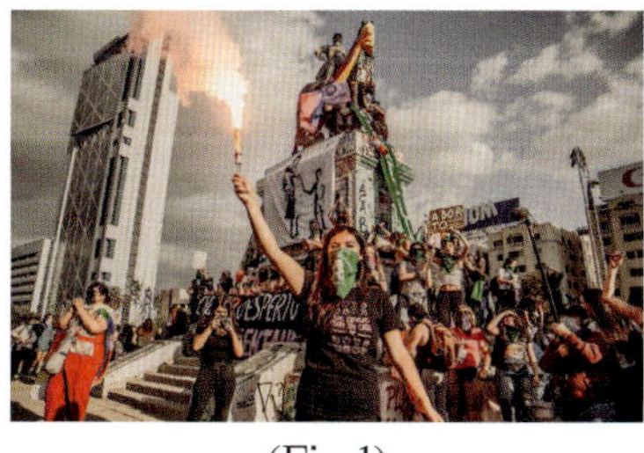

(Fig. 1)

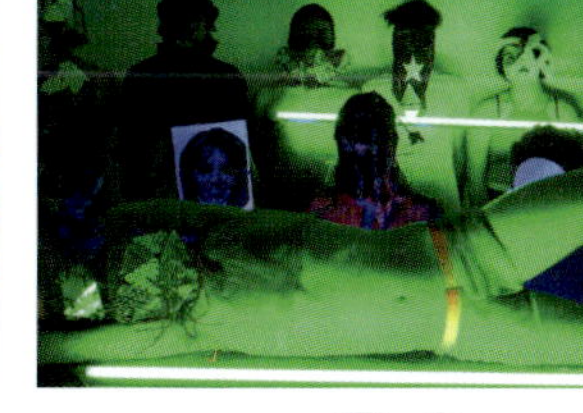

(Fig. 2)

To translate is to betray

The translation of El Manifiesto Capucha into English is inevitably inscribed in tension. The global hegemony of certain languages in the worldwide exchange of ideas, contains within itself the colonial violence with which this same 'global' has been constructed. We still remember that it was in the same year, 1492, in which Columbus accidentally came across these lands, that Antonio de Nebrija presented to the king his *Gramática de la Lengua Castellana*,—the first grammar of a modern

Fig. 1. March against Sexist Violence in Plaza Dignidad, 25 November 2019. Photo by Karla Riveros.

Fig. 2. Capucha Press Conference, 1 February 2020. Photo by La Escuela Nunca y los Otros Futuros.

European language to be published in print —with the explicit aim of facilitating the Conquest.*8 We also remember that Malinche was the Nahuatl translator who enabled Hernan Cortés to organise the betrayals for the occupation of Tenochtitlán.*9 With this tension in mind, our challenging task of translation begins.

Once translation is assumed to be necessary, betrayal is inevitable. The search for solidarities in other parts of the planet in order to continue thinking about the construction of spaces of resistance and political struggles for emancipation, obliges us to assume this treacherous contradiction with a dose of enthusiasm.

Clarification: translation is impossible. The use, in El Manifiesto Capucha, of terms

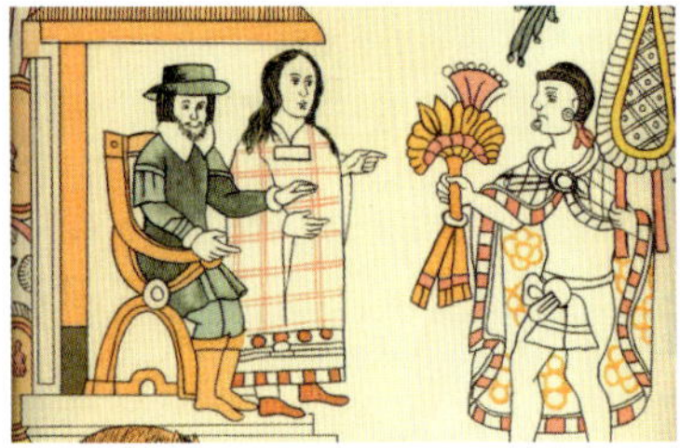

(Fig. 3)

that break the binarism of the Spanish language,*10 of local terms and slang, as well as word plays, are intertwined with the lack of experience of the translators in a work like this.*11 We hope that our enthusiasm will do what our incapacity prevents.

Fig. 3. La Malinche translates the conversation between the four ranking *tlataloque* or 'speakers' of the Tlaxcalteca and Hernán Cortés, Lienzo de Tlaxcala, 1552. The Tlaxcalteca and the Spaniards organize their alliance against the Aztec empire.

La Escuela Nunca y los Otros Futuros
El Manifiesto Capucha
* **footnotes & references**

*1 The square was originally established in 1875 as Plaza La Serena. In 1928 it adopted the name Plaza Baquedano to honor Manuel Baquedano (Commander-in-chief of the Army during the War of the Pacific) and is also commonly known as Plaza Italia. In the context of the 2019–2021 protests, the people have renamed the square as Plaza de la Dignidad (Dignity Square).

*2 Historically, the traditional space for demonstrations in Santiago was the Plaza Bulnes. On 11 September 1975, to commemorate two years after the military coup, the military installed the 'Flame of Freedom' monument there. From then on, this space was permanently guarded by the repressive forces, which naturally led to the demonstrations moving to what we now call Plaza Dignidad.

*3 Between October 2019 and March 2020, according to data from the National Human Rights Institute there have been a total of 2349 allegations against the military and police for cases of physical, sexual or psychological violence.

*4 Since October 2019, the square has constantly been filmed by the cameras of Galeria Cima and transmitted live in their Youtube Channel. https://www.youtube.com/watch?v=9yo7CUpQGoU.

*5 *La Escuela Nunca y los Otros Futuros* is an experimental, latinoamerican, para-institutional, anti-bureaucratic, deeply personal, non-hierarchical, collective, independent, free and open school. A school to learn, not to teach. A generative and non-productive space. A collective experience of thinking together critically. More info at laescuelanunca.org/.

*6 @dragstracta organized a workshop for the production of masks.

*7 *Capucha* in Spanish refers to the element that covers your head and face, making you explicitly unrecognizable, usually worn by political activists. While in English, the hooded figure is one whose head and face is implicitly unrecognizable, and often brings to mind a character in a fairytale.

*8 'After Your Highness has subjected barbarous peoples and nations of varied tongues, with conquest will come the need for them to accept the laws that the conqueror imposes on the conquered, and among them our language; with this work of mine, they will be able to learn it, as we now learn Latin from the Latin Grammar', Antonio de Nebrija, *Gramática de la lengua castellana*, 1492.

*9 'Without the help of Doña Marina (La Malinche) we would not have understood the languages of New Spain and Mexico', Bernal Díaz de Castilla in *Historia verdadera de la conquista de la Nueva España*, 1632. Today, The Royal Spanish Academy defines 'malinchista' as having 'attachment to what is foreign with contempt for what is one's own'.

*10 In Spanish every adjective, noun, and article are all either masculine or feminine. To speak Spanish in a gender-neutral way, it's common for example to write *Latinx* or *Latine* as a gender-inclusive version of *Latino* and *Latina*.

*11 This text was translated at the end of July 2021, 17 months after it was written. This attempt of translation has been done by a group of 3 people. None of them, professional translators. Two of them did not participate in the original writing. We all prefer to maintain anonymity.

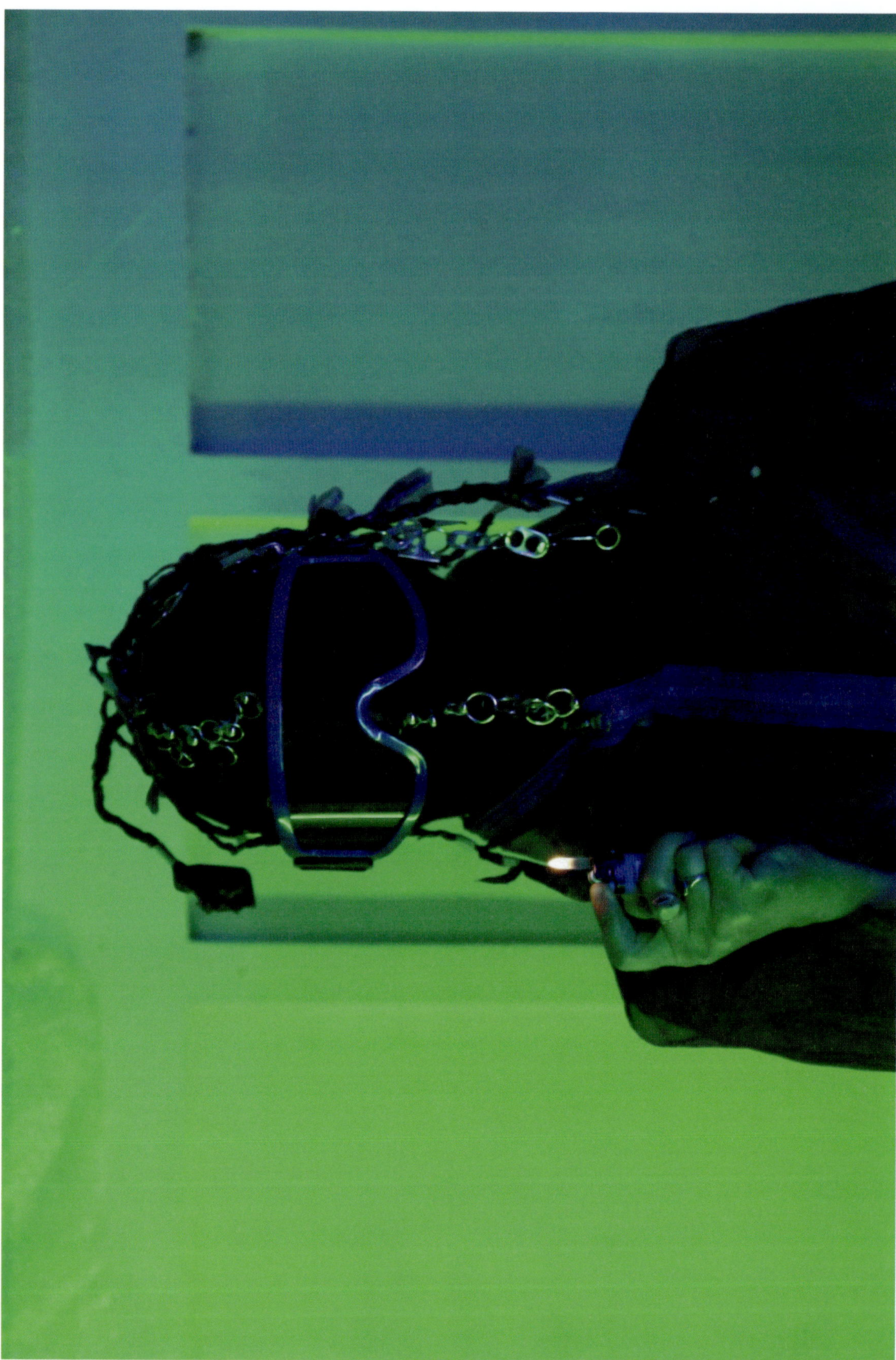

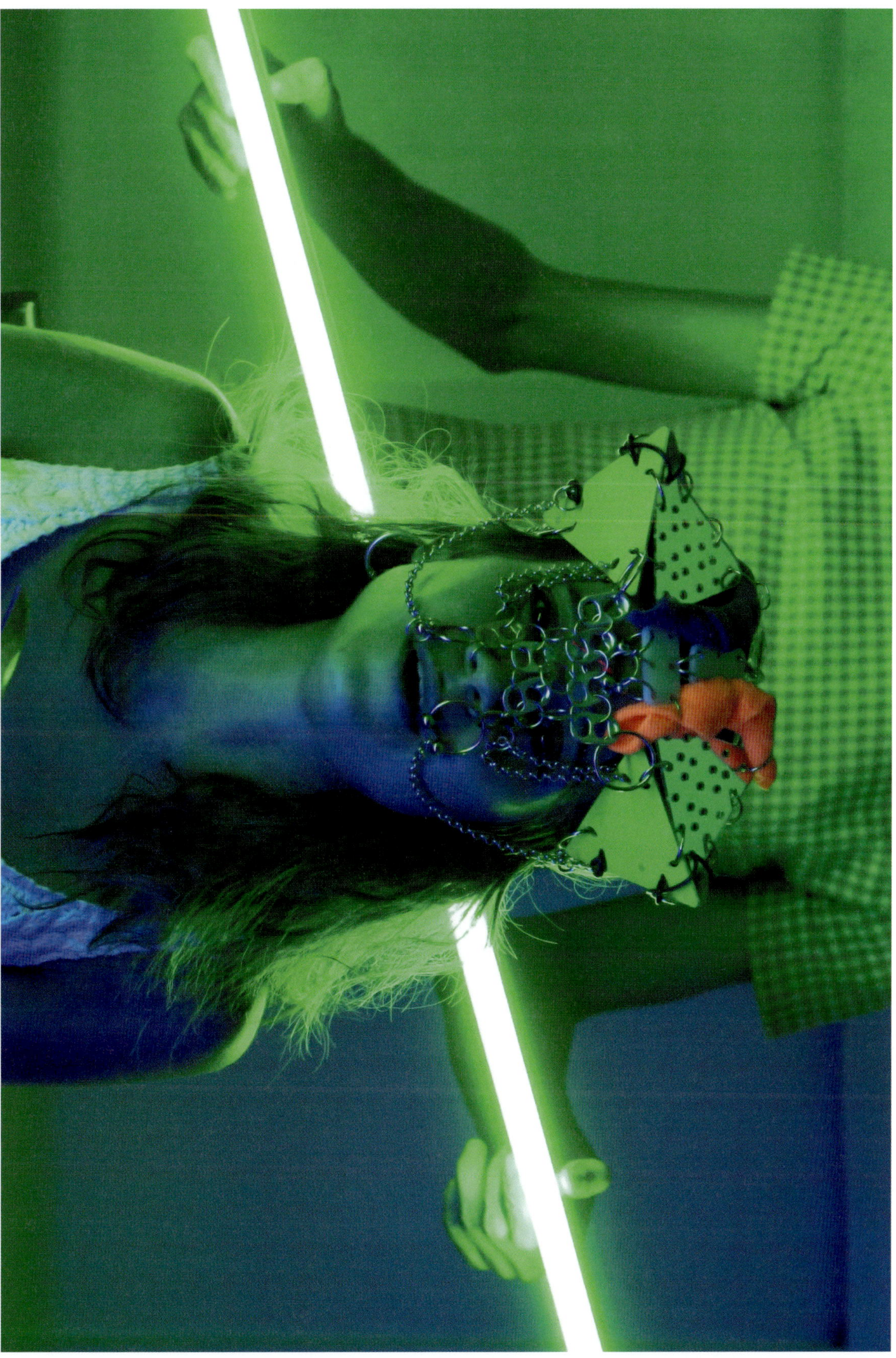

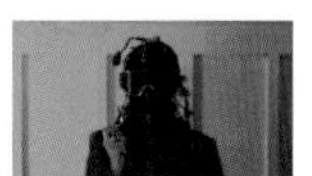

[ES]

Lxs aquí presentes
celebramos en este acto
un proceso infinito de apertura
a la desconstitución constituyente.

Nos paramos,
nos acostamos,
nos revolcamos,
nos abrimos paso
sobre el presente, el pasado y el futuro
para hacer de esta acción
una rasgadura en el presente neoliberal.

Con la fuerza de nuestrxs muertxs,
con la imaginación mutante de lxs no nacidxs,
festejamos la construcción de un territorio Otro
donde podamos vivir y perder la forma.

[EN]

Those present here
celebrate in this act
an infinite process of opening
towards a constituent deconstitution. *12

We stand up,
we lie down,
we roll around,
we make our way
over the present, the past and the future
to make of this action
a tear in the neoliberal present. *13

With the strength of our dead, *14
with the mutant imagination of the unborn,
we celebrate the construction of an Other territory
where we can live and lose our form.

*12 The protests in Chile in October 2019, have resulted in, among other things, a constitutional initiative to overthrow Chile's current constitution, created in 1980 under the civilian-military dictatorship. On 15 November 2019, ten political parties signed an 'Agreement for Social Peace and the New Constitution', that initiated a constitutional process that has recently elected the members of the Constitutional Assembly.

*13 Chile was the first Neoliberal experiment. Long before the famous policies of Ronald Reagan in the US and Margaret Thatcher in the UK, in 1974, during the first period of the civilian-military dictatorship, the first measures in favour of privatisation of services and reduction of state powers were adopted. The 'Miracle of Chile' was a term used by economist Milton Friedman, in an interview in 2008, to describe the reorientation of the Chilean economy during the 1980s and the effects of the political and economic policies.

*14 We are not sure to which dead the text refers. They could be the dead of the Conquest, the dead of the multiple repressions by the lords, the dead and disappeared of the military dictatorship of Augusto Pinochet, the dead in democracy due to police and military repression in Araucanía, or even the dead of the social protests that took place in various cities of the country when this manifesto was written.

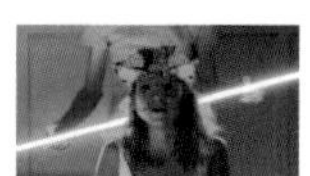

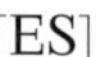

[ES]

Rechazamos la constitución
de una nueva constitución.
Celebramos su redacción infinita
como acto performativo.

Escribimos mientras nos infectamos,
nos movemos como proceso desconstituyente
de escritura y reescritura,
de borrado y control zeta,
de ensayo y creación.

Renunciamos al nombre propio,
llamamos a perder la identidad,
a perder la cara,
el género,
la nación,
a devenir capucha,
carne,
sangre,
organismo vivo y múltiple.

[EN]

We reject the constitution [*15]
of a new constitution.
We celebrate its infinite drafting
as a performative act. [*16]

We write as we become infected, [*17]
we move as a deconstitutive process
of writing and rewriting,
of erasure and zeta control,
of rehearsal and creation.

We renounce the proper name,
we call to lose the identity,
to lose the face, [*18]
the gender,
the nation,
to become *capucha*,
flesh,
blood,
living and multiple organism.

*15 When this manifesto was written, the constitutional process was just a flimsy pact between various political parties. At the time of this translation, the constitutional process has advanced significantly: a few weeks ago (15 and 16 of May 2021) the election of the members of the Constitutional Assembly was held, with an overwhelming defeat of the forces of the right that govern the country. Indigenous seats, gender parity and a resounding triumph of various popular and progressive forces were achieved.

*16 Various performances had taken to the streets. Undoubtedly, the best known was the one performed by the feminist collective LASTESIS, which ended up being reproduced in public spaces all over the world. The lyrics of the performance speaks for themselves: 'The patriarchy is a judge / That judges us for being born / And as women we are / punished / By the violence you don't see // The patriarchy is a judge / That judges us for being born / And as women we are punished / By the violence we have seen // The crime is femicide / The judges let the killers go / They make the women disappear / The crime is rape // And the fault it wasn't mine / Not where I went or how I dressed / And the fault it wasn't mine / Not where I went or how I dressed // We know the rapist is you / We know the rapist is you / It's the cops / The judges / It's the state / The President // It's the state that's our oppressor / It's the rapist government / It's the state that's our oppressor / It's the rapist government // We know the rapist is you / We know the rapist is you // Sleep very soundly / Girl so innocent / And don't you worry / About the bandit / Your loving cop / Sees your sweet smile / And watches over you/ While you dream // We know the rapist is you'. Extracted from the original version translated by Sarah Plant.

*17 At the time of this writing in January 2020, the infectious spread of COVID-19 was only just beginning to be known in China. There were still months to go before its arrival in Western countries. It entered Chile at the beginning of March of that year.

*18 The loss of the face could be understood as an intentional disidentification process, such as the use of hoods in the context of protests. But it also could be related to the multiple mutilations and eye damage that the police forces exercised on members of society.

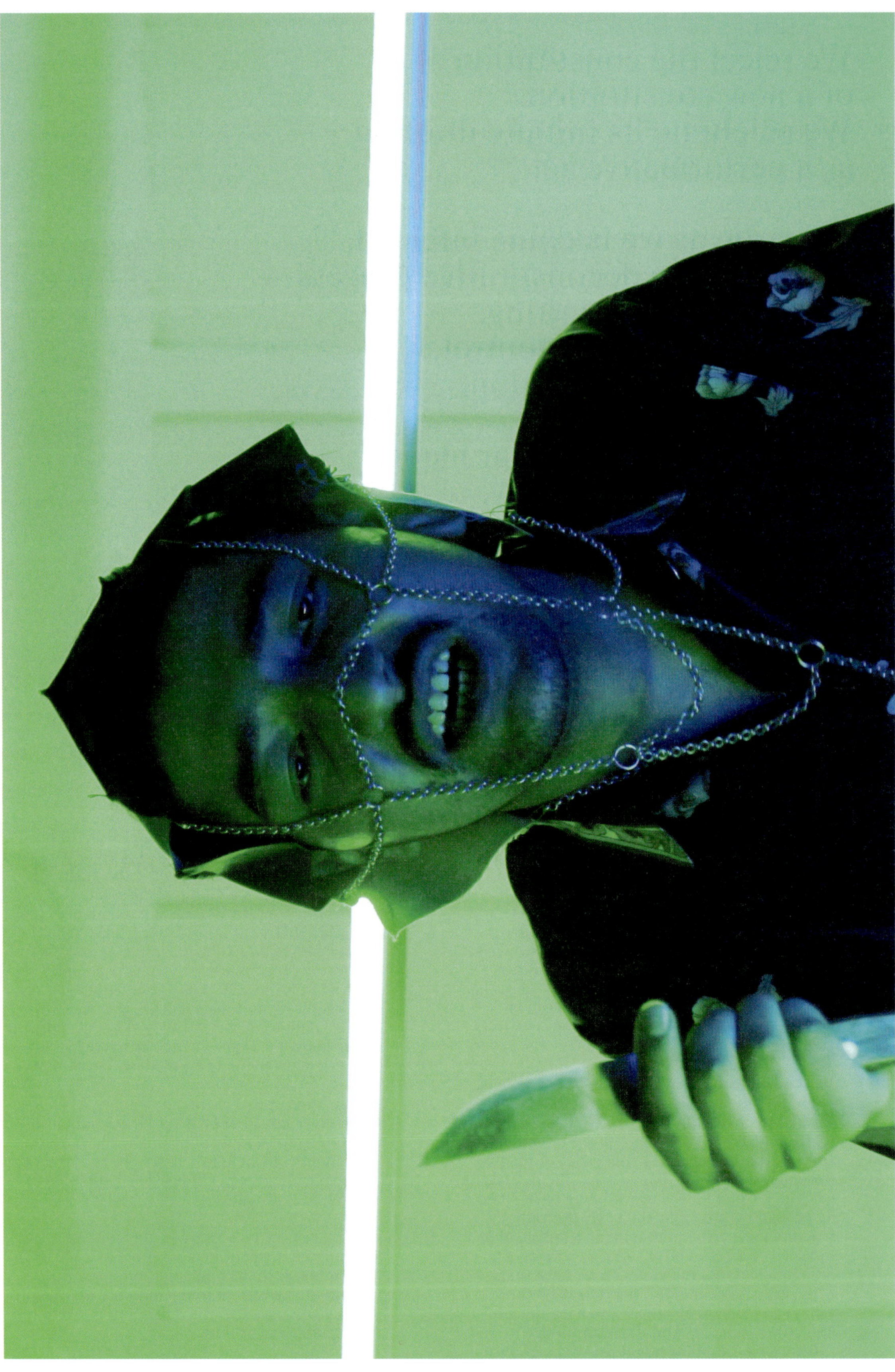

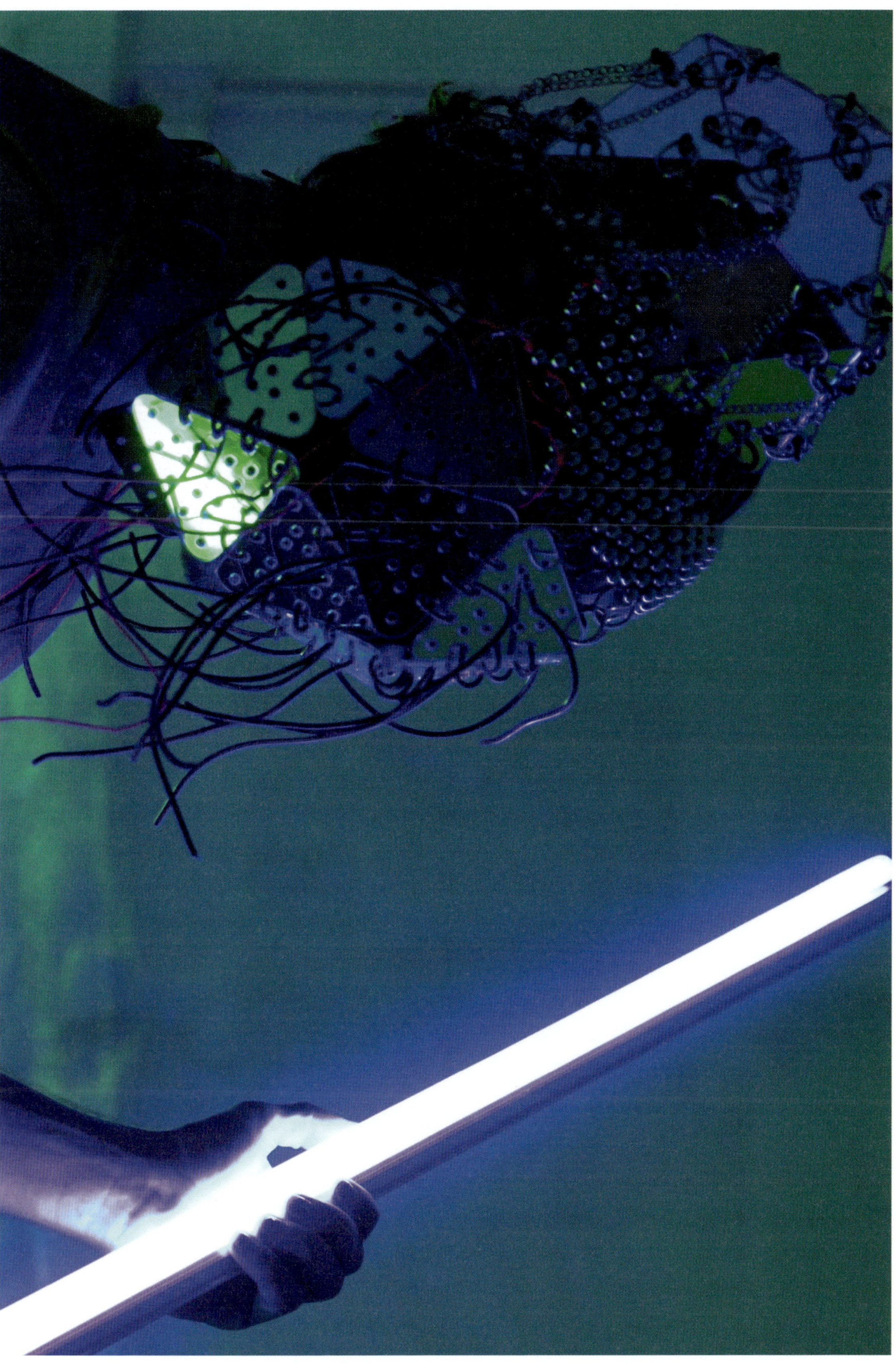

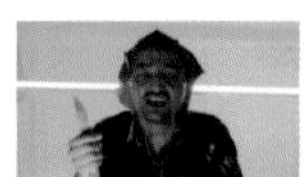

[ES]

Llamamos a todxs lxs anonimxs,
lxs desertores,
lxs caídxs,
lxs anormales,
lxs desencajadxs.

Llamamos y somos llamadxs a gritos por esas voces,
para matar al padre,
a la patria,
al patrón,
al patrimonio
y al patrullaje.

Para desertar de cualquier régimen de normalidad
que pretenda reducir nuestras potencias.

Acá, juntxs, armamos la nueva matria.

Sobre las ruinas de la antigua plaza italia
un nuevo territorio se organiza.

[EN]

We call on all the anonymous,
the deserters,
the fallen,
the abnormal,
the misfits.

We call and are called out by these voices,
to kill the father,
the fatherland,
the boss,
the patrimony
and the patrol. *19

To defect from any regime of normality
that seeks to reduce our powers.

Here, together, we build together the new *matria.**20

On the ruins of the old Plaza Italia
a new territory is organised.

*19 In Spanish, father *(padre)*, fatherland *(patria)*, patron—or boss—*(patrón)*, patrimony *(patrimonio)*, and patrol *(patrullaje)* form a family of words. They all share the root 'patr-'.

*20 *Matria* is the feminine substantive of *Patria* in Spanish. The traditional and most used translation to English of *Patria* means 'homeland or country'. *Matria* brings an idea of a non-masculin territory.

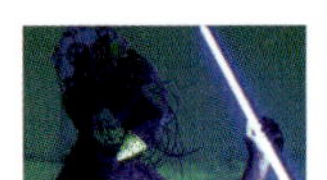

[ES]

Antiguamente,
fue el nodo central de la conexión metropolitana,
centro estratégico de la distribución del capital.
Infraestructura moral del ordenamiento
de los flujos de la mercancías.

Espacio jerarquizado a partir de una rotonda,
símbolo urbano del avance moderno
y sus lógicas de organización eficiente
y autorregulación controlada del territorio.

Sobre la vereda sur: los accesos principales al metro,
orgullo infraestructural del experimento neoliberal.

Hacia el oriente: la fálica torre corporativa,
controladora de los flujos de información
y homenaje al consumismo
de la caducidad programada.

[EN]
In the past,
it was a central node of the metropolitan connection,
strategic centre of capital distribution.
Moral infrastructure for the organisation
and flow of goods.

Hierarchical space based on a roundabout, *21
urban symbol of modern progress
and its logic of efficient organisation
and controlled self-regulation of the territory.

On the south sidewalk: the main access to the subway,
infrastructural pride of the neoliberal experiment. *22

To the east: the phallic corporate tower, *23
controlling the flow of information
and homage to the consumerism
of programmed expiration.

*21 'The roundabout organised the protest in concentric circles, a geometric order that exposed the crowd to itself, helping a political collective in becoming', quoted from the urban and architectural analysis of the revolts of the Arab Spring in *The Roundabout Revolutions*, Eyal Weizman, 2015. There is an attraction between revolutions and the circular movement of traffic circles.

*22 The first subway line in Santiago was inaugurated during the military dictatorship on 15 September 1975. On 1 October 2019, a 30 chileans pesos (0.041 US dollars) increase in Metro fares triggered a series of massive social demonstrations. The slogan 'it's not 30 pesos, it's 30 years' reflected a turning point in the country's history, highlighting the anger of the vast majority of the population in relation to the precarious living conditions.

*23 The Telefónica Tower is a skyscraper located in front of Plaza Dignidad. Its shape resembles a cell phone from the nineties. It was owned by the multinational telecommunications company Movistar for their operations center in the country. Since the demonstrations started it was covered in graffiti, many windows were destroyed and its west wall (over 140 meters high) was used as a canvas for light projections with political statements.

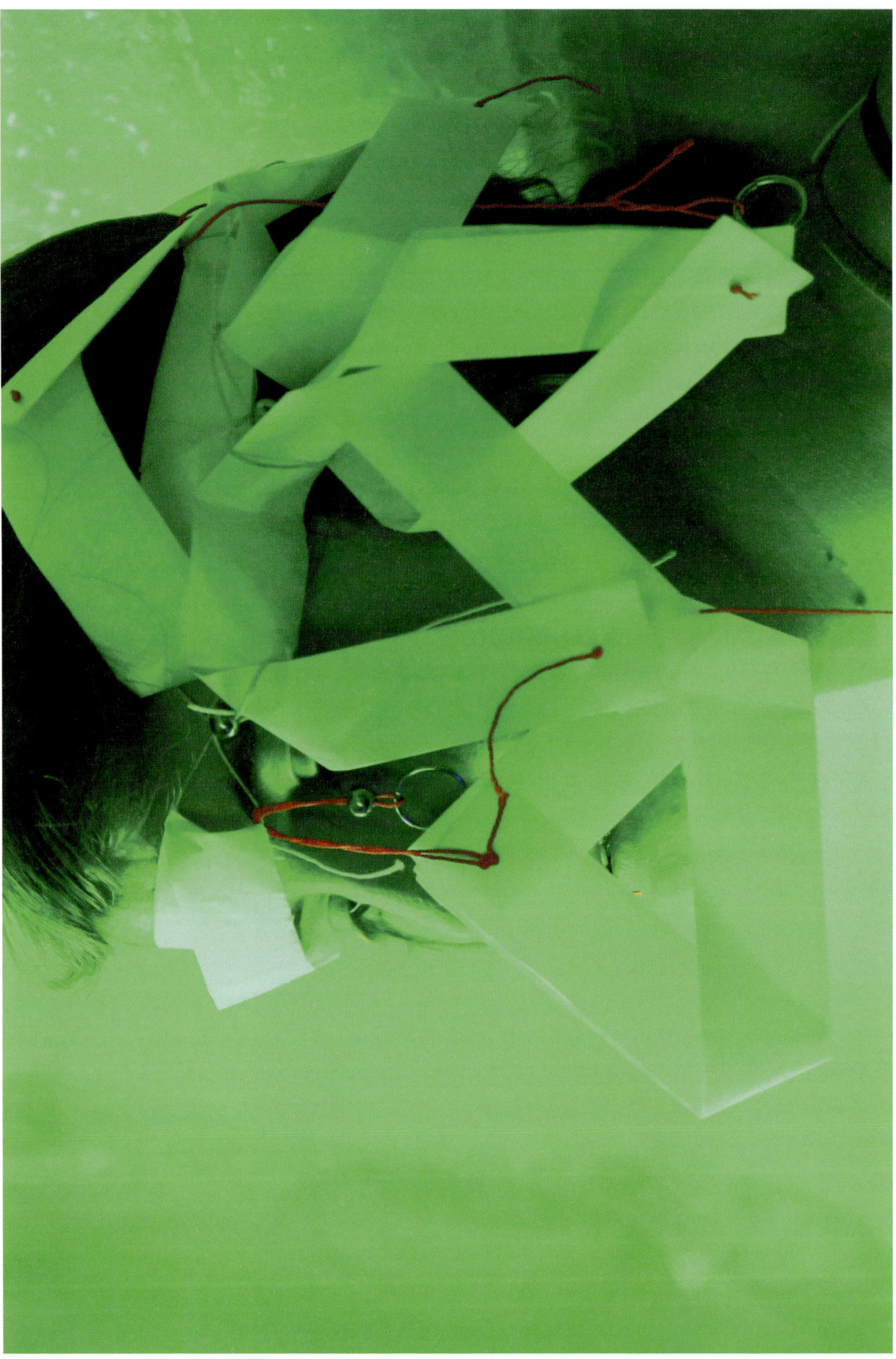

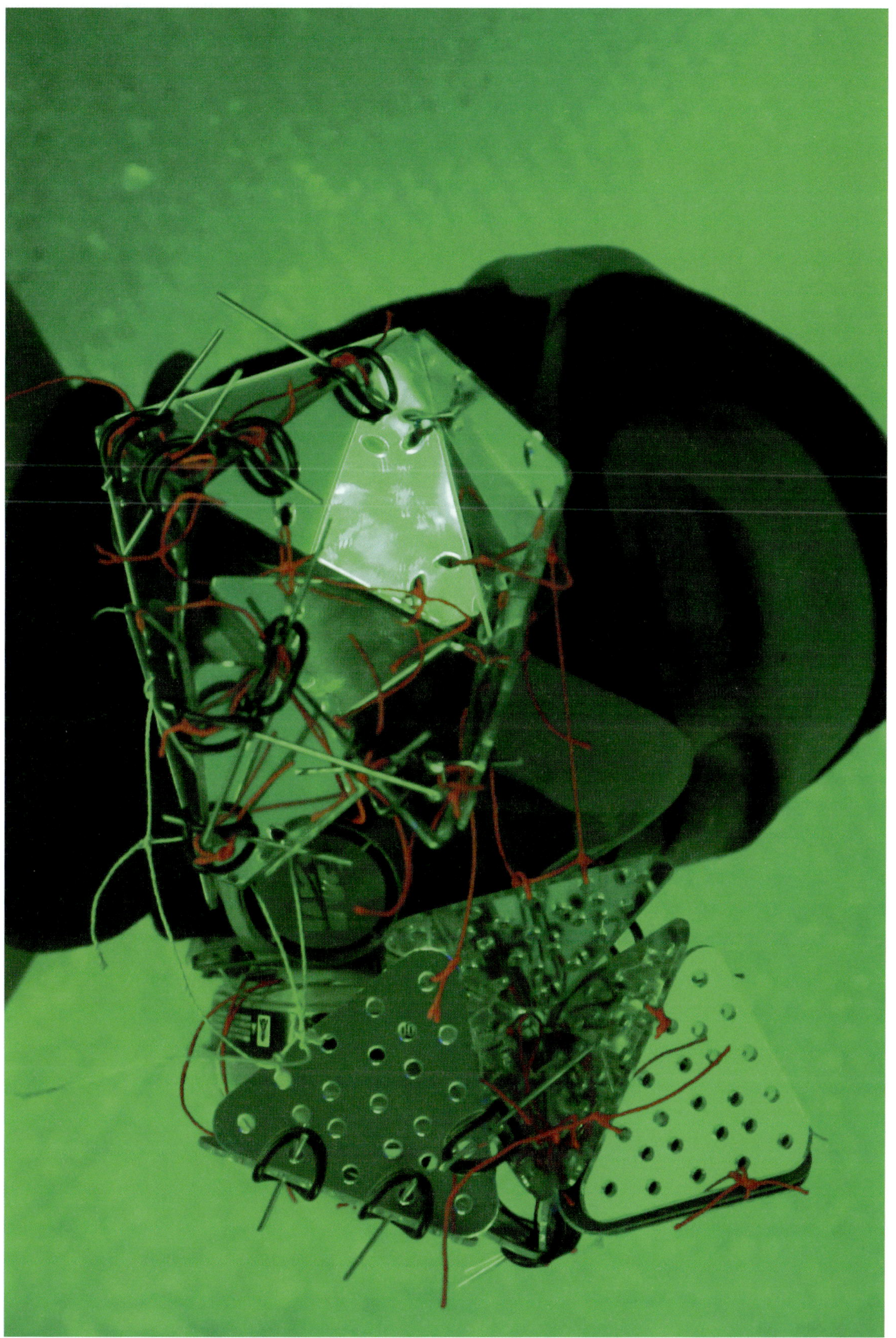

[ES]

Entre las ruinas de un proyecto totalizador
tiramos piedras contra ese poder
que se había vuelto arquitectura, espacio y ambiente.

Contra ese poder que organizaba nuestros movimientos,
nuestros comportamientos y nuestros deseos.

Contra el machirulismo de ese poder vuelto
hierro y hormigón,
es que lxs cabrxs enfiestadxs
ocupan las plazas y las grandes alamedas.

[EN]

Among the ruins of a totalising project
we threw stones against that power
that had become architecture, space and environment.

Against that power that organised our movements,
our behaviors and our desires.

Against the *machirulism* [*24] of this power turned into
iron and concrete,
is the partying guys
occupying the squares and the great avenues. [*25]

*24 The word *machirulo* is used colloquially to refer to a man who boasts of being undisguisedly *macho*. This neologism is frequently used in feminist vocabulary in a derogatory sense. It is considered that the word derives from the union of the terms *machista* (a man who acts in an overbearing or violent way towards women) and *chulo* (ruffian, pimp).

*25 The original phrase in Spanish 'las grandes alamedas' could refer to Salvador Allende's famous phrase, said on 11 September 1973 minutes before he died when the Government Palace was bombed by the military. The original phrase is '... keep on knowing that, sooner than later, the great avenues will open again, where free men can pass, to build a better society ...'

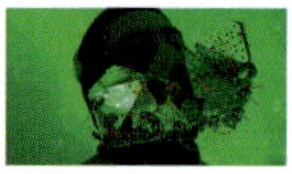

Se perdieron vidas pero la vitalidad crece,
se perdieron ojos pero crecemos en una visión lateral,
estrábica, autónoma y sudaka.

Día tras días,
barricada tras barricada,
en un tiempo circular y cósmico,
alzamos las ciudades del fuego:
nuevos sentidos de circulación,
múltiples, abiertos, no-fascistas.
Nuevas formas de lo común,
de la complicidad,
del cuidado,
del goce,
de la amistad,
del tiempo
y la presencia.

Ahora todo está al revés.
El tufillo a lacrimógena que desde octubre
flota entre la moneda y la dignidad
no es otra cosa que la asfixia de la antigua vida mula.

[EN]

Lives were lost [*26] but vitality grows,
eyes were lost but we grow a lateral vision,
strabismic, autonomous and *sudaka*. [*27]

Day after day,
barricade after barricade,
in a circular and cosmic time,
we raise the cities of fire:
new senses of circulation,
multiple, open, non-fascist.
New forms of the common,
of complicity,
of care,
of enjoyment,
of friendship,
of time
and presence.

Now everything is upside down.
The breath of tear gas that has been wafting since October
between *la moneda* and *la dignidad* [*29]
is nothing more than the asphyxiation of the old mule life. [*30]

*26 Between October 2019 and March 2020, 34 people have been officially reported dead as a result of the demonstrations.

*27 The word *sudaka* or *sudaca* is, according to the definition of the Dictionary of the Spanish language of The Royal Spanish Academy, a degrading expression used to refer to the natives of South America.

*28 Palacio de La Moneda, or simply La Moneda, is the government palace of the President of the Republic of Chile. In Spanish, *moneda* means coin.

*29 The English translation for 'la dignidad' is 'dignity'. Here it refers to Plaza de la Dignidad (Dignity Square).

*30 The use of the word *mula* in Spanish can refer to a mammal born of two different equids (a donkey and a horse), and is also used colloquially (like in this case) to refer to a deceitful or untrustworthy person or thing.

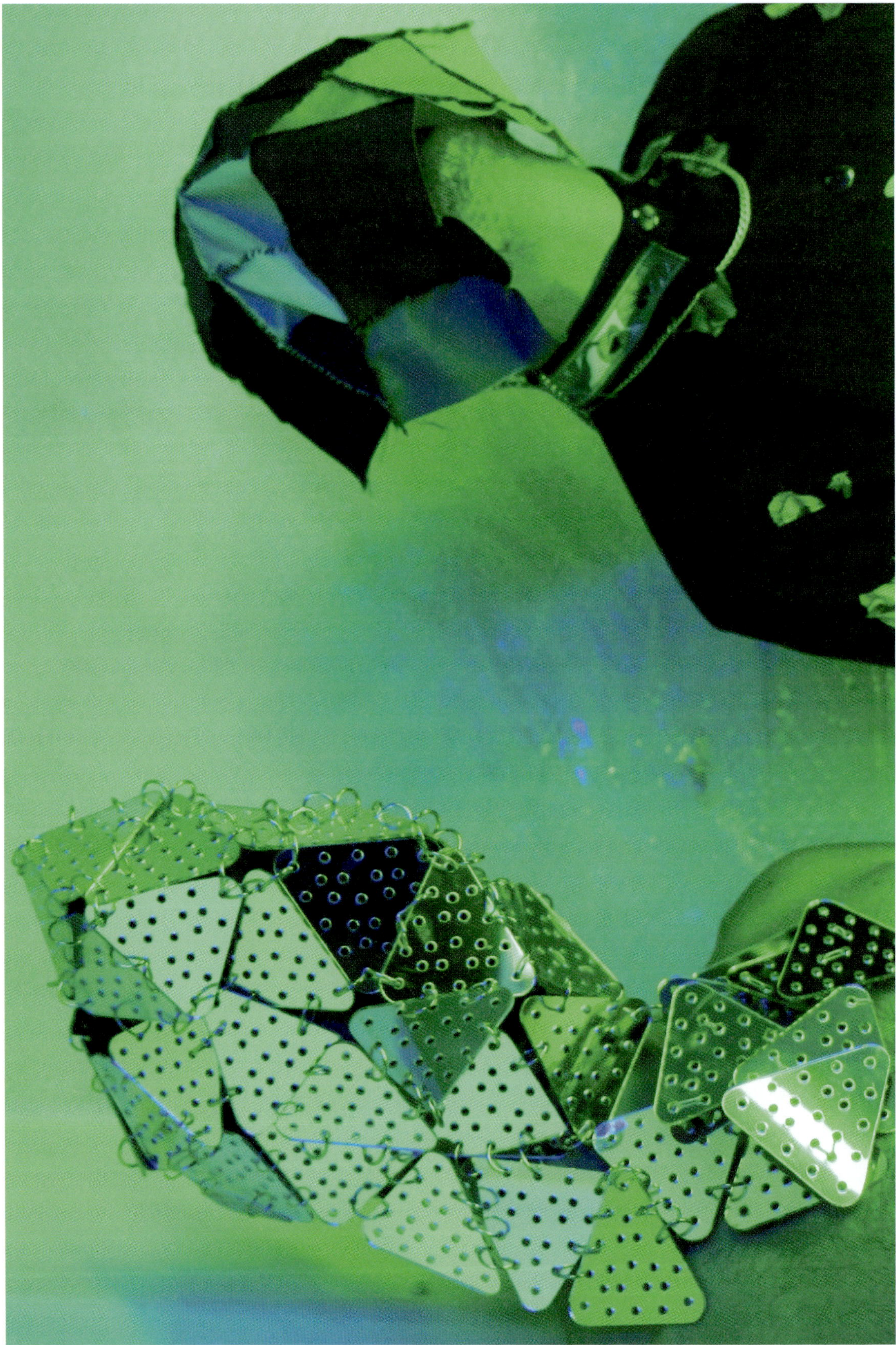

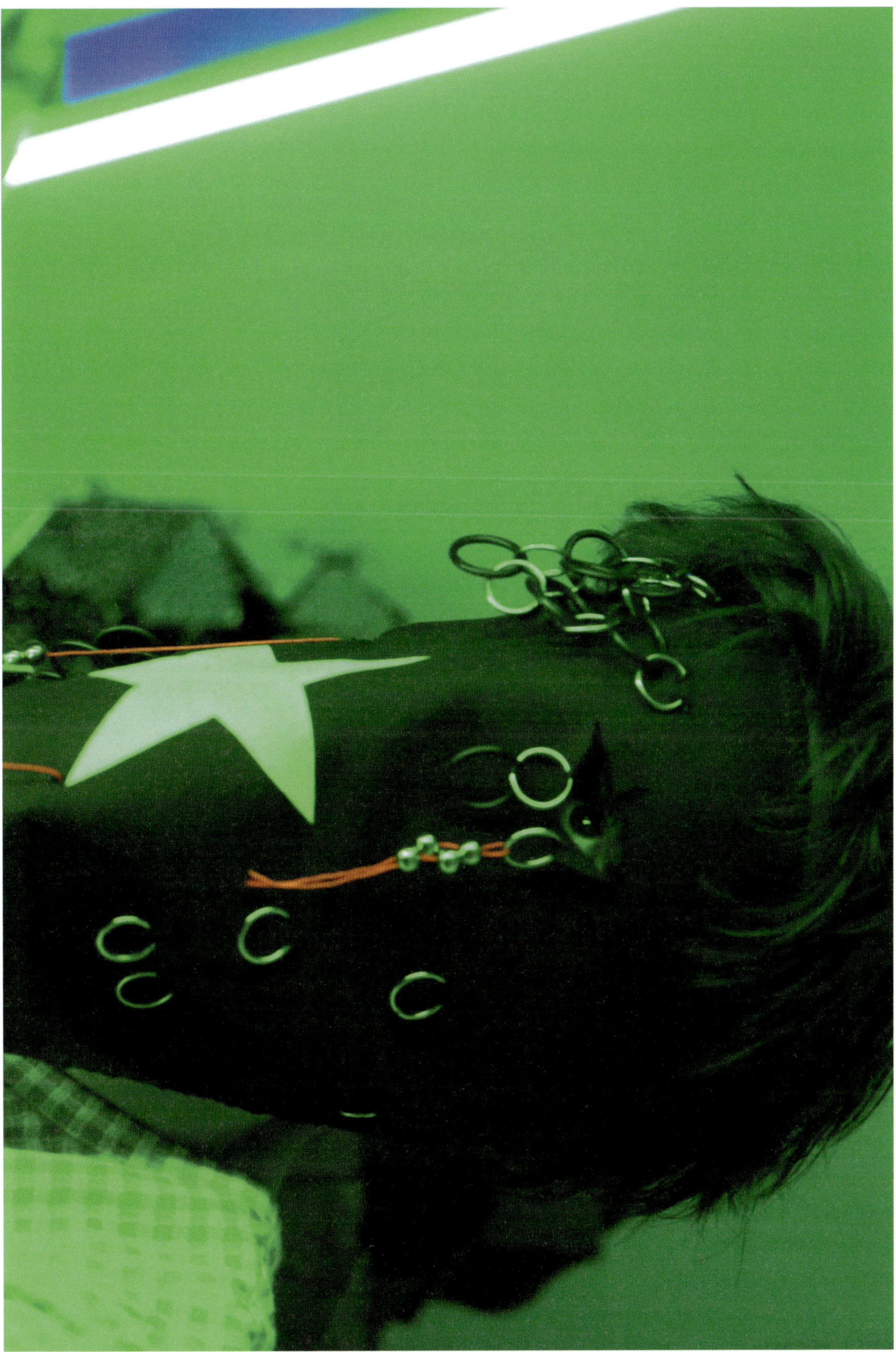

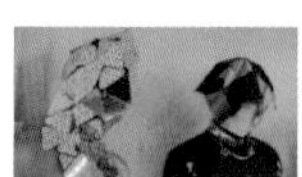

[ES]

Ahora las cosas están más claras:
si todavía quieren mantener sus bancos,
sus malls y supermercados,
qué asco,
resguárdenlos bien weones,
cúbranlos con esa chapa bien gruesa
y si tanto les gusta su plata
enciérrense en sus bóvedas.
Nos gusta cuando te blindas
porque estás como ausente.
Igual los vamos a saquear.

[EN]

Now things are clearer:
if you still want to keep your banks,
your malls and supermarkets,
how disgusting,
protect them carefully, you assholes,
cover them with that thick sheet of metal [*31]
and if you like your money so much,
lock yourselves in your vaults.
We like it when you shield yourselves
because you are as if absent. [*32]
We are still going to loot them.

*31 The use of metal sheets to protect the facades of supermarkets, banks, pharmacies, McDonalds, shopping malls, pension fund centres and corporate buildings, owned by a few economic groups, reached such a level that, during those days, finding an available blacksmith in Santiago was more difficult than robbing a bank.

*32 This phrase could refer to the poem of Pablo Neruda, 'Me Gustas Cuando Callas'. The original verse is 'Me gustas cuando callas porque estás como ausente' (I like you when you are quiet because you are as if absent).

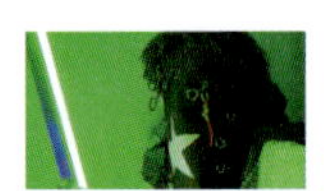

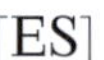

[ES]

Declaramos el nacimiento
del Territorio Autónomo de la Dignidad.

Este territorio no nació a la luz de un reloj.
No hay certificado de nacimiento.
No hay registros de su día y hora.
Fue parido en la noche oscura,
en la invisible niebla de la lucha,
en el incierto momento
en que el tiempo se prolonga continuo.

A la luz temblorosa de una fogata,
sin padre ni madre,
confundido con las ruinas
de aquello contra lo que se levanta.
Con sus antiguas baldosas y sus muebles
construimos barricadas,
con sus fachadas armamos
campos contra los blindados,
en sus parques
hacemos crecer jardines de romero y marihuana,
sus avenidas se vuelven laberintos de buses quemados,
sus puentes devienen campamentos
de deudores expiados de sus culpas.

[EN]

We declare the birth
of The Autonomous Territory of Dignity.

This territory was not born by the light of a clock.
There is no birth certificate.
There are no records of its day and hour.
It was given birth to in the dark night,
in the dense fog of struggle,
in the uncertain moment
when time is continuously [*33] prolonged.

In the trembling light of a campfire,
without father or mother,
confused with the ruins
of that against which it rises.
With its old tiles and furniture
we build barricades,
with its facades we set up
camps against the armoured vehicles, [*34]
in its parks
we grow gardens of rosemary and marihuana,
its avenues become labyrinths of burned buses, [*35]
its bridges become camps
of debtors expiated of their guilt. [*36]

*33 This continuity does not seem to refer to the continuity of the productive time of hegemonic capitalism where the same is repeatedly fabricated, but to the continuity of the vital and cosmic cycles where difference is repeatedly created.

*34 The massive use of armoured vehicles by the police force during the protests was striking. So much so that their zoological names have become part of our colloquial language. *Zorrillo* (skunk): armoured vehicle that fires tear gas. *Guanaco* (type of camelid that spits): armoured vehicle that shoots water at high pressure. *Cuca* (maybe from cuco, some kind of childish imaginary monster, but we like to think it also could be from 'cucaracha' that means 'cockroach' in English): patrol vehicle.

*35 Although the burning of buses has a historical association with an act of struggle, in recent years it has been linked with the unfulfilled promise of the new integrated transportation system and its role in urban segregation. That is why it is not surprising that the protest in the turnstiles of the city's subway has unleashed mass demonstrations.

*36 In Chilean society connections between economic relations and religion are articulated with surprising ease. We allow ourselves to speculate that the high level of indebtedness of the population (data from Fundacion Sol shows that, in 2020, half of the Chilean workers (4 million) are in default of their debts) is rooted in the construction of Catholic guilt as a mechanism for controlling souls.

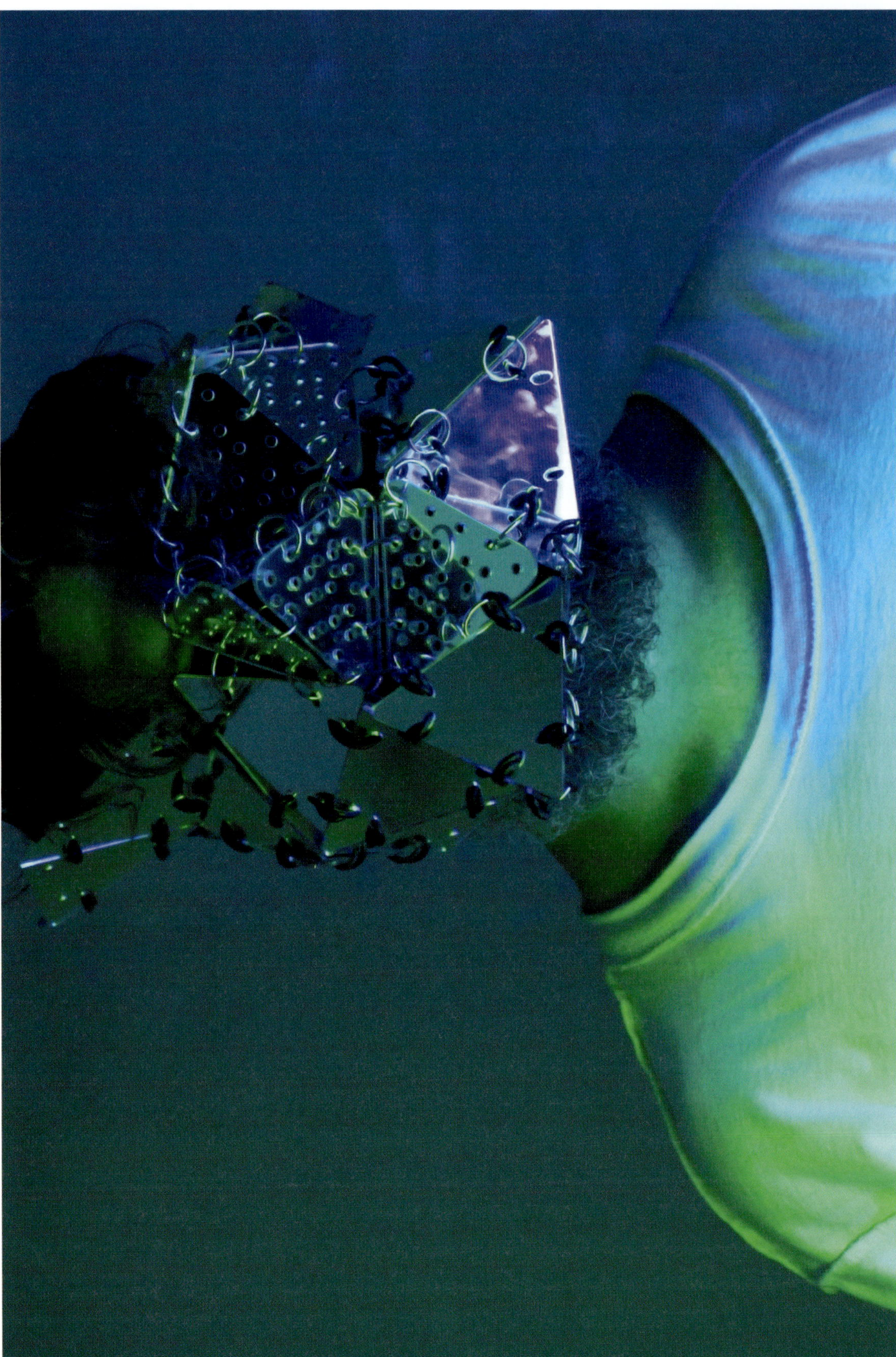

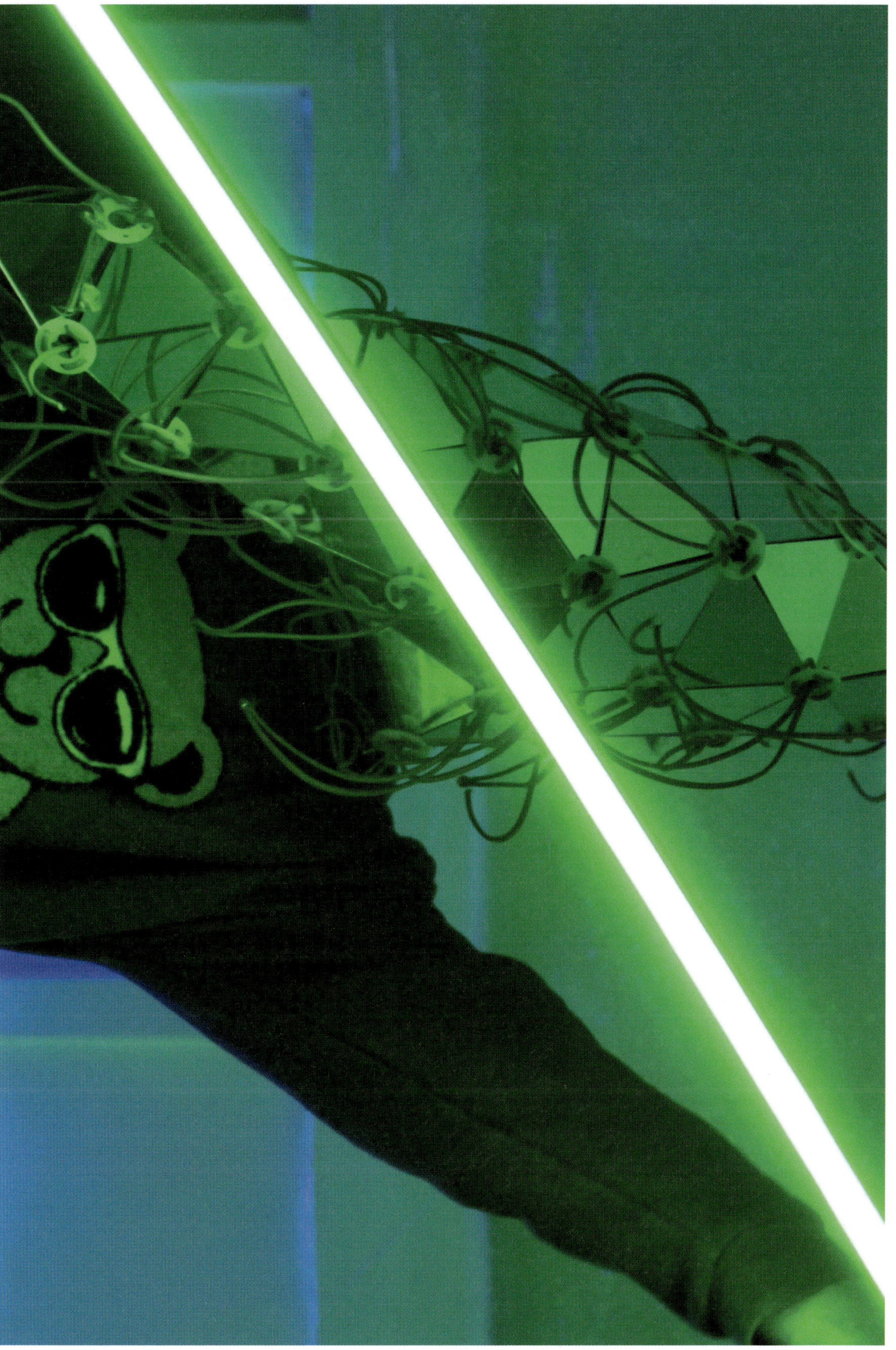

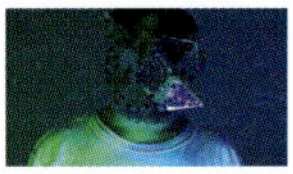

Levantamos el asfalto para hacer respirar la tierra,
para volverla permeable a la lluvia y sus espíritus.
Levantamos las calles para dejar que la tierra,
la lluvia y el fuego
nos cuenten relatos ancestrales para vivir mejor,
para imaginar una justicia no winka,
una cuerpa colectiva,
un lenguaje no binario,
un inconsciente rebelde,
un amor transexual, orgiástico y multiespecie.

Nuestro territorio es una frontera sin interioridad,
puro umbral y transformación.
Es un vivir en el borde.
Un gran obstáculo al desarrollo sin fin.

Nuestras fronteras son móviles y permeables,
tendientes a desaparecer,
sedientas de acoger,
de coger,
de festejar y aprender
de las formas de vida
que resisten a este régimen de mierda hace siglos.

[EN]

We lift the asphalt to make the earth breathe,
to make it permeable to the rain and its spirits.
We raise the streets to let the earth,
the rain and the fire
tell us ancestral stories to live better, [*37]
to imagine a non-*winka* [*38] justice,
a collective body,
a non-binary language, [*39]
a rebellious unconscious,
a transsexual, orgiastic and multispecies love.

Our territory is a frontier without interiority,
pure threshold and transformation.
It is a living-on-the-edge.
A great obstacle to endless development. [*40]

Our borders are mobile and permeable,
tending to disappear,
thirsty to welcome,
to catch,
to celebrate and learn
from the forms of life
that have been resisting this shitty regime for centuries.

*37 The consideration of the land as a living subject, its link with the spirits and the stories of the ancestors, seems to be linked in this text to the multiple struggles of indigenous peoples, both on a continental and Chilean level. The use of the *Wenüfoye* (Mapuche flag) in social demonstrations since 2019 highlights these relationships.

*38 *Winka* is a term from the Mapudungún language used by the Mapuche, to refer to white people, and more specifically to the Spanish conquerors of the 16th century.

*39 Binarism is a structural condition of the Spanish language.

*40 The idea of unlimited development marks the Latin American territory, going from the dispossession of the land to the indiscriminate extraction and exploitation of its natural resources.

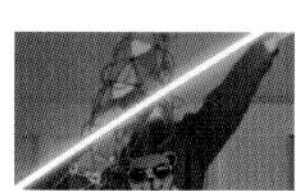

[ES]

No queremos imponer una nueva norma.
No queremos erguir una identidad
en contra de la que abandonamos.
No buscamos la independencia.
No es este un trámite político
en dirección a una nueva identidad nacional,
ni la cristalización de un nuevo mapa del poder,
de una línea punteada con un color a un lado,
y otro al otro.
No deseamos ni paz ni armonía.
Ni higiene ni salud.
Queremos vivir deseantes,
comunales, mamarrachas, en tensión.

Nos expandimos convulsionando,
para adentro y para afuera,
inventando ritos de pasajes
que nos permitan perder la forma.

[EN]

We do not want to impose a new norm.
We do not want to erect an identity
against the one we have abandoned.
We do not seek independence. [*41]
This is not a political step
in the direction of a new national identity,
nor the crystallisation of a new map of power,
of a dotted line with one color on one side
and another on the other.
We desire neither peace [*42] nor harmony.
Neither hygiene nor health.
We want to live desiring,
communal, *mamarrachas*, [*43] in tension.

We expand convulsively,
inwardly and outwardly,
inventing rites of passages
that allow us to lose our shape.

*41 Struggles for independence mark the founding milestones of modern American nations. Today, the history of those days is being rewritten and its military heroes are being knocked down from its horses and pedestals.

*42 The repeated call for peace has been a rhetorical device of the conservative sectors to censor the struggles that seek to change both the material distribution of wealth and the symbolic distribution of power.

*43 *Mamarracha(o)* is a term that usually refers to a person who lacks formality and composure and does not deserve to be taken seriously or treated with respect.

Lidia Morawska

Masks: To disguise your identity, or to protect you from what is in the air?

As a child growing up in Poland, masks had only one purpose: to represent the different characters who knocked on our door after Christmas and during the carnival period, demanding treats. I liked the Turoń, a scruffy looking horned animal, but preferred not to look at the Devil or Death. Interestingly, the Angel did not usually wear a mask, but had a nice, friendly face and big wings. Over time, I discovered that masks are used in many different parts of the world for different purposes, and that they are symbols of rich cultural practices.

My fascination with masks increased when my older daughter Alina developed a keen interest in the masks I brought back from my travels. She now has a large collection of these masks decorating her living room. I always carefully assess each mask before I buy it to ensure that it was made to be used for local cultural practices, rather than a mass-manufactured tourist souvenir. I like to buy masks from a local who knows the history behind them, and who can tell me what they represent, how they are or were used, and whether the tradition is still alive.

Is there a connection between this type of mask and the masks used to protect the wearer from pollution in the air, or to protect others from pathogens exhaled by an infected mask wearer? Their purposes could not differ more, which is seen in the parts of the face they cover. Masks for cultural traditions always cover the eyes, leaving just small holes to see through, with the intent of concealing the identity of the wearer and allowing them to assume a different personality. They often have openings for the nose (to breathe) and the mouth (to talk). Masks used for protection never cover the eyes (except in the case of full protective equipment), but always cover the mouth and nose. The different designs indicate the significant differences in their objectives and the roles they play. Here we take a closer look at those used for protection from pathogens and pollution and their recent entry into our everyday life.

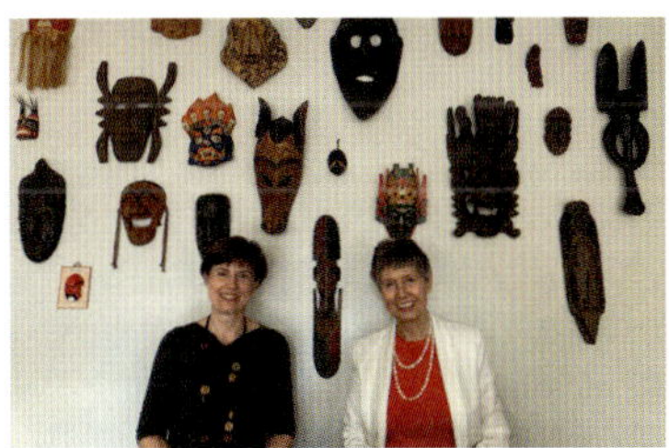

(Fig. 1)

Fig. 1. Dr Alina Morawska (left) and Dr Lidia Morawska (the author) with Alina's mask collection from around the world.

Masks in research

It was only when I led a research project to quantify the fraction of inhaled particles that are deposited in the lungs that masks became a research tool in my work. It is extremely difficult to gain insight into what happens in our respiratory tract during inhalation, when particles of different sizes are deposited with different probabilities in different parts of the airways, or, during exhalation, when new particles are generated there. As we noted in our recently published commentary, 'we know more about the surface of Mars from direct images, including the dynamics of the impact of airflow and the Martian wind, than we know about the surface of the lung of a living person'.[*1] This is because there are no means to obtain direct empirical information from the surface of the respiratory tract of a living person. To study the process of inhalation, we compare the characteristics of inhaled air with those of exhaled air, and then draw conclusions about what fraction of particles was deposited in the respiratory tract. Then, we employ modelling to apportion what fraction was deposited in which part of the respiratory tract. Why is it important to know this? The particles deposited in the upper parts of the respiratory tract may cause irritation, leading to inflammation, with all its ensuing health consequences. However, particles deposited in the deeper parts of the tract may enter the blood system and then be carried to different parts of the body, resulting in other health implications.

What is the role of masks in such studies? We use masks because we need to know exactly what was inhaled and what was exhaled, without any interference from the background air or interactions between the inhaled and exhaled air streams. In that study,*[2] our volunteers wore modified masks that allowed them to breathe air with well-defined characteristics from an experimental chamber with the exhaling valve closed, and then exhale with the inhaling valve closed. One important conclusion we drew from that study was that masks do not fit all faces equally well. We devoted a great deal of effort to ensuring a perfect fit, without which our results would have been meaningless.

Some years later our team conducted another study, this time to investigate the effectiveness of masks in preventing particles containing a pathogen from being emitted by infected people into the air. The focus of that study was on a bacterium, *Pseudomonas aeruginosa*, the most common pathogen in the airways of people with cystic fibrosis. It is a dangerous pathogen to chronically harbour in the lungs: infected people not only experience a decline in pulmonary function and quality of life, but their life expectancy is also reduced. Therefore, any measures that can reduce cross-infection with *Pseudomonas aeruginosa* help, and masks are considered to be one such measure. But which masks? Do these people need to wear N95 respirators? Or are simple surgical masks sufficient for minimizing the release of respiratory particles carrying the bacteria? In two papers that we published on this topic, we concluded that both surgical masks and N95 respirators were effective in reducing the release of particles carrying *Pseudomonas aeruginosa* during coughing, however, surgical masks had the advantage of being more comfortable to wear.*[3]

These studies made me realise that putting a layer (or more) of fabric in front of your nose makes breathing more difficult. We breathe in and out twelve times a minute; the additional effort imposed by wearing a mask in this most fundamental function makes life more difficult.

Reasons why people wear masks

Wearing masks became common in Asian countries to prevent infection transmission during the SARS1 epidemic. No one was wearing masks in Chinese cities up until early 2003, the year in which SARS spread throughout the world. People were scared, and authorities recommended many measures to prevent SARS transmission, including the use of masks. And thus they entered everyday life as a means to protect people against airborne infectious agents. Of course, this type of protection has long been used in health care to protect medical staff from contracting infections from patients, and to protect vulnerable patients from infection via medical staff.

Even after the SARS1 epidemic, people continued using masks in Asia as the practice had become fully socially acceptable. However, this was not the case outside Asia. Over time, I noticed that precaution against potential infection was not the only reason people wore masks. Another important application emerged, against another threat to human health: air pollution. Severe air pollution events were becoming more frequent and everyday levels of air pollution were increasing, particularly in large urban agglomerations in developing countries. Masks offered some level of protection. But eventually I realised that there were numerous situations when the reason for wearing masks was unclear—on days with no obvious air pollution, or when there were few people around in outdoor settings to spread infection. In a beautiful park in Beijing, full of spring blossoms, people were wearing masks, apparently out of a fear that plant pollen would trigger allergies. I also learnt that they became fashionable in some cultures: transparent and beautifully ornamented masks worn by young women in Lhasa would surely not protect against anything. On the other hand, when I saw a masked man walking around a ski resort in Japan, I wondered if it were possible they were being used as face warmers. There was no air pollution; in fact, the air was of rare clarity. There is no pollen in the subzero winter environment, and the person was walking away from a congregation of people. With distance and dilution, not to mention temperature, infection would be highly unlikely, if not impossible.

There are numerous situations that cause experts to wonder why members of the public wear masks, most likely due to the public's false perceptions about risks and preventive measures. On the flip side of this, as we will see, there are also situations of real risk that are not effectively mitigated by masks due to other factors.

How masks stop particles

Apart from the use of masks as fashion statements, it is laudable that people are using masks for protection against infection or air pollution. However, one concern is that masks may not offer much or enough protection. This concern stems from an understanding of the mechanisms by which masks remove particles present in the air, or, in other words, an understanding of particle dynamics.

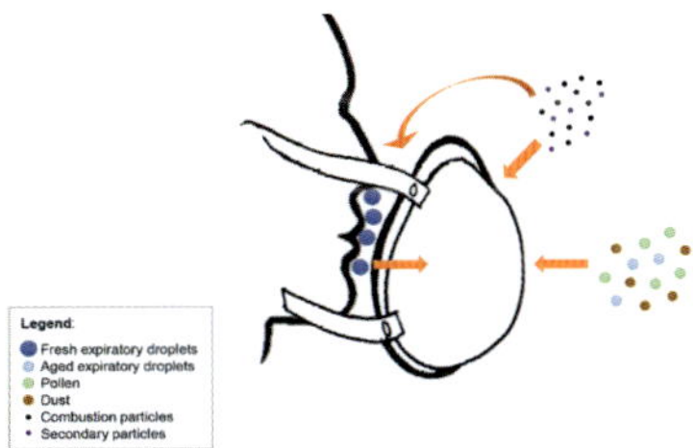

(Fig. 2)

Acting as protection against the spread of infection, the mask is supposed to stop infectious agents from the mouth or nose of an infected person penetrating through its material, or conversely, to stop infectious agents from the air coming through the material to the mouth or nose of a person who does not want to be infected. Infectious agents are bacteria or viruses that are typically contained in the liquid material of respiratory particles. These particles are larger immediately after exhalation and smaller when aged in the air, after some of their liquid content has evaporated. Still, they are relatively large compared with other particles in the air, and typically range from under one micrometre to several to several tens of micrometres. Such large and therefore heavy particles have a high inertia and are deposited by impact or intercepted by the fibres of the mask material.

In contrast, most particles in polluted urban air typically originate directly from combustion or are formed in the air in a process of vapour condensation (and are called secondary particles). These particles are two to three orders of magnitude smaller than the respiratory particles, most of them are smaller than 0.1 µm (and called ultrafine particles), and they are filtered by the material of the mask through diffusional deposition. Being light, they have very little inertia; they follow the flow of the air and do not impact on the fibres, but may diffuse towards them.

Is this difference in the filtration mechanism between large and small particles of different origin significant? It is! Even relatively thin or less dense masks will efficiently remove the larger particles, but their efficiency will be lower for small particles. In practical terms, this means that masks provide more protection against infectious agents than against air pollution (Fig. 2). Notable exceptions are desert dust, pollen, and pollen spores, which are large particles (up to 100 µm) that can be filtered efficiently.

It is important to mention that a mask will filter only the particles, but not the gaseous components of air pollution. In a dense haze, in addition to particles, there are hundreds of toxic gases and vapours that will not be filtered by a mask.

A mask is only effective if it is properly fitted, with no gaps allowing air to flow between the mask and the face. If the fit is not perfect, although a good fraction of larger particles will be captured, most of the small particles will get through to the breathing zone. This is due to the ability of small particles to follow the airflow around obstacles and, therefore, to pass through small openings. In contrast, larger particles, with greater inertia, are more likely to be deposited by impact on the edges of the opening (between the face and a poorly fitting mask), and not enter the breathing zone.

Fig. 2. Particle dynamics: transport of particles of different origins and sizes through or around the mask.

Can we assume that in most cases masks are properly fitted? I would argue that the opposite is the case unless the mask is fitted by a professional. The quality of the fit depends on the type of a mask; proper respirators provide a better fit than typical surgical masks.[*4] The fit also depends on the shape of the face. In our research work we encountered people for whom it was extremely difficult to correctly fit a mask. In addition, a mask will not fit well on a bearded face. And finally, it depends on the behaviour of the wearer: whether the wearer is diligent in correctly applying the mask, how long the mask is worn (e.g., allowing it to get wet after prolonged wearing changes its filtration characteristics), and how many times the mask is taken off (and perhaps not correctly re-applied). The behavioural aspects are important, particularly considering that wearing a mask is uncomfortable, and the better the mask is in terms of density and fit, the greater the discomfort.[*5] It is more difficult to breathe with a mask, especially when it is hot (like on a hot hazy day in Beijing). Carbon dioxide may build up in the mask (causing sleepiness),[*6] the tone of the voice changes when speaking through the mask, and the mask prevents the wearer from snacking or drinking without removing it.

The discussion so far has demonstrated the complexity of the problem and the many factors that need to be taken into account to assess whether a mask wearer is protected, including the size (source) of the particles, the type of mask, and the face shape and behaviour of the wearer. It comes as no surprise that it is difficult to quantify the performance of masks, either in a population or for an individual.

Masks and COVID-19

Pre-COVID-19, there was already much discussion about whether to wear a mask or not and the level of protection offered by masks; we commented on this in 2019. [*7] More research has been done on the performance of masks against the spread of infection than against air pollution. However, some studies demonstrated the limited protection offered by masks against air pollution on a population basis. Just before COVID-19 struck there was, for the first time, a discussion about wearing masks in Australia. The reason? Bushfire smoke blanketing several Australia cities for weeks at a time (Fig. 3), making breathing not only difficult, but hazardous to health.[*8]

Together with a team of colleagues, we were planning a review paper on mask-related topics when COVID-19 arrived. This shifted my priorities, and I soon realised that the number of papers on masks mushroomed—everybody seemed to have an expert view on this topic, and experts were writing reviews or commentaries on the many mask-related issues. For example, is there any benefit in wearing home-made masks?[*9] In fact, masks seem to have been one of the most discussed topics during the pandemic.

It turned out that the topic of masks was not only one of the most discussed topics during the pandemic, but also one of the most controversial. In March 2020, Dr. Mike Ryan, executive director of the World Health Organization Health Emergencies program stated: 'There is no specific evidence to suggest that the wearing of masks by the mass population has any potential benefit'.[*10] Was it because of an old medical dogma that the virus is not airborne, and therefore there is no risk if the distance of 'one arm length' is maintained, and therefore masks are not needed? Or because

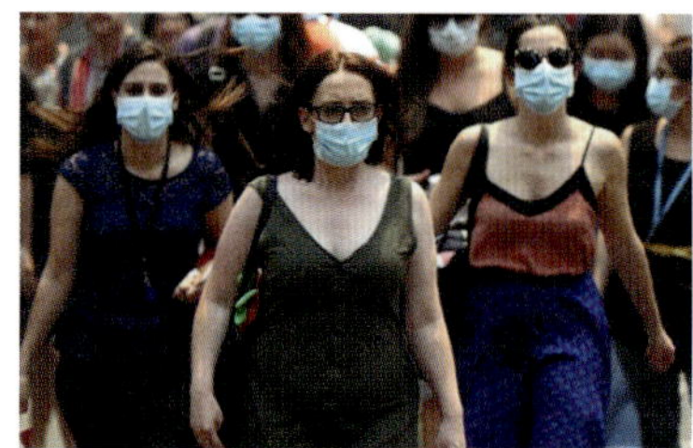

(Fig. 3)

Fig. 3. People wearing face masks to protect from smoke haze as they cross a busy city street in Sydney, Australia. Smoke haze hung over the city for several weeks as bushfires burned across New South Wales in 2019. (Getty)

of an insufficient supply of them worldwide? Eventually the WHO changed their advice completely and recommended wearing masks stating: 'Non-medical, fabric masks can be used by the general public under the age of 60 and who do not have underlying health conditions'.[*11] Masks became mandatory in most countries around the world.

Despite this, healthcare workers were still fighting for their right to access adequate masks (N95 respirators, not surgical masks) to protect them from the risks they were facing while caring for infected people. While surgical masks are adequate in community exposure situations (as I explained above), they are not suitable for situations with high concentrations of virus-laden particles in proximity to infected people. After more than a year of the pandemic, a big victory was won by healthcare workers in Australia: the Infection Control Expert Group (ICEG) and National COVID-19 Clinical Evidence Taskforce jointly agreed on updated recommendations to protect health care workers from COVID-19 infection. This includes advice on when to use face (surgical) masks, P2/N95 respirators and eye protection.[*12]

At the same time, there was some excessive mandating of mask wearing: during the outbreaks of the past few months, some Australian state governments (as well as the governments of many countries) have mandated wearing masks outdoors. But outdoors the concentration of the virus is insignificant, and therefore the risk of infection is close to zero,[*13] unless one stays very close to an infected person, in which case even short exposure can lead to infection, particularly with the Delta variant.[*14] Some states, such as Queensland during the March 2021 outbreak, took a more rational approach, 'It is strongly recommended you wear a mask outdoors if you are unable to stay more than 1.5 m distance from other people, such as busy walkways and thoroughfares.' In other words, there is no need for masks if distance can be maintained.[*15]

While wearing masks indoors is important, and is considered a personal responsibility, it is not always a viable solution—we cannot dine with masks on, for example! This leads to comical situations when we are ushered to the tables in restaurants with masks on, to take them off at the table. Will the virus take a break when we are dining? Clearly, scientific evidence is not the basis for public health authorities in decision-making on airborne infection transmission. There is another critical measure missing: sufficient and effective ventilation to lower the risk of respiratory infection transmission indoors. Mandating adequate ventilation is much more complex than asking people to wear masks. In Australia, as in many other countries, ventilation is not yet part of the discussion or the package of intervention measures for infection control, despite calls from scientists that highlight the importance of this issue.[*16] What is in the best interests of public health fades away in the face of old dogmas, mixed with politics, entangled with economic and other vested interests—these are what dictate the course of action taken and shifts the responsibility for infection prevention away from government to individuals. In this case, masks win and ventilation loses.

Masks in the future

Even if ventilation is fully embraced as a key measure to protect against infection, masks will also remain part of this equation—humans will always emit pathogens, and protection from pathogens will always be necessary. However, I hope masks will be less necessary for protection against air pollution, as we look forward to a future without anthropogenic air pollution. The transition to clean energy has already started. In our lifetime, electric or hydrogen fuelled vehicles will roam city streets and country roads, and the electricity and hydrogen for these cars will be generated in a clean way, without fossil fuels. Likewise, women in the villages of Indonesia, Pacific Island countries or India will no longer need to bend over open fires when cooking meals for their families, exposing babies carried on their backs to smoke, as cleanly generated electricity will be used for cooking everywhere. Unfortunately, airborne pollution will not be a phenomenon of the past; we will be plagued by climate change related air pollution for a long time, as recently concluded by the Intergovernmental Panel on Climate Change (IPCC) in its sixth report—from more frequent fires and dust storms, as we have already experienced in Australia.[*17] But as explained above, masks will not protect us against bushfire smoke.

I strongly hope, however, that masks will continue to be used for cultural practices, as they have been over centuries and millennia. While we have a different and much improved understanding of the world around us than did our forebears who initiated the traditions, we are strengthened as humans by maintaining traditions. Let us cherish this tradition of covering faces for all the reasons this has been done in the cultures of the Indo-Pacific region and beyond.

Lidia Morawska
Masks: to disguise your identity, or to protect you from what is in the air?
* **footnotes & references**

---

*1 L. Morawska and G. Buonanno, "The Physics of Particle Formation and Deposition During Breathing," *Nature Reviews Physics* 3 (2021): 300-301.

*2 L. Morawska, W. Barron & J. Hitchins, "Experimental Deposition of Environmental Tobacco Smoke Submicrometer Particulate Matter in the Human Respiratory Tract," *American Industrial Hygiene Association Journal*, 60 (1999): 334-339.

*3 R. E. Stockwell, M. E. Wood, C. He, L. J. Sherrard, E. L. Ballard, T. J. Kidd, G. R. Johnson, L. D. Knibbs, L. Morawska & S. Bell, "Face Masks Reduce the Release of Pseudomonas Aeruginosa Cough Aerosols When Worn for Clinically Relevant Periodsm," *American Journal of Respiratory and Critical Care Medicine* 198 (2018): 1339–1342; M. E. Wood, R. E. Stockwell, G. R. Johnson, K. A. Ramsay, L. J. Sherrard, N. Jabbour, E. Ballard, P. O'Rourke, T. J. KIDD & C. E. WAINWRIGHT, "Face Masks and Cough Etiquette Reduce the Cough Aerosol Concentration of Pseudomonas Aeruginosa in People with Cystic Fibrosis," *American Journal of Respiratory and Critical Care Medicine* 197, (2018): 348-355.

*4 V. Offeddu, C. F. Yung, M. S. F Low & C. C. Tam, "Effectiveness of Masks and Respirators Against Respiratory Infections in Healthcare Workers: A Systematic Review and Meta-analysis," *Clinical Infectious Diseases* 65 (2017): 1934–1942.

*5 B. V. Shenal, L. J. Radonovich Jr, J. Cheng, M. Hodgson & B.S. Bender, "Discomfort and Exertion Associated with Prolonged Wear of Respiratory Protection in a Health Care Setting," *Journal of Occupational and Environmental Hygiene* 9 (2012): 59-64.

*6 A. T. Johnson, "Respirator Masks Protect Health but Impact Performance: A Review," *Journal of Biological Engineering* 10 (2016): 1-12.

*7 W. Huang & L. Morawska, "Face Masks Could Raise Pollution Risks," *Nature* 574 (2019): 29-30.

*8 L. Morawska, "From Face Masks to Air Purifiers: What Actually Works to Protect Us from Bushfire Smoke?" *The Conversation*, December 12, 2019, https://theconversation.com/from-face-masks-to-air-purifiers-what-actually-works-to-protect-us-from-bushfire-smoke-128633.

*9 A. P. Sunjaya & L. Morawska, "Evidence Review and Practice Recommendation on the Material, Design, and Maintenance of Cloth Masks," *Disaster Medicine and Public Health Preparedness* (2020): 1-5.

*10 J. Howard, "WHO Stands by Recommendation to Not Wear Masks if You Are Not Sick or Not Caring for Someone Who is Sick," *CNN*, March 31, 2020 (accessed June 23, 2021) https://edition.cnn.com/2020/03/30/world/coronavirus-who-masks-recommendation-trnd/index.html.

*11 WHO, "Coronavirus Disease (COVID-19): Masks," WHO, December 1, 2020, https://www.who.int/emergencies/diseases/novel-coronavirus-2019/question-and-answers-hub/q-a-detail/coronavirus-disease-covid-19-masks.

*12 The Infection Control Expert Group (ICEG), *Guidance on the Use of Personal Protective Equipment (PPE) for Health Care Workers in the Context of COVID-19* (Australian Government, Department of Health, June 10, 2021).

*13 L. Mannix, "Little Evidence to Support Outdoor Mask-Wearing Rule, Scientists Say," *The Age*, June 11, 2021, https://www.theage.com.au/national/victoria/no-evidence-to-support-outdoor-mask-wearing-rule-scientists-say-20210611-p58087.html.

*14 G. Cortellessa, L. Stabile, F. Arpino, D. E. Faleiros, W. van de Bos, L. Morawska and G. Buonanno, "Close Proximity Risk Assessment for SARS-CoV-2 Infection," *Science of the Total Environment* 794 (November 2021), https://doi.org/10.1016/j.scitotenv.2021.148749.

*15 Queensland Government, *"COVID-19 Update,"* Queensland Government, accessed June 23, 2021, https://www.qld.gov.au/health/conditions/health-alerts/coronavirus-covid-19/current-status/urgent-covid-19-update.

*16 L. Morawska, J. Allen, W. Bahnfleth, P. M. Bluyssen, A. Boerstra, G. Buonanno, J. Cao, S. J. Dancer, A. Floto & F. Franchimon, "A Paradigm Shift to Combat Indoor Respiratory Infection," *Science* 372 (2021): 689-691.

*17 L. Morawska, T. Zhu, N. Liu, M. A. Torkmahalleh, M. de Fatima Andrade, B. Barratt, P. Broomandi, G. Buonanno, L. C. B. Ceron, J. Chen, Y. Cheng, G. Evans & Gavidia, "The State of Science on Severe Air Pollution Episodes: Quantitative and Qualitative Analysis," *Environment International* 156 (November 2021).

94

Juan Elvira

Face politics and the micro-architectures of immunity

You're in a crowd of people. People's voices, gestures and body language can be read instantly. Together these form a communicative atmosphere in which the face is the central element. We know if someone is friendly or hostile by looking at their face: it is an assemblage that communicates the other's will, at least within the limits of cultural bias.

In the attention economy of contemporary cities, an exhausting amount of impulses and individual signs saturate and shape our everyday experiences. Cities are places of high optical demands and low communicative efficacy. Yet, there is a kind of perception where no cognitive effort is required, where communication is direct and the optical demands are low.[*1] This happens when experiencing nature, where a series of stimuli patterns capture our attention. This is called non-semantic information and the human face is one such source. While semantic information requires mechanisms of codification, these are not necessary in this instance. The traits and gestures of the human face conform to a non-semantic physiognomic landscape, in the Humboldtian sense.

Content and form are inseparable in a face. For Georg Christoph Lichtenberg, physiognomy is the practice of reading character and emotional states through the individual's form, in particular that of the face. The physiognomic presupposes a particular relationship between interior and exterior, where one is a direct correlate of the other. We can also see this relationship expressed in architectural terms. Rowe wrote that until the nineteenth century, architecture had a face or main facade, something that the modern movement tried to unmask by revealing inner structures. Architects still talk about the physiognomy of classical orders.

Let's come back to that crowd of people. Things have changed. Everyone's faces are covered with masks (Fig. 1). When confronted with air that is infused with components—tear gas, pollution, viruses, all kinds of external anomalous agents—that threaten our coexistence with our atmospheres, a rich set of techniques are deployed to make this coexistence possible. Together they compose a set of micro-architectures that are essential in the mediation between us and our environment. In doing so, they make visible those emerging conflicts between human life and the environment while simultaneously negating the face (the fundamental vehicle in a social milieu). A mask is the face of a face. Physiognomic mediation, whatever the kind, engages interior and exterior spaces, as well as psychological (facial expressions) and atmospheric (the environment) elements. In light of this, the human head is one of the principal terrains of biopolitics.

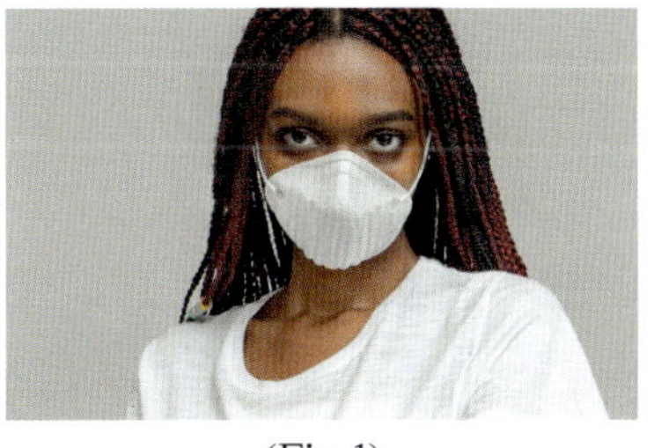

(Fig. 1)

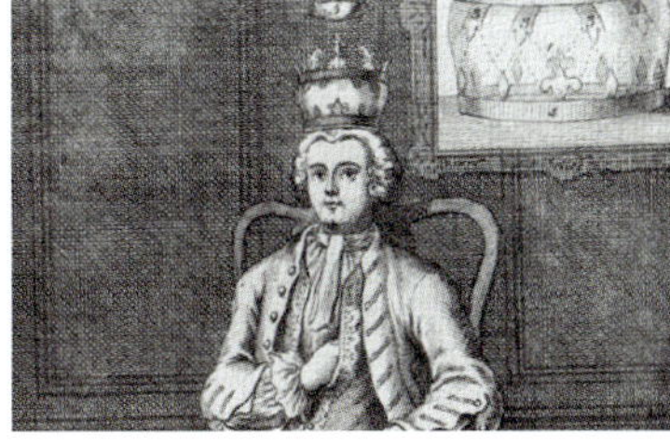

(Fig. 2)

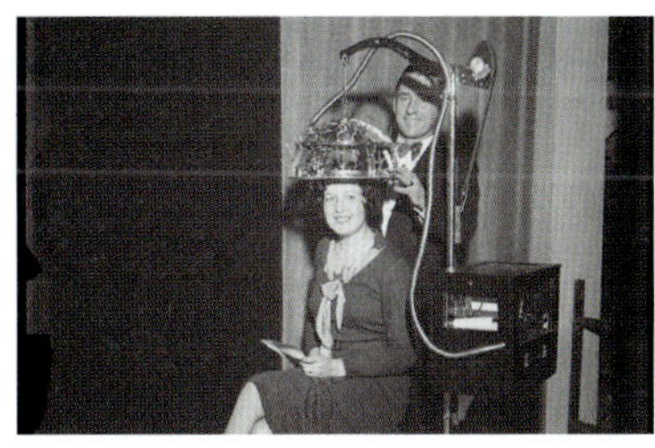

(Fig. 3)

Fig. 1. COVID mask.

Fig. 2. *Beatification Device.* Engraving by Georg Matthias Bosse (in Benjamin Rackstraw, *Miscellaneous Observations,* (London: 1748).

Fig. 3. *Woman Seated With a Psychograph, a Phrenology Machine, on Her Head.* Photo by Harris & Ewing, United States of America, 1931 (Harris & Ewing photograph collection at the Library of Congress, https://www.loc.gov/item/2016879401/).

Technologies of the head

The construction of architectural apparatus that preserve and manipulate our most intimate sphere has a long tradition. Although these technologies experienced an intense development in the 60s, the manipulation of the human sensorium and psychological atmospheres have been the aim of different micro-architectures since ancient times. In the eighteenth century, several electrical apparatuses anticipated the mind expansion devices developed in our time. This is the case of the *Beatification* built by Georg Matthias Bosse in 1784 (Fig. 2), which allowed for the staging of spiritual superiority in the form of auras produced by electrified crowns.[*2] The experimenter, usually a man, sat in a chair and received a light metallic headdress. Like a saint's *nimbus* or halo, a 'continual flux of fire'[*3] emanated from it, which inspired in the receptor feelings of greatness. Beatification was inscribed within the social prestige and genre politics of the time, where electricity stressed the power and spirituality of the male personality.

Following the theories of nervous fluid, which aligned mental activity with electrical fluxes, some devices were designed with the purpose of regulating the cerebral 'electrical charge' in order to balance the patient's mind. In the chapter dedicated to 'Pathogenic atmospheres' in *Les vibrations de la vitalité humaine*, [*4] researcher Hippolyte Baraduc described one of his inventions. The 'apparatus for cerebral de-condensation' was a metallic cylinder placed over the patient's head with the purpose of 'de-electrifying' it. Years later, a similar device called 'personality reading phrenologic robot'[*5] (Fig. 3) was presented in society. A helmet equipped with a grid of metallic bars placed perpendicular to the head sent electrical impulses from the head to a receiver, which in turn printed a report. Obviously, these were proto-scientific devices born from a hesitant discipline, but through their rituals and intentions they were steps towards the cerebral activity apparatus invented later in the century.

Technologies of the head also served another purpose: the mediation of our external environment. Diving helmets (Fig. 4) or oxygen masks (Fig. 5) are well known for making otherwise inhospitable environments accessible. Air mediation also encompasses atmospheric therapy, like the apparatus described by Lawrence Wright in his history of the bed. Conceived at the beginning of the twentieth century, it's a funnel-like gramophone placed in a bed headboard and connected to the exterior, which meant that opening windows was no longer necessary for providing fresh air to the sleeper, and it also prevented noises and unwanted air currents.[*6]

Other devices were contrived to create an atmosphere of concentration. An extreme example of this was the *Isolator* (Fig. 6), built in 1925 with the purpose of preserving emotional balance and the improvement of personal space. Its author was Hugo Gernsback, electric engineer and editor of the *Electrical Experimenter* and *Science and Invention*. Covered in felt, it rested on the shoulders of the user, completely covering the head, and allegedly provided the conditions for efficient work. Two eye slits allowed for the reading of a single line at a time. The *Isolator* also featured an oxygen intake connected to an external tank.

With the popularization of mass media devices, head architectures would implement the emission and reception of information as part of their features. Gernsback is also the author of the *Teleyeglasses* (1936) (Fig. 7), an audiovisual prototype with stereoscopic image and bifocal lenses that would open up the myriad of technologies that we know today. Information technology also extended to educational models, reinterpreted as individual interfaces, which is the case of the *Shoulder Carrell* (Fig. 8) designed by architect Charles Colbert in 1968.

The idea of an architectural medium specifically designed for the individual

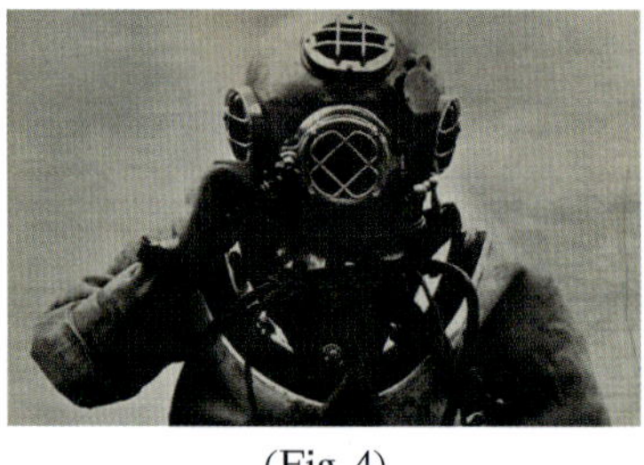

(Fig. 4)

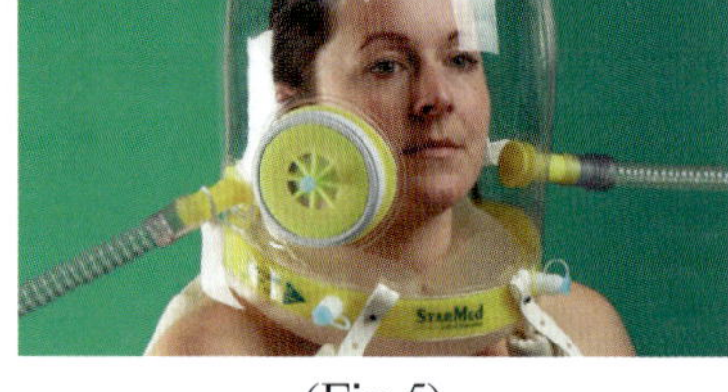

(Fig. 5)

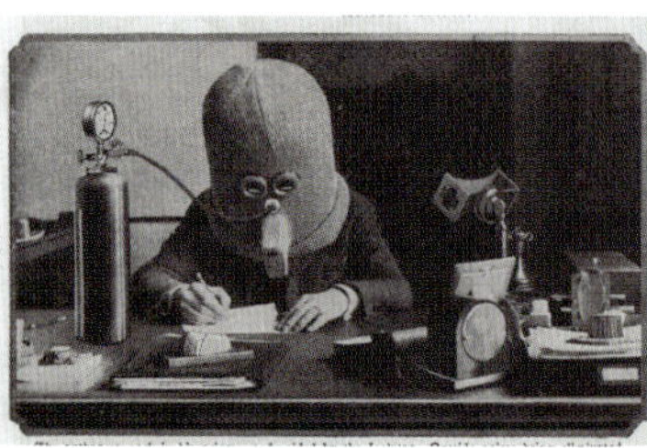

(Fig. 6)

Fig. 4. *Mark V Standard Diving Dress*, US Navy, 1930.

Fig. 5. The StarMed CaStar Hood by Intersurgical.

Fig. 6. Hugo Gernsback, *The Isolator*, 1925 (in *Science and Invention* 13, no. 3, July 1925).

sensorium was detailed for the first time in Kisho Kurokawa's *Capsule Declaration* (1969). Taking space suits and modern automobiles as key references, the architect wrote:

> The capsule is a cyborg architecture. Man, machine and space build a new organic body which transcends confrontation. As a human being equipped with a man-made internal organ becomes a new species which is neither machine nor human, so the capsule transcends man and equipment. Architecture from now on will increasingly take on the character of equipment. This new elaborative device is not a 'facility', like a tool, but is a part to be integrated in a life pattern and has an objective existence. [...] The human being in the capsule and the film which protects his life constitute a new existence which did not exist in the past.[*7]

Kurokawa envisions architecture as an amplified body. Although he is only referring to a technological expansion, it clearly anticipates proposals such as Haraway's cyborg twenty years later, a 'new species' whose features are constantly upgraded. Kurokawa proposed the integration of the individual and technological additions, which provided protection and conditioned the atmosphere in an unprecedented assemblage.

All the aforementioned devices led to the most influential moment in the speculative design of the human sensorium. Jet pilot cabins (Fig. 9) and astronaut suits (Fig. 10) would be the spatial paradigm every architect would look at in awe in the 60s. Likewise, space suits were the definitive life-support devices, with an innovative synthesis of life-supporting systems. Radical architecture would experience a progressive reduction in scale, achieving a closer fitting or casing of the individual's sensorium. Pneumatic units would wrap cities, parties, families, couples and finally heads in order to create a self-sufficient ambience, isolated from the exterior and perfect on its own terms. All of these were driven by technological optimism and the longing for atmospheric autonomy. The architects of Archigram would develop some of the most remarkable examples in this direction, such as the *Radical Portable Ambient* (1966), *Suitaloon* (Michael Webb, 1967–68), and *Cushicle* (Michael Webb, 1967). These comprised a transitional moment that would lead to the creation of progressively smaller spheres, like the *Info-gonks* (1968) (Fig. 11), an educational glass and headset.

Architects' research looked at the helmet as the spatial format for the creation of new artificial ambiances. In Italy architect Ugo la Pietra intensely explored this field, with projects such as *Immersioni* and *Audio Casco* (1968). Nonetheless, the Viennese radical avant-garde created the most interesting and boundary-shifting experiences. Hans Hollein, Haus Rucker-Co, Raimund Abraham, Walter Pichler and others explored this field in an urgent manner and with an initially optimistic trust in technology. The extension of physical and mental capacities through technology would be the perfect tool for emancipation and the exploration of the inner self. It would also

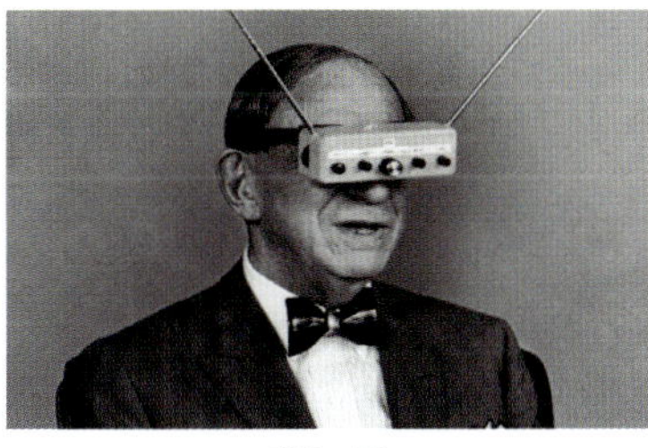

(Fig. 7)

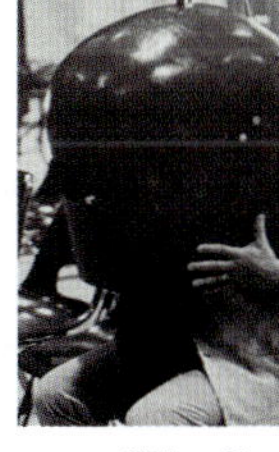

(Fig. 8)

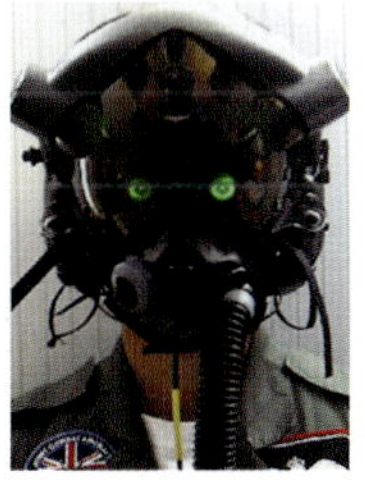

(Fig. 9)

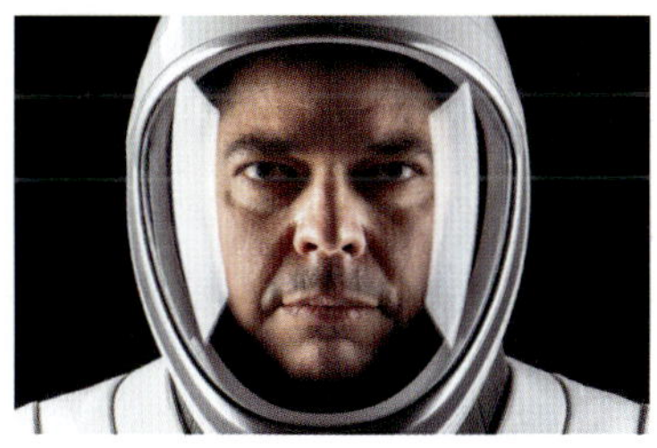

(Fig. 10)

Fig. 7. Hugo Gernsback, *Teleyeglasses*, 1936 (in *Life Magazine*, 1963).

Fig. 8. Charles Colbert, *Shoulder Carrell*, 1968.

Fig. 9. The Gen III Helmet Mounted Display System (HMDS) by Collins Aerospace.

Fig. 10. The Spacesuit Helmet by Space X (in Elisabeth Howell, "New SpaceX Spacesuits Get Five-Star Rating from NASA Astronauts", Space.Com, June 10, 2020, https://www.space.com/spacex-spacesuits-five-star-astronaut-review.html).

open the way for a radical critique of the architectural conventions of the moment.

Haus Rucker-Co's proposals dealt with these issues in several projects, problematizing perception by kinetic, optical and acoustic techniques, and progressively introducing a critical vision that was far from optimist. In their projects from the late 60s, alienation and disorientation were sought for effect, such as in the case of the *Environment Transformers* (1968), where individual devices pursued estrangement from reality. Things were seen differently while wearing them, in the figurative and the literal sense. *Flyhead* (Fig. 12) diverted sound and sight inputs with dual filters and stereophonic sound, provoking a distancing from reality. In *Drizzler* (Fig. 13), a PVC helmet combined fluorescent strata with a motor that rotated a disk in front of the face. This provoked perceptual bewilderment and the fragmentation of the visual field. Finally, the *Viewatomizer* (Fig. 14) used pulsating plastic lenses to induce an 'effect of alienation' by blurring of peripheral vision.

Coop Himmelb(l)au's projects aligned with Haus Rucker-Co.'s interests, in projects like *Astroballoon I* (1969) (Fig. 15). The architects used ongoing scientific research and medical equipment to register and amplify the user's heartbeat with the aim of inducing relaxation. Coop Himmelb(l)au contacted Dr. Haider from the Institute of Environmental Health in Vienna, which researched the impact of high-density habitats on its dwellers, testing some of their ideas in a device that initially was going to be a more artist-oriented installation. Electroencephalography devices were used to measure the subject's brainwaves and alpha-wave frequencies to induce progressive relaxation.[*8] They opened up techniques similar to today's biofeedback devices, like Muse company (Fig.16), or Fitbit devices that incessantly register our physiological constants.

Other appliances focused on the tracking of the individual's physiognomic landscape. In *Gesichtsraum / Soul Flipper II* (1971) (Fig. 17) 'the facade of a person's moods'—as described in the architect's project description—is objectified by registering facial expressions and translating them in a sound and light effect 'column'. A translation between the so-called *gesichtsraum* or 'face space' denoted an interest in the communicative features of the face and how to re-elaborate that information in an abstract haptic space. A smile produces bright colours, a sad expression infuses space with pale blue.

The interest in the face as an architectural topic expressed by Coop Himmelb(l)au can also be traced in the article *The tower of Babel revisited* (1993). This text is primarily the reaction to the failure of the Ronacher Theatre in Vienna. After a long process, the municipality decided that it wasn't going to build it: it was a weird project, even uncanny for some. From here, a discourse on fear and architecture developed, with claims that architecture was dead and no spatial concepts would survive, something they believed would lead to the decadence of society. Most significantly, a fragment of Bob Dylan's *Desolation Row* lyrics can be found at the beginning of the text:

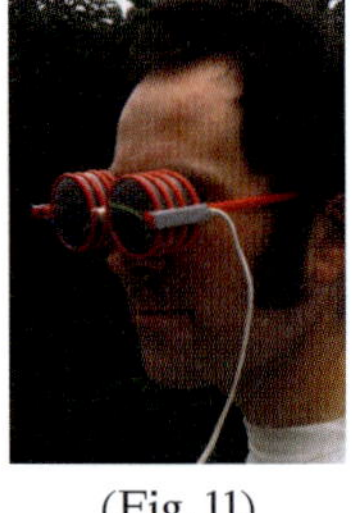

(Fig. 11)

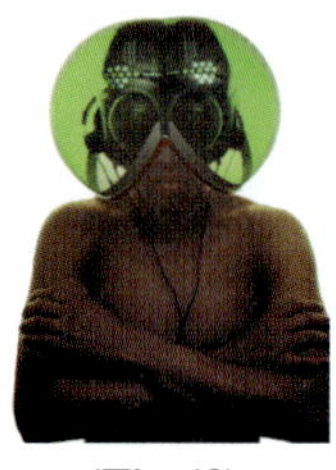

(Fig. 12)

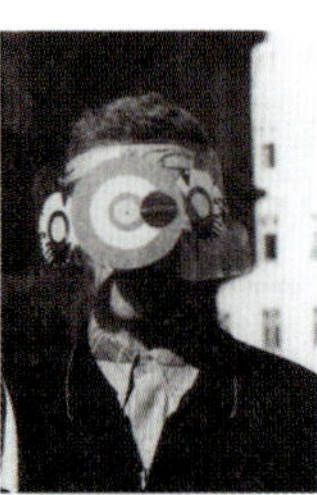

(Fig. 13)

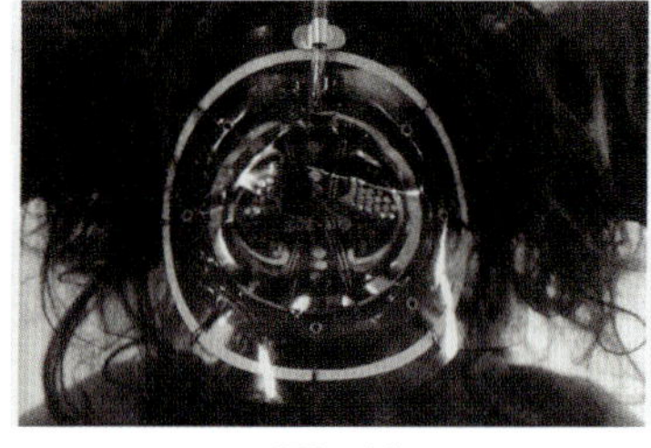

(Fig. 14)

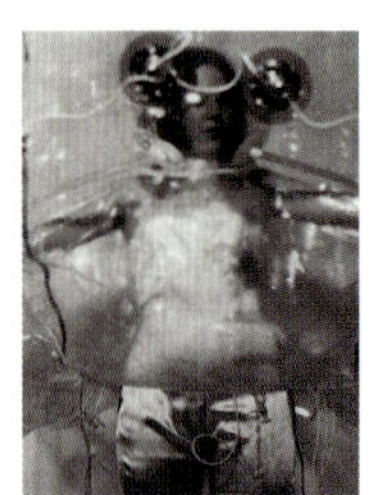

(Fig. 15)

Fig. 11. Archigram, *Info-gonks*, 1968.

Fig. 12. Haus Rucker Co., *Flyhead*, 1968. Photograph by Ben Rose.

Fig. 13. Haus Rucker Co., *Drizzler*, 1968. Photograph by Gert Winkler.

Fig. 14. Haus Rucker Co., *Viewatomizer*, 1968. Photograph by Gert Winkler.

Fig. 15. Coop Himmelb(l)au, *Astroballoon I*, 1969. Photograph by Erwin Reichman. (Coop Himmelb(l)au Archives at Galerie nächst St. Stephan, Vienna).

Yes, the people that you mentioned, I know them, they 're quite lame.

I have to rearrange their faces and give them all another name.

The quote is accompanied by a fragmented and partially cut model, both images representing dislodged facial structures. At the end of the article, the project *The Dissolution of our Bodies in the City* is introduced. The city must embrace individuals and live and breathe again: 'Our eyes became towers, our foreheads bridges, our faces landscapes, and our bodies the plan'.*9 A photograph of the architects' faces (Fig. 18) is marked, cut and its fragments reordered. Exposed to it, our gaze isn't able to rearrange the physiognomic map.

The devices shown so far imply a separation between two realms, the outside environment and the internal psychological experience. It aims to mediate them. This experience, the qualification and modification of the lived experience at will, was described as 'The Walkman Effect' by Shuhei Hosokawa in 1984.*10 New connections with our surroundings are established depending on what is listened to at a particular moment. The user of a walkman, an iPod (2001) or Google-glasses (2013) (Fig. 19) can choose between intersubjective contact or isolation at will. Contemporary works like *The Objectuals* (2003–2010) (Figs. 20, 21 & 22) by Hyungkoo Lee advance this research. *The Objectuals* visually manipulate our face features, generating a mutant physiognomy in the era of cosmetic surgery, and artificially changing the emotional atmosphere and the capacity of communication of the face-object. They are composed of interchangeable lenses that enlarge or reduce certain areas of the face, attached to a transparent sphere. *Floating Eye* (2001) (Fig. 23) by Hiroo Iwata builds an extra corporeal experience of sorts, where a technical gizmo changes our eye level. What we see is us from above, an image transmitted from a camera installed in a floating balloon.

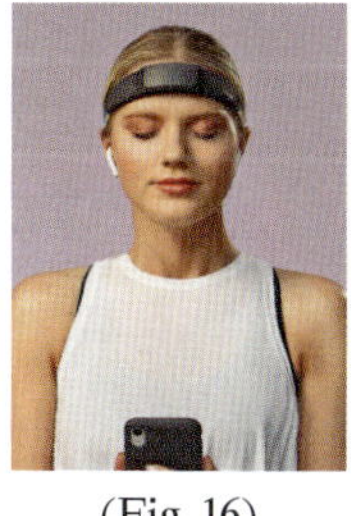

(Fig. 16)

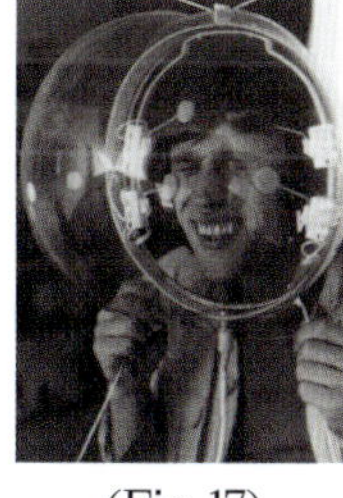

(Fig. 17)

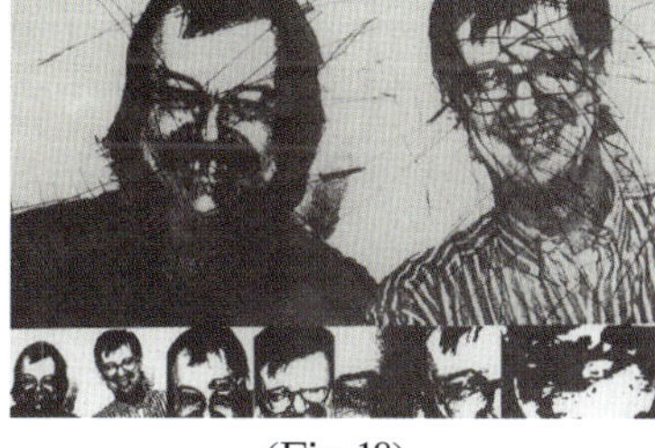

(Fig. 18)

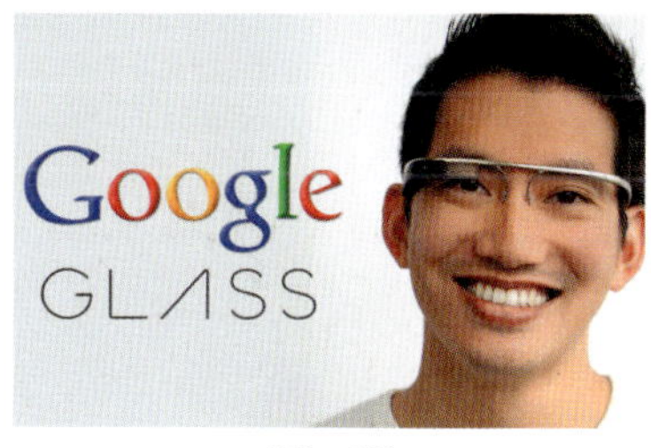

(Fig. 19)

Fig. 16. Muse S biofeedback sleep and meditation band by InteraXon.

Fig. 17. Coop Himmelb(l)au, *Gesichtsraum / Soul Flipper II*, 1971. Photograph by Peter Schnetz. (Coop Himmelb(l)au Archives, Basel).

Fig. 18. Coop Himmelb(l)au, *The Dissolution of Our Bodies in the City*, 1988 (in *Coop Himmelblau: Die Fascination Der Stadt / The Power of the City*, Oliver Gruenberg, Robert Hahn and Doris Knecht, eds. (Berlin: Georg Büchner Buchladen, 1988)).

Fig. 19. Google Glasses advertisement, 2012.

Anthropotechnics and immunity

Being conceived as tools for emancipation, these machines are also instruments of control, micro-spaces of immersion, power and confinement, whether that was the intent or not. Masks and helmets either mediate with an environment that is not enough—and thus serve to expand worlds from the mental and physiologic point of view—or simply save us from an atmosphere that is not compatible with our organism. Reviewing Walter Pichler's mental expansion devices, critic Werner Hoffmann arrived to a sombre conclusion: 'The connections inside these spaces suggest a variety of familiar possibilities such as gas chambers and electric chairs'.*11 The effects of such tools for 'personal instruction' also have a problematic side.

To understand the full implications *archi-cephallics*, it is necessary to introduce the techniques of improvement of the individual. For Michel Foucault, the body is the inevitable mediator between politics and life. But the dominion of biopolitics doesn't end here. It operates in the contact areas of both the individual and species spheres, to protect, reinforce and reproduce it.*12 Triggered by these fundamental ideas, philosopher Peter Sloterdijk developed the concept of 'anthropotechnics' in *Rules for the human park* (1991) and *You must change your life* (2009), and further elaborated upon this in the Spheres cycle. He translated Foucault's distinction between government techniques over the population (biopolitics) and the techniques of self-government ('aesthetics of the existence') as improvement of the world *(Weltverbesserung)* and self-improvement *(Selbsteversserung)*. Sloterdijk also adopted Arnold Gehlen's concept of *technique as compensation*. Human history isn't understood in terms of adaptation, but through the artificial creation of environments that are suited for social and individual

The urban medium penetrates us with all its components (chemical, electronic, energetic or telematic), cancelling the distinction between our interior space and the outside. Bio-power has suffered a process of atomization and ambientalization (in the terms introduced by Gilles Deleuze in *Postscript on the societies of control*, further analyzed by Byung-Chul Han through psychopolitics) in the shape not only of atmospheric manipulations but also in the networked technologies that permeate our habitats. In other words, the anthropogenic project consists in the adoption of 'explicit measures for symbiosis with "the invisible"'.*13

Of all the immunological shells, the mask could be considered the minimum anthropogenic assemblage. Likewise,

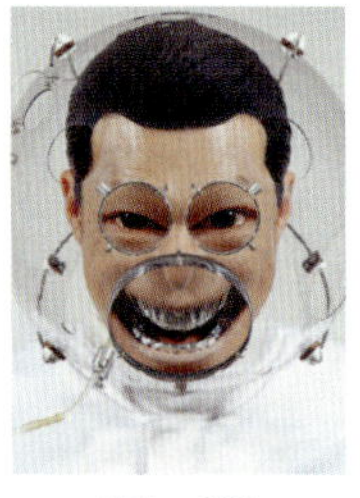

(Fig. 20)

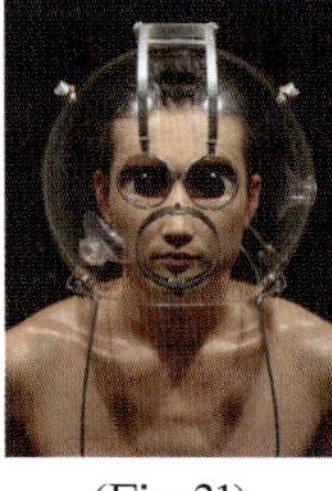

(Fig. 21)

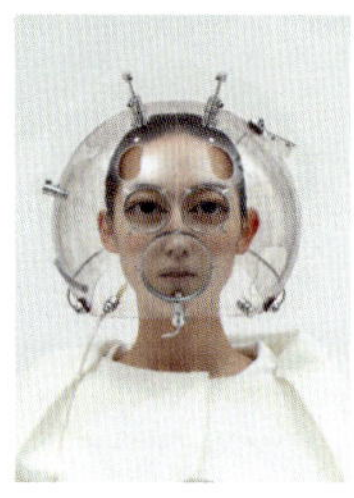

(Fig. 22)

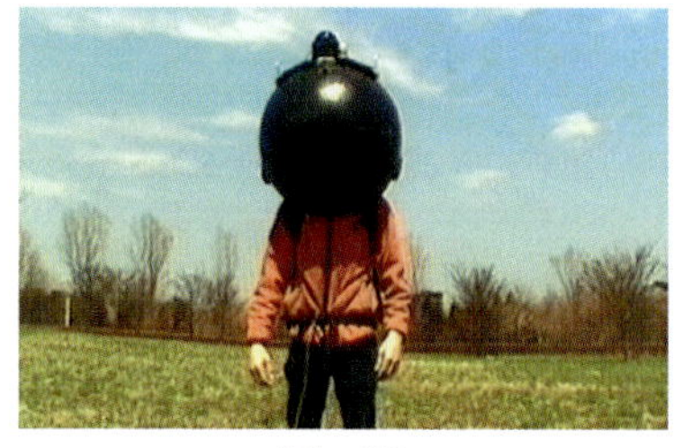

(Fig. 23)

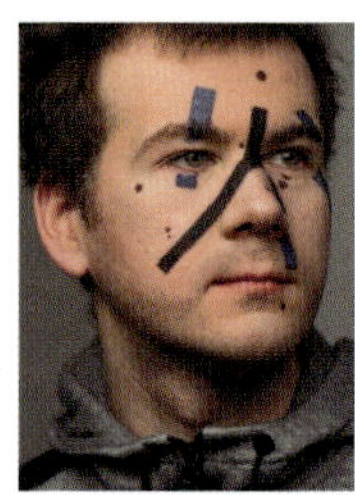

(Fig. 24)

development—responding to something that is lacking and the need to achieve new balance. Animals' needs are met through an intimate relationship with their surrounding environment, something that does not occur with humans, who are always at a distance with their own biological identity. Humans must develop an alternative nature to make up for being an organism that cannot thrive in the environment in which it was originally born. This is the origin of an enormous adaptive capacity.

Society is an immunological project. Immunity is triggered by a protective response in the face of a risk, either an epidemic, a legal affair, the erection of militarized frontiers or a cyber attack. This is another key concept to consider when analysing the technologies of the head, because the immune system operates at the point where the body encounters otherness.

Fig. 20, 21, 22. Hyungkoo Lee, *The Objectuals*, 2003–2010.

Fig. 23. Hiroo Iwata, *Floating Eye*, 2001.

Fig. 24. Grigory Bakunov, *King's New Makeup, Makeup Against Facial Recognition*, 2017.

a certain hairdo or makeup cancels the capacity for a face recognition system to function properly (Fig. 24, 25). Anaesthetic masks stop the processing of pain. Gas masks (Fig. 26) are the antidote to chemical warfare. Ambient terror blurs the difference between violence against persons and violence against the environment. These examples of creation of atmospheres of control make explicit the fragility of both our medium and our organism. The violence against what surrounds us triggers acts of resistance and adaptation.

Furthermore, the body defeats a poison not by expelling it, but by making it part of the body. The modified environment negates the masked, but they don't completely negate that environment back. The assimilation of the environment implies a will to coexist. Likewise, immunity is not a strategy of frontal opposition. The rhetoric of immunity cannot be limited to the idea of a defensive mechanism in the face of an external attack. This is Donna Haraway's thesis: by using metaphors of war and conflict, the immune system is represented as mutually exclusive and conflicting, a representation that contributes to the misrecognition and limitation of the self and the other. The strategized take on the self can be traced in the hygienist fear for the other. Where masks and gloves prevent the individual from the assimilation of uncontrolled and non-sterilized biomes, the sphere of the individual is privileged. But immunity and community share a deep relationship. There is no community without some kind of immunity apparatus (or, you don't wear a COVID mask to protect yourself but to protect others).

Haraway proposes a model for immunity where the body is an integral field of variable coexistences in the following terms:

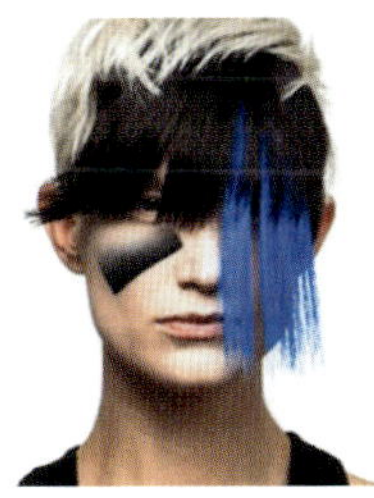

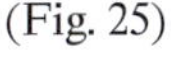

(Fig. 25)

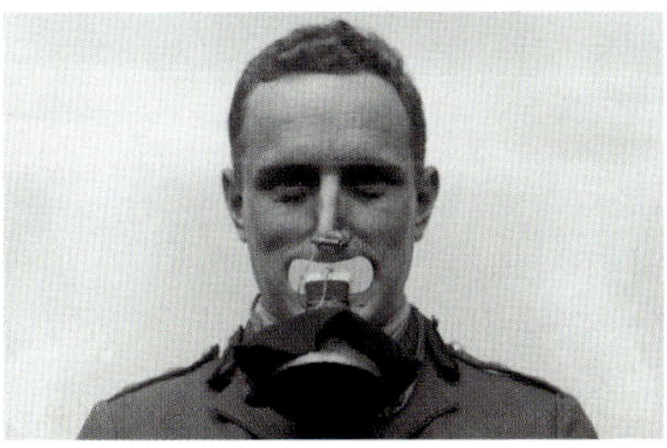

(Fig. 26)

> The immune system is a historically specific terrain, where global and local politics; Nobel Prize-winning research; heteroglossic cultural productions, from popular dietary practices, feminist science fiction, religious imagery, and children's games, to photographic techniques and military strategic theory; clinical medical practice; venture capital investment strategies; world-changing developments in business and technology; and the deepest personal and collective experiences of embodiment, vulnerability, power, and mortality interact with an intensity matched perhaps only in the biopolitics of sex and reproduction.*14

Fig. 25. Adam Harvey, *CV Dazzle, Computer Vision Dazzle Camouflage*, 2010.

Fig. 26. German gas mask taken by Canadians in Lens. There is no protection for the eyes, just a mouthpiece. Photograph, September, 1917. (Library and Archives Canada, http://central.bac-lac.gc.ca/.redirect?app=fonandcol&id=3397853&lang=eng).

The self is permeable. It can engage with other human and non-human agents. Within this dynamic, engagements can be favourable or fatal.*15 The body is understood as a work in progress, open to exchange with its environment. On the other hand, in an environment saturated with pollution or in the battle against a new resurgence of an epidemic, the masked crowd won't escape but go on. Head architectures can isolate individuals under air-tight conditions or they can introduce new modes of negotiation with our medium. They make us situated individuals who operate within this set of engagements (sometimes dangerous, sometime the source of joy and pleasure). They adapt to a modified medium by incorporating new assemblages that make that engagement possible.

Technologies of enchantment

In the book *Immunitas, the protection and negation of life*, philosopher Roberto Esposito stresses the degree in which the mask embodies the idea of compensation. He cites J. Svagelski for that purpose:

> Compensating *[compenser]* is like dressing a wound. In order to be dressed, the wound is covered up and masked; it may remain under the dressing but that does not make it disappear. The dressing soothes the wound, eases the pain (after all, compensation has a consolatory function), aids in healing, but at the same time, it draws attention to the wound, giving it a different reality. On the other hand, all masks unmask. In other words, one thing that compensates for another alters it, and while seeking to hide it, actually puts it on display and places it in the realm of difference.*16

In this analysis of head anthropotechnics, the technologies described are not just driven by efficacy. Masks—the face of a face—are not only technical devices. They also need to compensate for the absence of non-semantic information, that of our traits and gestures. This analysis cannot stop at the mere adoption of the medical device. Other components like decorations or even proto-magical devices deserve delving into, all of them a means of creating an additional impact and drawing attention to the concealment taking place.

From the nineteenth century on, anthropologists agreed that the personal systems of ornamentation in primitive communities were highly relevant, socially and spatially. Their masks were not only objects able to reproduce the human face but to evoke other creatures or objects, normally to inspire certain emotions in others. Thus, the purpose of technologies of the self exceeds their function.

Enchantment and fascination are key components in the micro-architectures designed for the individual. Anthropologist Alfred Gell distinguishes three fundamental technical categories. The first one is the 'technology of production', the conventional use of technology. The second is the 'technology of reproduction', which is focused in the consecution of human generations, its learning, domestication and reproduction. Finally, the third category is the 'technology of enchantment'. Any artistic, ornamental, rhetoric or social practice aimed at the creation of conformity in others in relationship with their intentions or projects belongs to this category. Here an element of invention and fantasy is key when bringing technical ideas to fruition.

> Human beings entrap animals in the mesh of human purposes using an array of psychological techniques, but these are primitive by comparison with the psychological weapons which human beings use to exert control over the thoughts and actions of other human beings. The technology of enchantment is the most sophisticated we possess.*17

Tools are complex technical sequences that go beyond the satisfaction of basic needs but also for pleasure and adornment. They create a sequence of purpose whose aim is 'to control and modify human psychological responses in social meetings'.*18 Therefore, techniques—the creation and use of tools—cannot merely be described as a survival activity. Technology is not only composed of artefacts but also of the social activity that allows for the transmission of technical knowledge, its fabrication and use. Its objectives are shaped by social context. Techniques make up the bridge that links a series of elements at hand (our body, certain materials or environmental features) with the purposes it aims for. The deliberate and intelligent reorganization of such elements allows for the channelling of the causal properties of a technical system, leading to a result whose features and capacities cannot be achieved otherwise.

The face is a source of fascination (Latin *fascinationen*, which stands for 'bewitch, enchant'). Also, Latin *facies* stands for 'appearance, form, figure', or 'form imposed on something', which is related to *facere*, to make.*19 Gell describes something in between a mask and an architectural facade, a place where faciality and fascination meet, in order to illustrate the way such technologies of enchantment operate. In most of technical assemblages engaged within social milieus, psychological warfare and magical efficacy are related. The first example offered by Gell is a certain canoe prow-board that can be found in the Melanesian Trobriand Islands (Fig. 27). These prows are virtuously carved in sinuous motifs that can be identified as a face where two 'eyes' are displayed prominently. Like the eye-like spots that feature on the wings of a Caligo butterfly, the display of eyes is a recurrent mimetic action that provokes uncanny feelings (Fig. 28). The prows are the first element to be perceived by the overseas partners of the Trobriand people. Overwhelmed by such instrument of persuasion, they will surely offer more valuable products. In Gell's words, they seek 'the demoralization of an opponent in a contest of will power'.*20 The Trobriand prows are technical assemblages aimed at the puzzlement and upsetting of the spectator. They are the decorated interface that mediates with the others.

Technologies of the head are the basic terrain for biopolitics. They link our internal fluids with the external atmospheres; they modify our appearance, manipulate our internal space and also amplify our abilities, updating our organism to operate in incompatible environments. Masks and helmets link both the social and the individual with their immediate surroundings. Such technical assemblages lie in the contact point between these two material fields, both of which are subject to biopower and thus polarized between the liberating, the protective and the submissive.

Technology is driven by the will to persuade others, the more so when our fundamental means for communication, the face, is impeded. The compensation for such a lack is one example of the human technologies of the self.

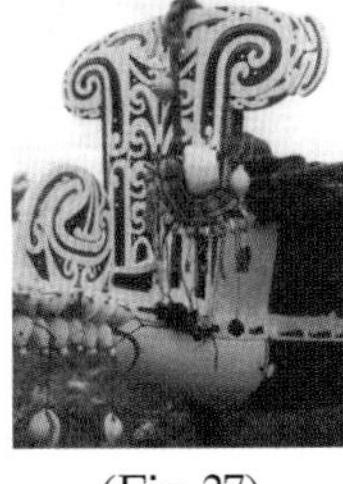

(Fig. 27)

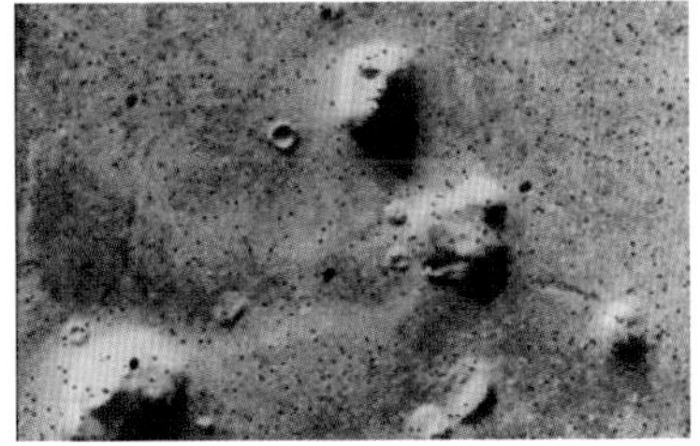

(Fig. 28)

A review on the evolution of head technologies or architectures reveals rich material assemblages that range from the medical device to the symbolic facial accoutrement. All of them have provided the foundations for future technologies of the self. Folk decorations, prosthesis, insertions and the superimposition of subtle layerings mobilize other politics of the face. They not only allow the construction of the personal identity but the strengthening of the communal. The decorated means of immunity transcends the pharmaceutical function, opening up for new technical means of intersubjectivity. Archi-cephalics are both biopolitical assemblages and technologies of enchantment.

Fig. 27. Trobrian canoe prow-board. Photograph by Shirley F. Campbell. 1971 (in Alfred Gell, *The Technologies of Enchantment and the Enchantment of Technologies* (London: Routledge, 1999)).

Fig. 28. Cydonia Mensae Mars relief called 'the face of Mars' for its pareidolic resemblance. Photograph by Viking 1 Mission, NASA, July 1976.

Juan Elvira
Face politics and the micro-architectures of immunity
* **footnotes & references**

*1 Malcolm McCullough, *Ambient Commons. Attention in the Age of Embodied Information* (Cambridge Massachusetts: MIT Press, 2013), 36-37.

*2 Things haven't changed much for the company Bose, which today sells high end headphones with sophisticated noise cancellation technologies.

*3 Benjamin Rackstrow, *Miscellaneous Observations, Together with a Collection of Experiments with Electricity. With the Manner of Performing them. Designed to Explain the Nature and Cause of the Most Remarkable Phenomena thereof: with Some Remarks on a Pamphlet Entitled 'A sequel to the experiments and Observations Tending to Illustrate the Nature and Properties of Electricity.' To which is annexed, A Letter, written by the author on the Academy of Sciences at Bordeaux, Relative to Similarity of Electricity to Lightning and Thunder* (London, 1758).

*4 Hippolyte Baraduc, *Les Vibrations de la Vitalité Humaine* (Paris: Librarie J. B. Baillière et Fils, 1904), 200.

*5 A common discipline in nineteenth century psychiatry, which established a correlate between the shape of the skull and mental traits. It has been fully dismissed.

*6 See Laurence Wright, *Warm and Snug: The History of the Bed* (London: Routledge and K. Paul, 1962).

*7 Kisho Kurokawa, "Capsule Declaration," in *Metabolism in Architecture* (London: Studio Vista, 1977), 75-85.

*8 Victoria Bugge, "On Astroballoons and Personal Bubbles," *E-flux*, last modified April 2018, https://www.e-flux.com/architecture/positions/194841/on-astroballoons-and-personal-bubbles/.

*9 Wolf Prix, Rainer Michael Holzer, Helmut Swizinski (Coop Himmelb(l)au) & Coop Himmelb(l)au, "The Tower of Babel Revisited", *ANY*, no. 0 (May/June 1993): 28.

*10 Shuhei Hosokawa, "The Walkman Effect," *Popular Music* 4 (1984): 165-180.

*11 Werner Hoffman, "On Walter Pichler," *Protokolle '68*, 1968.

*12 Roberto Esposito, *Immunitas: The protection and negation of life* (Cambridge: Polity Press, 2011), 153.

*13 Peter Sloterdijk, *Terror from the Air* (Los Angeles: Semiotext(e), 2009), 109.

*14 Donna Haraway, *Simians, Cyborgs and Women: The Reinvention of Nature* (New York: Routledge, 1991), 205.

*15 Donna Haraway, *Simians, Cyborgs and Women*, 225.

*16 J. J. Svagelski, *L'idee de Compensation en France* (Lyon: L'Hermès, 1981), cited in Roberto Esposito, *Immunitas: The Protection and Negation of Life* (Cambridge: Polity Press, 2011), 93.

*17 Alfred Gell "Technology and Magic," *Anthropology Today 4*, no. 2 (1988): 6-9.

*18 *Ibid.*

*19 E. H. Gombrich, "On Physiognomic Perception," *Daedalus* 89, no. 1, (Winter, 1960): 228-241. Gombrich makes an analysis of the physiognomic turn and its limits: "The physiognomic approach may lead to the suicide of criticism" (p. 237).

*20 Alfred Gell, "The Technologies of Enchantment and the Enchantment of Technologies," in *Anthropology, Art, and Aesthetics*, ed. by Jeremy (Oxford: Clarendon Press, 1994), 44.

106

Matthew Connors
If We Burn

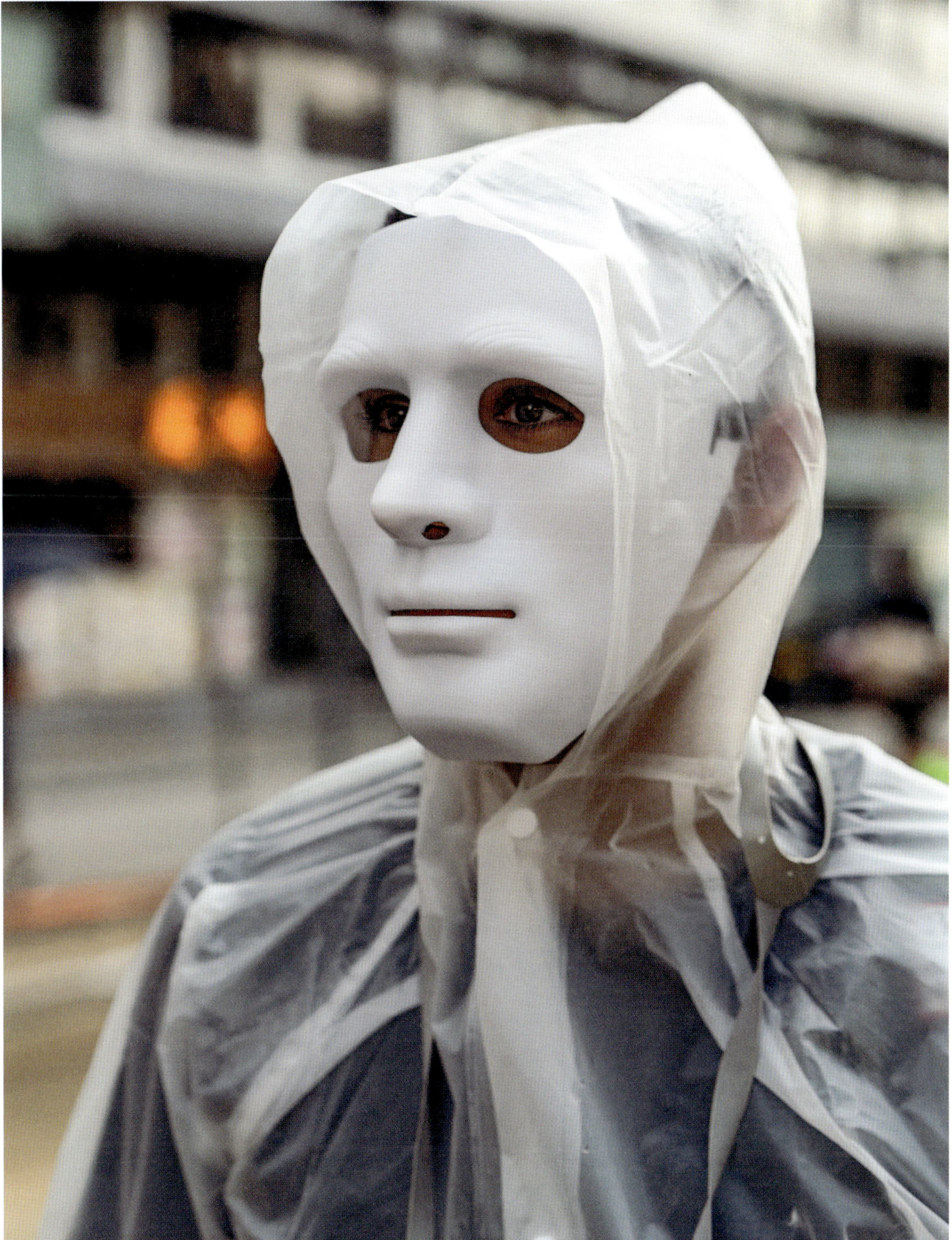

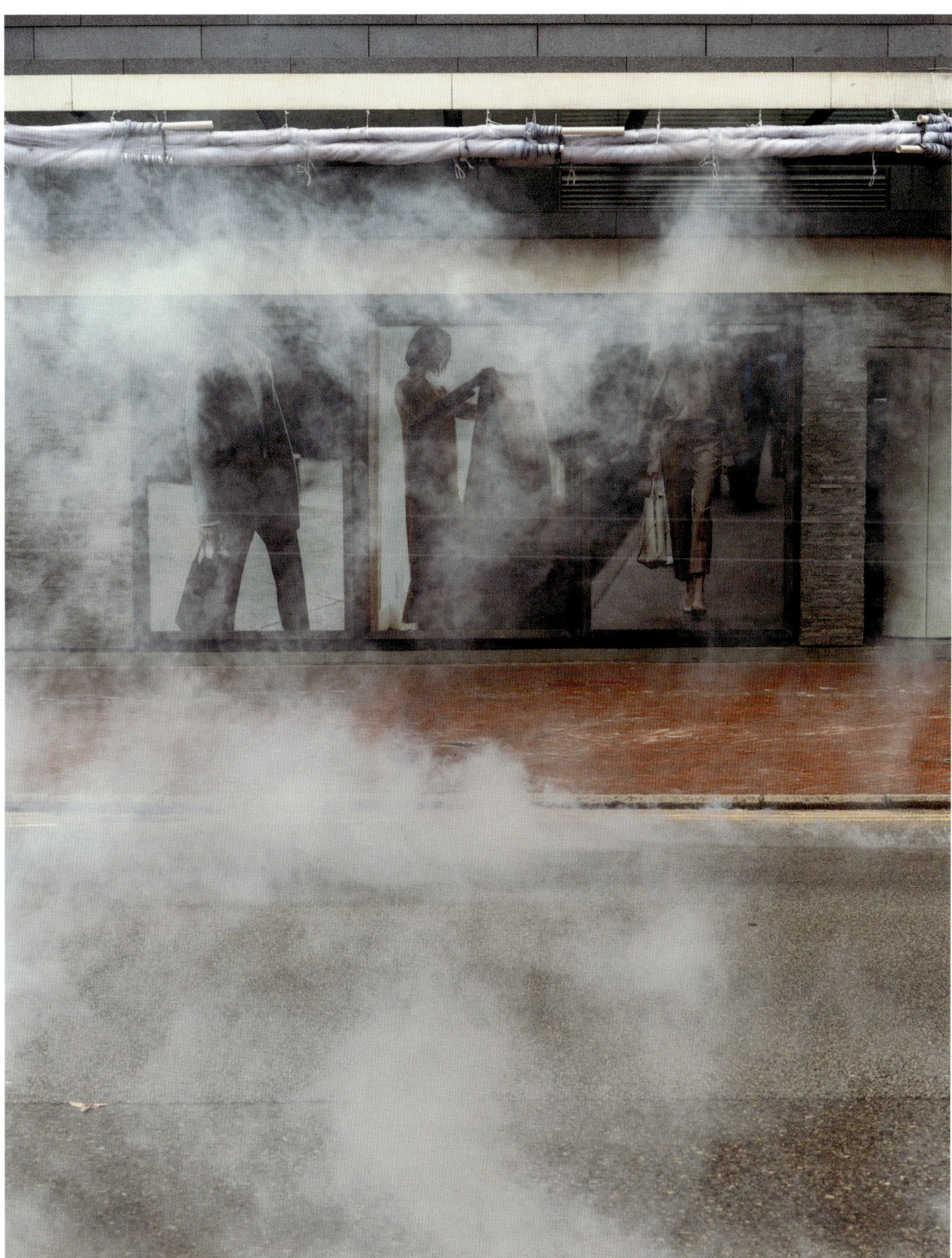

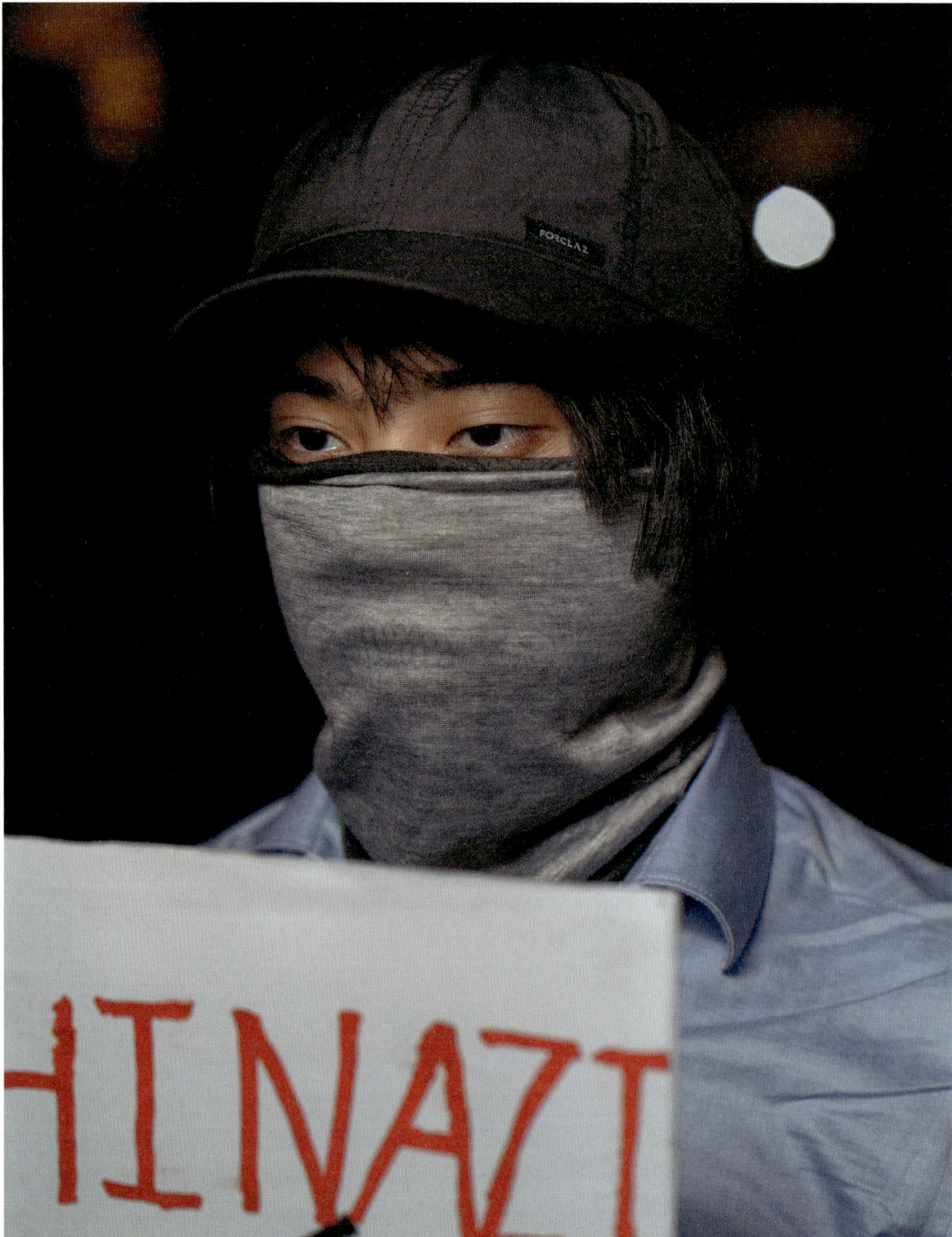
FORCLAZ
HINAZI

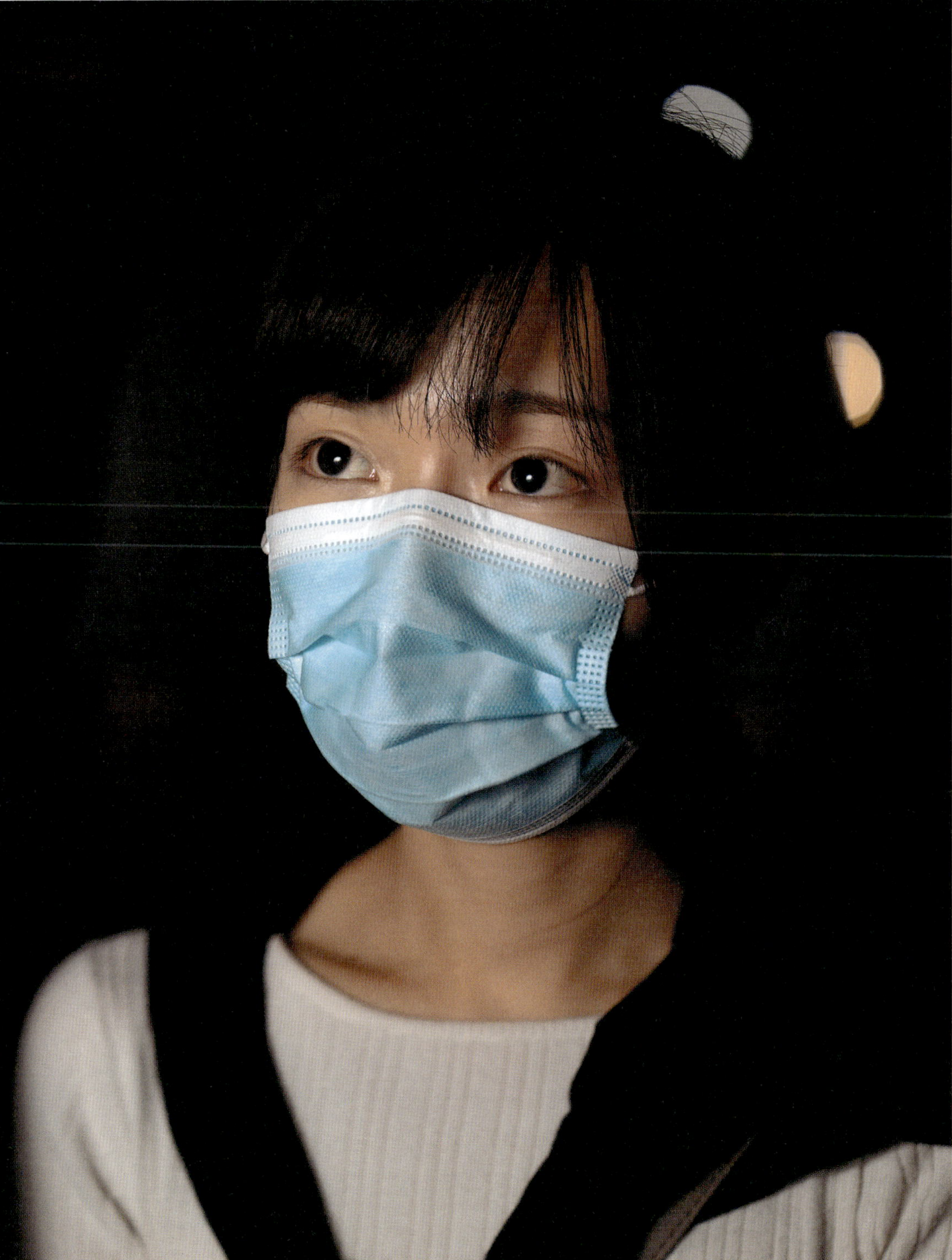

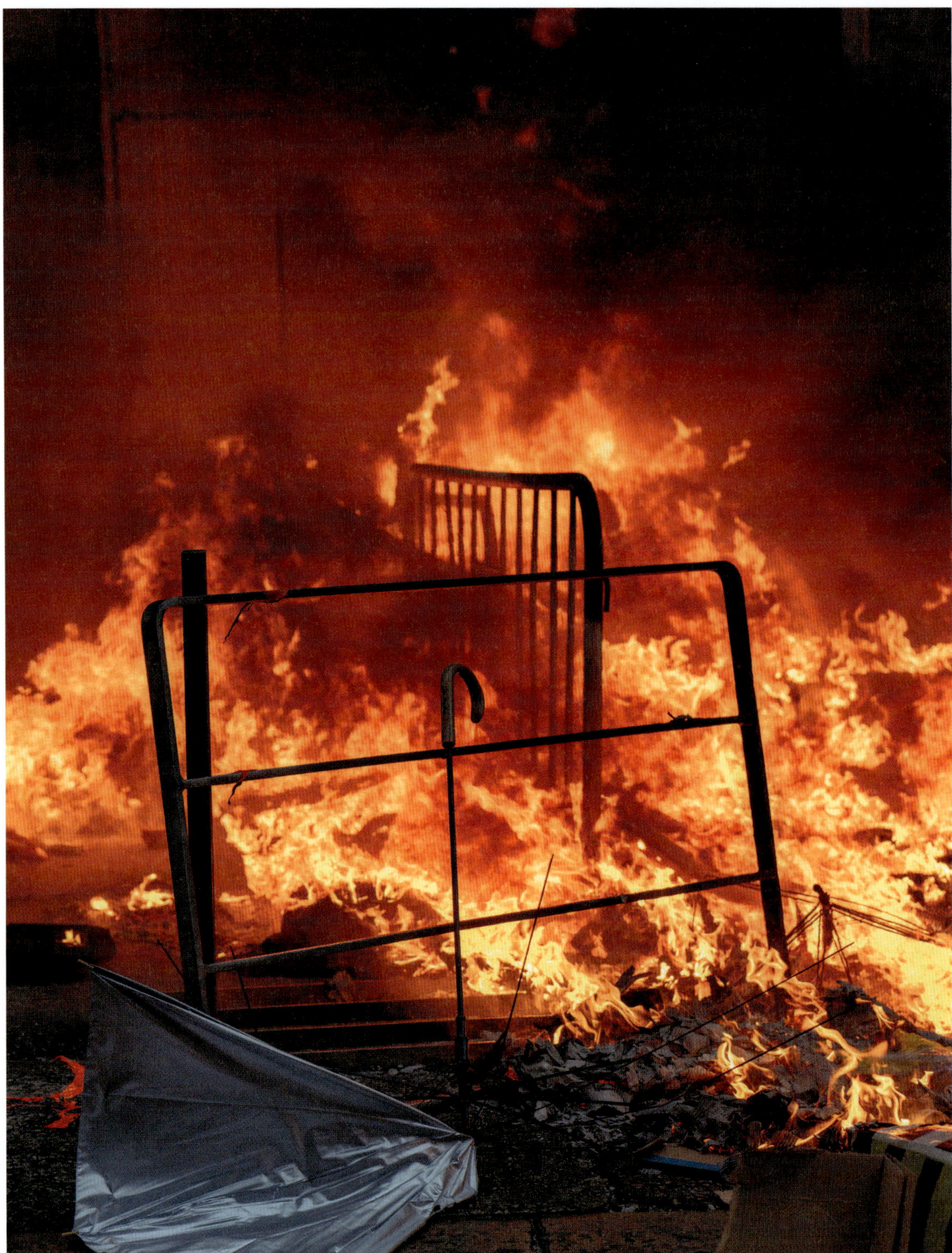

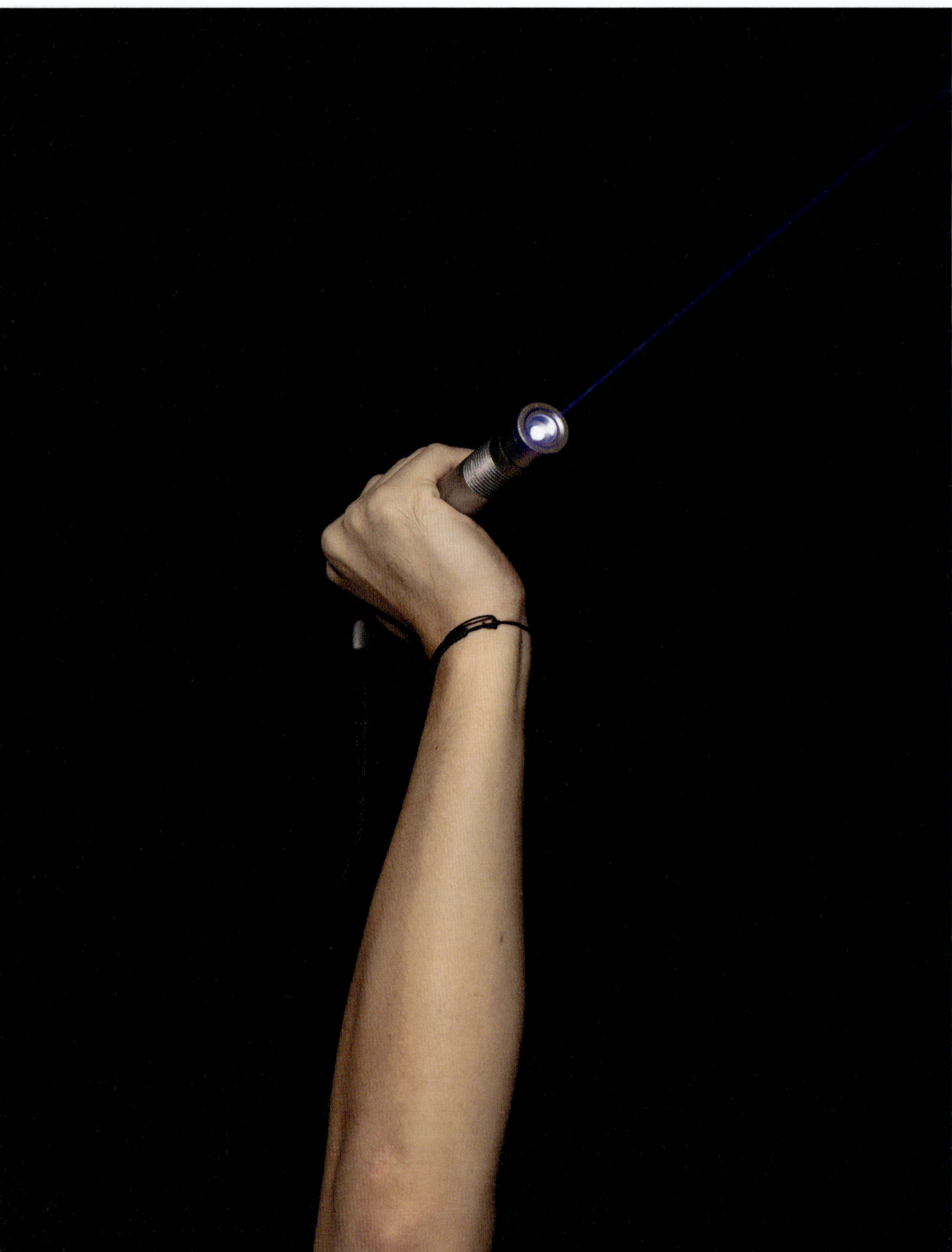

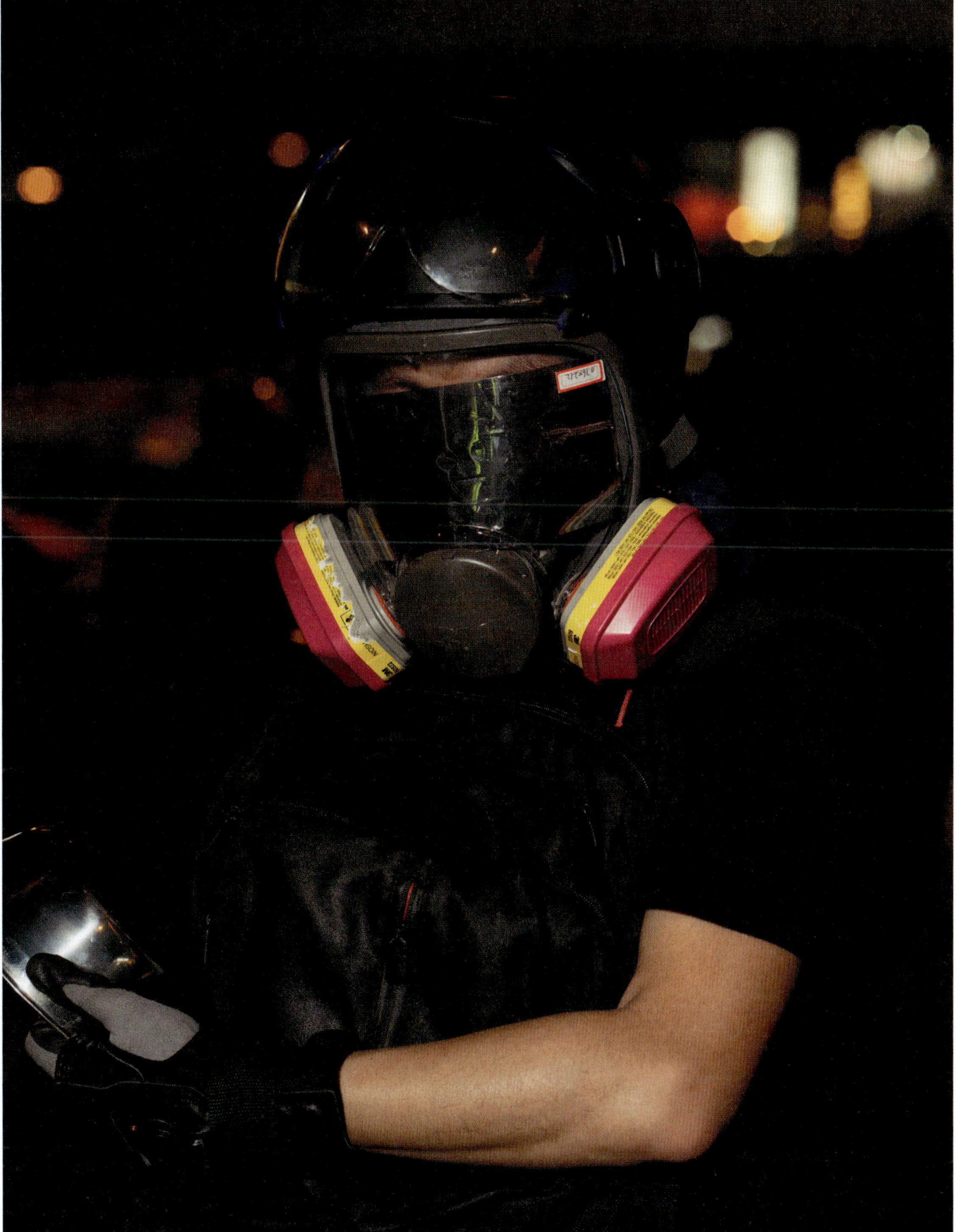

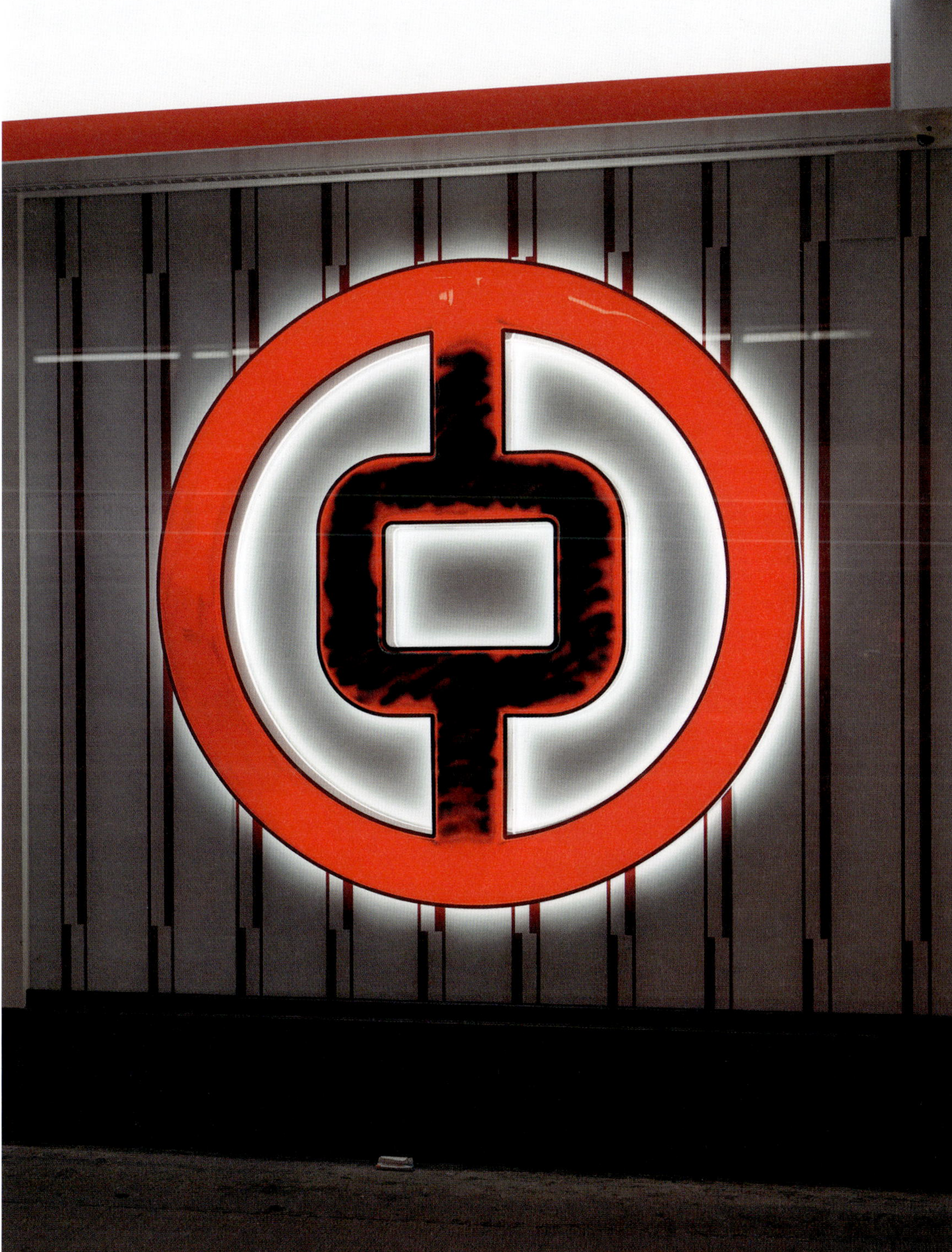

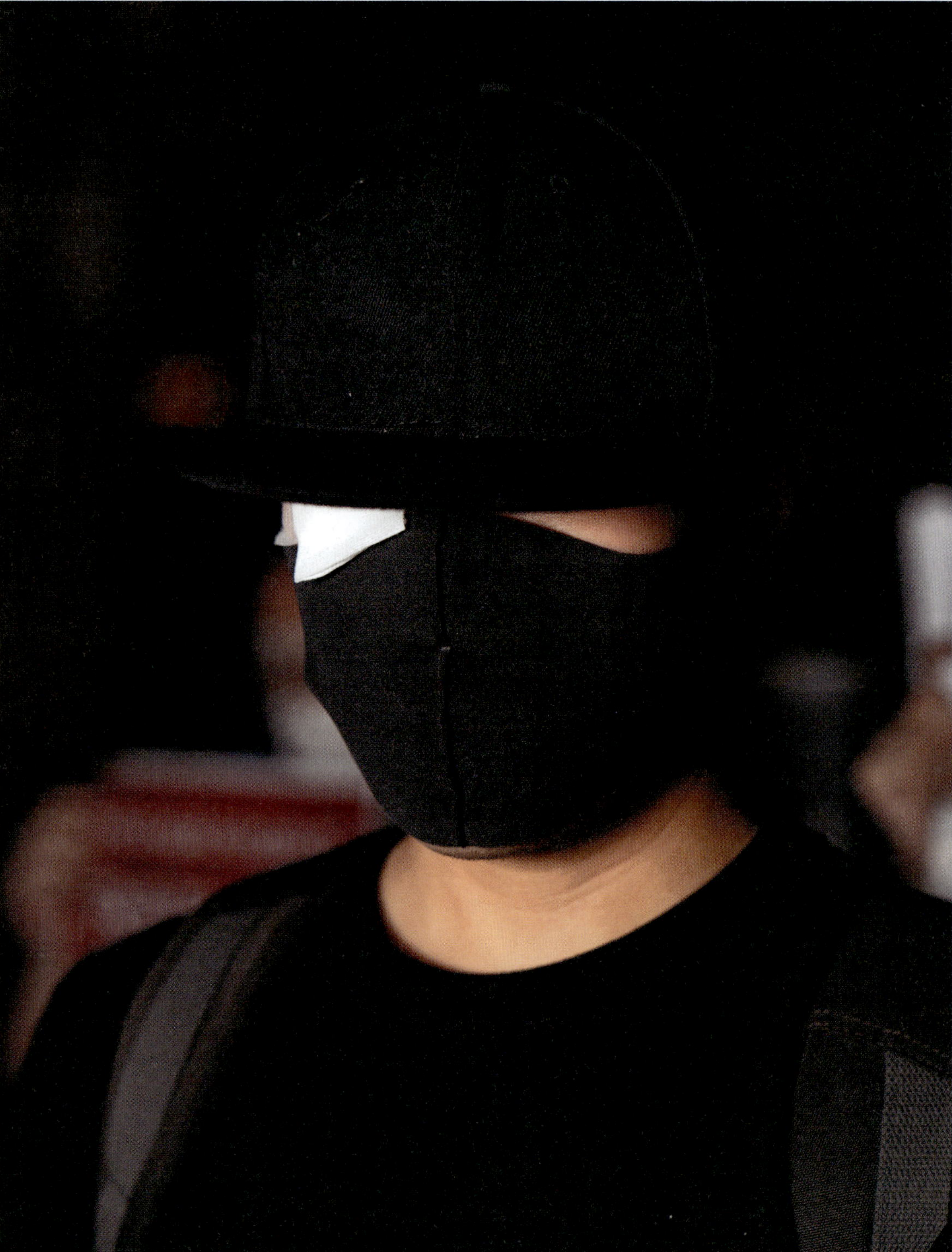

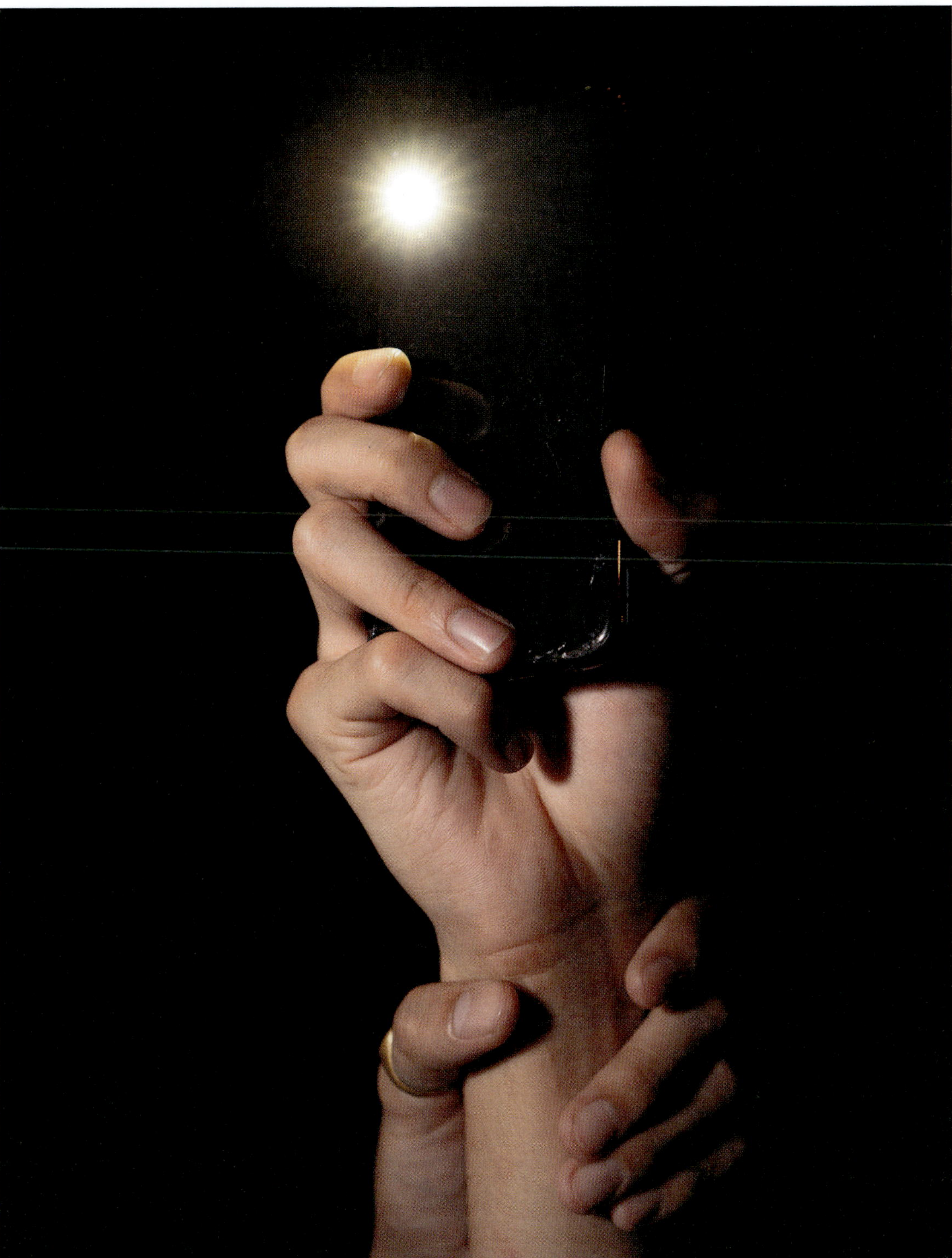

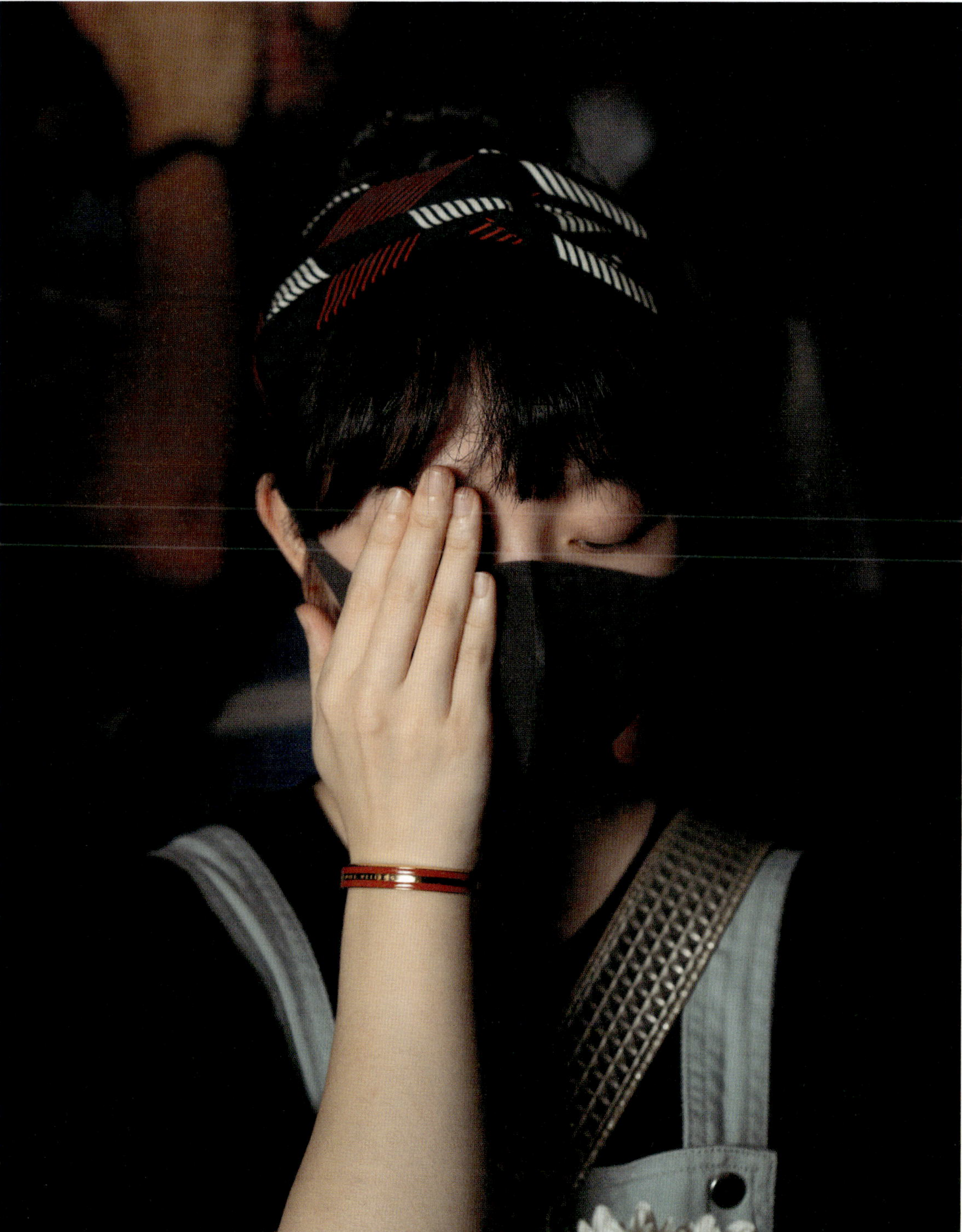

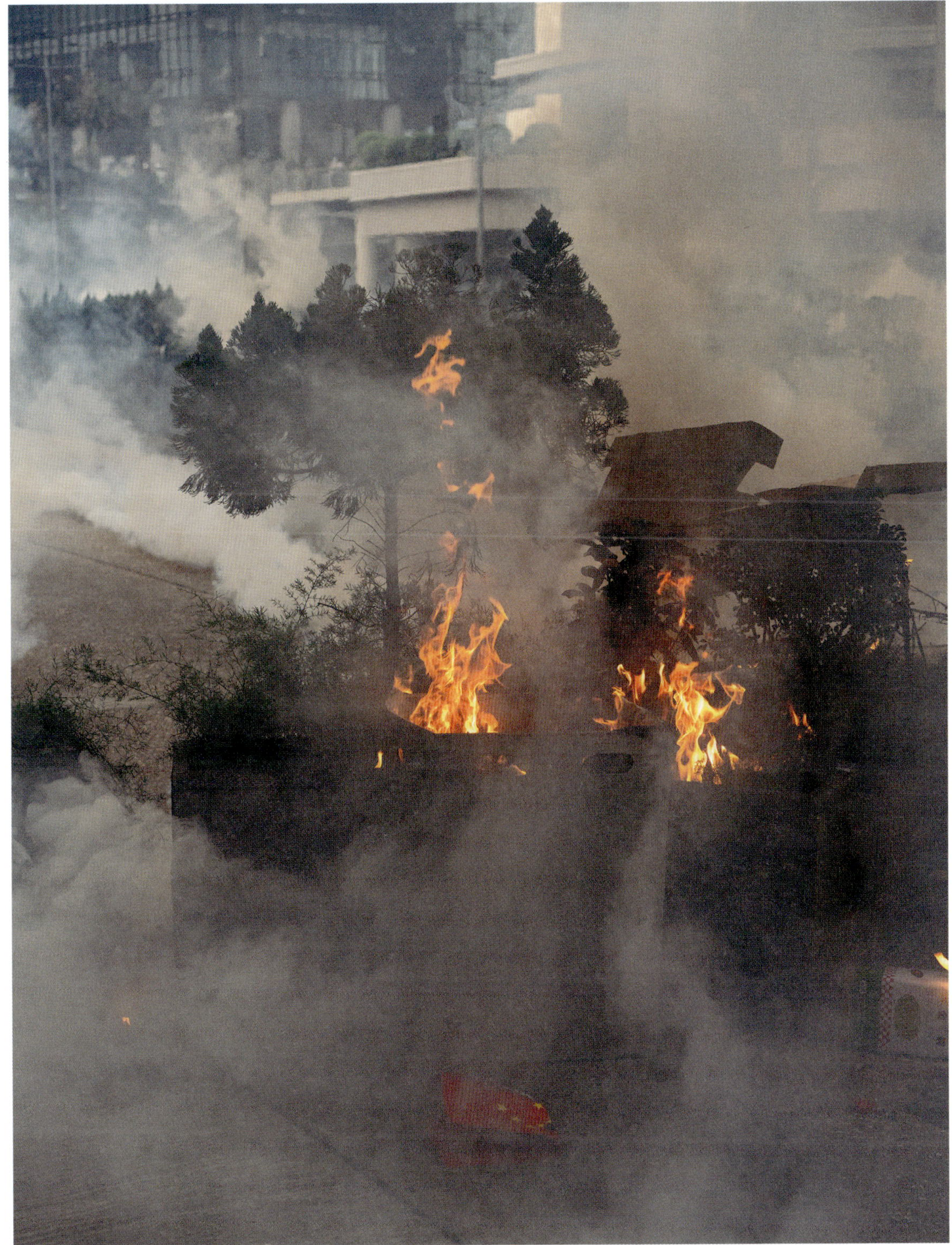

124

Ricarda Bigolin

At least you won't know how I really feel: Masking performance & obstructed agency

Sociologists study and create frameworks for the way people present and perform themselves to each other, as well as for understanding body language and gestures. These frameworks are hindered by the normative standards of daily mask wear in our present times (standards that will likely be in play for the foreseeable future). A key signifier for reading social situations is appearance, which includes the clothes we wear. These denote social status, gender, occupation, and age, as well as the social state or 'scenario' we might be in, such as going to work or exercising.*1 Whilst signifiers of social status might not be rendered less visible by the use of face masks, concealing a large area of the face alters how we communicate with each other and our body language as part of this.

Let us take a look at some of key examples of these sociological frameworks to get a better understanding of the impact of wearing masks. Erving Goffman based a model for understanding how we interact in social scenarios with each other on dramaturgy. Goffman made reference to theatrical compositions, dialogue and stage directions—that is, there is an on-stage aspect to behaviour, where we act in face-to-face encounters.*2 Nick Crossley builds on this and views embodiment as the subsequent awareness of our own location (our understanding of our body in a spatial plane) and point of view (the way this body projects into and to the world).*3 Crossley also make notes of 'body techniques', a concept originated by Marcel Mauss that refers to the highly developed body actions and gestures which are ingrained and or learnt via culture, gender or class. All of these readings of our interactions become problematic with face masks.

The adornment of either a small piece of cloth that is treated, non-woven and contains extruded fibres, or novel, desperate and destitute makeshift refashioned ones, alters how we perceive ourselves and our performance in the world. Are we seeking to protect or conceal? There's the potential for a little harmless deception. With such a proportion of the face concealed, one's innermost feelings can be covert or reframed—the mask might hide the extent of a flushed cheek, but frame darting eyes.

Another set of associations emerge from our everyday use of face masks in the codification of PPE (personal protective equipment), those of increased emotion, fear and global disruption as a result of the pandemic. Theories of affect and agency are often derived from 'the emotional contours of life during increasingly precarious times'.*4 Cultural theorist Sianne Ngai describes these flighty emotional states of envy and anxiety as 'ignoble feelings' in her book *Ugly Feelings*. They are referred to as a form of 'obstructed agency', situations where one is forced to a position of passive action.*5 The covering of the mouth obstructs key features, gestures and speaking, and the subject is pacified to an extent as their communication is truncated. Duct-taped mouths or masked victims of lascivious acts are dominated into submission, for example.

I will use the defined emotional states and 'obstructed' agency created by mask-wearing to pin down emergent personas of pandemic and post-truth times. In doing so I will sketch scenarios of masked interactions occurring somewhere in the Indo-Pacific region, mostly likely at 33.8688° S, 151.2093° E, Djubuguli, Sydney, Australia, sometime between five months and five years from now. Although it is not an entirely disembodied experience when we wear a mask, some of our sensory perceptions, embodied knowledge and spatial intelligence can be obscured. These personas show how masks might hinder or enhance our ability to influence others and to conceal things such as emotions, or general societal and political malaise.

I imagine these emerging contemporary performances, striding towards bizarre senses of self and embodiment, either tangibly masked or masked in other ways—framed by digital technologies such as through the limitations of video call. Are masks then limitations? What forms of agency emerge in this new time? The fictive personas that follow give life to my imaginings.

Zoom masks, technical glitches, influencer lighting and IRL

Every time I saw this person online, their face was motionless, never straight-on but pitched 3/4 to the screen. They only exposed one side (the good side), and were smoothly lit with influencer ring lights.

No unbecoming shadows, darkening of lines or wrinkles, just a smooth filter glow, prepped with Vitamin C serums, hydraulic acid boosters and the reclaimed drag makeup technique of contouring and highlighting now made famous by Kim Kardashian. They sat motionless, staring perhaps at their own image with the same affected posing as when looking in the mirror. (The rectangular frame of the screen also masks behaviour—we become tamed by our own video feedback.) There were never any sudden moves or gestures. Maybe they were frozen by a state of anxiety, induced by the chronic change of means of communication. Dozens of meetings passed and this person never once let diminish this frozen composure. No strong emotions, just feigned interests/ agreement. When I saw them in person, wearing a sun set *ombré* cotton cloth mask, awkwardness defined the experience as the whole body was proximate—it existed in space. They looked different without the even and flattering ring lights, but real emotions were still easily obscured by the mask.

With these various ways of masking ourselves, what will become of the way we relate to our image, and what will become of the way we relate to ourselves?

Masking an impression

In the waiting room, I was nervous. I felt clammy with the climate-controlled warmth, in the mild or not-really-winter Sydney *winter*. There was one other woman waiting there, presumably for the same reason: a job interview for front of house roles in one of the city's latest boutique hotels, *Hotel X*, another in a long line of this kind of hotel that seemed to open monthly regardless of the pandemic. I'd lost my last job during COVID-19 at a well-known restaurant to a former contender from *MasterChef*, which, despite investment from a group from the Arab Emirates, had failed with the lack of tourism in Australia. I was pretty desperate to get the job. Due to the nature of the industry and it being so much 'about the people' they said the interviews were in person, not onsite at the hotel but at a recruitment agency headquarters in the city. The instructions were that 'masks must be worn during the interview at all times'. I wondered if they were implementing this as a sign of things to come in hotel life for some time yet, if not forever. In the corporate waiting room, there was a reproduction Arne Jacobsen swan chair in black, which the other candidate was sitting on, scrolling through their phone. I had been googling about how to still look stylish whilst wearing a mask before the interview and the number one tip was to wear black. Some *YouTubers* said that this was a severe look, but others said that this was still chic and professional, and that you could enhance makeup on your eyes, as key place for more expression. Others talked about wearing matching sets to look professional, e.g. buying a matching set of mask and shirt. I didn't do that. I just went for a solid black cotton mask with a mostly black outfit.

My name was finally called by a lean, thirty-something woman in a knee-length skirt suit and silk blouse with a subtle print, and hair slicked back in a sleek ponytail. Her blue eyes were set with quite pronounced mink false eye lashes, and copper shimmery pigments on the eye lids making them look more steely blue, scrutinizing. She wore a fresh blue surgical face mask, the most common kind. Just moments before entering the building I saw a homeless person out of the front of *7-eleven* smoking a cigarette whilst wearing the same mask. It was not so fresh when he took a drag on the cigarette through the mask and exhaled smoke, which slowly released from above the ridge of the nose, where the mask does not fit so closely. These masks were always in the gutters, trodden on in the street, going down drainpipes, ending up in the oceans.

The interviewer cast a different image, one of corporate platitudes and hygiene, and good grooming. Once in the room, she sat down and crossed her legs in the way ladies are meant to with one leg in front of leg, calf in front of calf. After introducing the other panel members and the first few minutes of chit chat, she began the interview questions by moving forward in her chair. She suddenly pulled her mask down to reveal filled lips, pausing and looking at me. 'What personality trait do you believe would make you the ideal candidate for this role?', she asked. I didn't know if she was meaning for me to also remove my mask and do the same, as if to reveal a true identity. Instead, I just answered the question with a generic response but also added, 'I love working with people'. That couldn't seem insincere with such obstructed facial expressions.

"Extinction rebellion vigilante ruins fashion week: model wears shocking mask"

I knew I had to do it. I'd no longer be able to model but I had to do it. I was cast for a fashion show that was taking place outside in Circular Quay, across the cove with the Opera House as a backdrop. I wasn't a dedicated model, someone 'scouted' me one night at a rave in a warehouse in outer Eastern Sydney, looking quite sweaty and demented. I did it as it paid more than bar work. I was studying political science at UNS and the last year had made me angry and isolated—the ineffective leadership of our country combined with the world going woke and broke, and a religious fanatic/complacent fool heading our nation. He made late and dodgy decisions with the vaccine rollout, blamed the states for lockdowns whilst his wife had shares in labs that have the Australian license to produce AstraZeneca. I could no longer continue just reposting political memes or *Guardian* articles on Instagram stories. I felt the urge to do something with by body, to *do something* with myself. It was not well calculated, even though media coverage post event suggested so. I had a bandanna that was a print of an image of Scott Morrison or 'ScoMo', the Prime Minister of Australia, which exclaimed "SACK SCOMO" in bold printed letters at the top. I took it with me to the show. I didn't think too much about it. Only just planned to stuff it in the pocket of whatever I was wearing for the show. But once ready to walk in front of such an iconic Sydney vista, I didn't really think any more. Instead, the body took over and when I was doing the finale choreography right with the backdrop of the Sydney Opera House across the bay, I just pulled the bandana out of my pocket. The coastal breeze held it up like a flag and I held it up adjacent for the cameras to see as I walked then quickly fashioned it around my face as mask. There was a delay with the politically blazé fashion audience reacting/ unsure what to do but smartphones captured everything. Then two burly security men came running in and pulled me off the runway area along the pier. The next day a headline in Rupert Murdoch's Newscorp-controlled *The Daily Telegraph* read "Extinction Rebellion Vigilante Ruins Fashion Week".

Ricarda Bigolin
At least you won't know how I really feel: Masking performance & obstructed agency
* **footnotes & references**

---

*1 Erving Goffman, *The Presentation of the Self in Everyday Life* (New York: Knopf Doubleday Publishing Group, 1959).

*2 Goffman, *Presentation.*

*3 Nick Crossley, "Researching Embodiment by Way of 'Body Techniques,'" *The Sociological Review* 55, no. s1 (2007): 80-94.

*4 Hua Hsu, "Affect Theory and the New Age of Anxiety," *New Yorker,* March 18, 2019, https://www.newyorker.com/magazine/2019/03/25/affect-theory-and-the-new-age-of-anxiety.

*5 Sianne, Ngai, *Ugly Feelings* (Cambridge: Harvard University Press, 2005).

Peter Irga & Fraser Torpy

Understanding the impacts of air pollution on human experience: Two case studies

It has long been known that substances in the air can have adverse effects on human health. Today, with the impacts of climate change and human activity changing the world in untold ways, air pollution represents a considerable and global threat to our health.

Between 2005 and 2010, the death rate associated with exposure to outdoor air pollution increased globally by 4 per cent, by 5 per cent in China and by a staggering 12 per cent in India.[*1] The Organisation for Economic Co-operation and Development (OECD) has stated that outdoor air pollution exposure is predicted to become the leading environmental cause of premature death by 2050.[*2] In 2012 alone, it was estimated that approximately 7 million deaths were related to outdoor air pollution.[*3] Pollution exposure also has a negative impact on economies, with a reported ~USD$ 1.7 trillion spent on health-related costs in 2010.[*4]

Whilst a proportion of air pollution results from natural processes such as bushfire smoke, pollen release and surface dust, in cities large quantities of pollutants are produced from fossil fuel emissions, which comprise a mixture of solid particulate matter (PM) and gases, including oxides of sulphur (SO_x), oxides of nitrogen (NO_x), carbon monoxide (CO), carbon dioxide (CO_2), and ozone.[*5]

By examining industrial pollution in China and the pollution resulting from the recent Australian bushfires, we can see how our changing planet is influencing both man-made and biomass generated sources of air pollution. But first, it is important to have an understanding of the pollutants and their risk profiles.

The pollutants

Particulate matter (PM) encompasses a complex and diverse range of organic and inorganic particles that exist in either suspended solid or liquid phases. PM is defined by the particle aerodynamic diameter in µm, and is classed accordingly (PM_{10}, $PM_{7.5}$, PM_5, $PM_{2.5}$ or $PM_{<0.1}$). PM can be generated in ambient environments by human activities such as vehicle emissions, road dust, fossil fuels, industrial activities, and indoors from heating, cleaning activities and cooking.[*6] PM is widely recognised as one of the most dangerous pollutants for human health, with the smaller fractions of PM ($PM_{2.5}$ and $PM_{<0.1}$) being directly associated with over 2 million deaths per annum worldwide.[*7] Due to their small size, $PM_{2.5}$ and $PM_{<0.1}$ pose a greater risk to human health than larger PM classes as they can penetrate and embed into the alveoli and thus translocate into the blood, potentially transferring large volumes of toxic compounds.[*8] This is cause for concern worldwide, as mechanically ventilated commercial buildings generally have insufficient filtration capabilities to effectively remove PM of the smaller size fractions.[*9]

Nitrogen dioxide (NO_2) is a relatively reactive atmospheric gas and is often detected in indoor environments at concentrations that pose a threat to human health, as gas stoves and ovens are the major sources of NO_2 and other nitrogen oxides (NO_x).[*10] Vehicular emissions are the primary ambient source of NO_2, and thus concentrations are generally higher in dense urban areas.[*11]

Ozone is a secondary contaminant that is primarily formed in the troposphere from chemical reactions between various reactive agents.[*12] In some indoor environments, elevated concentrations are released from typical office and domestic equipment such as electrostatic air cleaners and photocopying machines.[*13]

Much like NO_2, sulphur dioxide (SO_2) is mainly combustion derived, however it is only produced in problematic concentrations when fuels containing sulphur, such as coal and oil, are burned. Indoors, kerosene-burning devices such as heaters and cooking stoves, and especially solid fuel cooking and heating appliances may be significant sources.[*14] However, in developed countries, elevated indoor SO_2 concentrations and resultant exposure have primarily been attributed to infiltration of ambient vehicular emissions.[*15] Globally, SO_2 emissions have fallen by up to 75 per cent in metropolitan and industrial areas, mainly due to the now widespread use of low sulphur diesel fuel,[*16] however in dense urban environments, ambient and indoor SO_2 remains an issue.[*17]

Carbon monoxide (CO) is a relatively unreactive gas that can pass freely through building envelopes and ventilation systems.[*18] In many cases, indoor concentrations are higher than those in ambient environments due to the use of combustion appliances such as gas cooking stoves and ovens, flueless gas and kerosene heaters or fireplaces, tobacco smoking and similar combustion processes.[*19]

Impact of industrialisation on the atmosphere: China

Developing countries suffer the most from poor air quality, with exceptional economic growth and industrialisation leading to high level air pollution, along with water contamination and land degradation.[*20] These serious environmental issues are thus the focus of considerable research and public attention.[*21] Although reductions in air pollution will clearly lead to improvements in human and environmental health, very little data is available on the public health benefits of air pollution control measures and policies, especially for developing countries.[*22] This issue is important since the disease burden associated with air pollution has increased in the past decade, especially in low-income and middle-income countries.[*23] Additionally, although air pollution is a universal issue, it causes the greatest harm in susceptible individuals who are exposed to high air pollution concentrations. People with chronic diseases (particularly cardiorespiratory illnesses), little social support, and poor access to medical services are most at risk from air pollution. In developing countries, such cases may largely go unreported.

The largest developing country, China, has been changing rapidly over the last three decades and its economic expansion is largely driven by the use of fossil fuels, which have led to a dramatic increase in emissions of both ambient air pollutants and greenhouse gases (GHGs).[*24] It is now the largest emitter of carbon dioxide,[*25] and a large emitter of methane and black carbon, the other two major GHGs contributing to global warming.[*26] Ambient air pollution and climate change are placing Chinese residents at significant risk health-wise.

With growing energy consumption and rapid urbanization, an increase in ambient air pollution is an inescapable reality. Even though ambient air quality in Chinese cities has remained stable or even improved slightly in recent years —an accomplishment achieved through the relocation of polluting industries, a switch to less polluting fuels, the enforcement of zoning regulations and stricter emission standards for mobile and stationary sources,[*27] better city planning, and increased investments in city infrastructure[*28]—China is still amongst the countries with the worst air quality globally. Megacities such as Beijing, Shanghai, and Chongqing are frequently among the cities with the highest levels of air pollutants in the world.[*29]

Additionally, the makeup of China's air pollution is changing. Coal is still the major source of energy, constituting about 75 per cent of all energy sources.[*30] Consequently, air pollution in China predominantly consists of coal smoke, with suspended particulate matter and sulphur dioxide the principal air pollutants.[*31] In Chinese cities, however, with the rapid increase in the number of motor vehicles, air pollution is gradually transforming from coal combustion-sourced to a mixed coal combustion/motor vehicle emission type.[*32]

In recent years, the 'grey sky' phenomenon caused by fine particles ($PM_{2.5}$ and smaller) has become an increasing public concern. This effect, which occurs predominantly in urban areas, poses a serious health risk to Chinese residents.[*33] $PM_{2.5}$ is not yet a routinely monitored air pollutant in most Chinese cities. China's reported annual average concentrations of $PM_{2.5}$ in the 2000s were in the range of 56 to 122 $\mu g/m^3$. In Beijing, for example, the annual average $PM_{2.5}$ concentrations in 2001–2004 ranged from 96.5 to 106.7 $\mu g/m^3$,[*34] which was approximately seven times the ambient air quality standard recommended by the US Environmental Protection Agency (15 $\mu g/m^3$) and ten times the WHO Global Air Quality Guideline (AQG) (10 $\mu g/m^3$). In Shanghai, the annual average $PM_{2.5}$ concentration in 2005 reached 56 $\mu g/m^3$, which was also much higher than the WHO AQG.[*35] There is an on-going plan to include $PM_{2.5}$ in air quality monitoring in Chinese cities.[*36]

So far, the information available on the health benefits of air quality improvements in developing countries is limited to modelling studies, although they do provide important information, especially with respect to China. For example, Wang et al., used county-level $PM_{2.5}$ and mortality data to estimate $PM_{2.5}$-associated disease burden in 2020 along with forecasts for 2030.[*37] They reported that the projected health benefit of the Air Pollution Prevention and Control Action Plan would be considerable, and could reduce the number of $PM_{2.5}$- elated premature deaths by approximately 130,000 (13.5 per cent) in 2020 and by 220,000 (22.8 per cent) in 2030. However, the health benefits resulting from air quality improvements could be potentially offset by the effect of population growth and an aging population. Thus, to reduce future disease burden, the implementation of more stringent measures for air quality improvement and public health protection are needed in China. Further, collaborative and focused efforts are needed to deal with a growing and aging population.

In Australia, human-generated sources of pollution pale in comparison to those from biomass sources: smoke from bushfires, wildfires and planned hazard reduction burns can contribute up to 43 per cent of the emissions over a yearly period.[*39] While bushfires and their associated emissions have always been part of Australia's history, the recent 2019–2020 bushfire season—known as the 'black summer'—wasthe worst in recent memory.

Both New South Wales and Queensland declared a state of emergency after new record property losses during this fire season. At least 2.7 million hectares in New South Wales burned, with widespread fires starting in September 2019—a much earlier start to the fire season than in previous

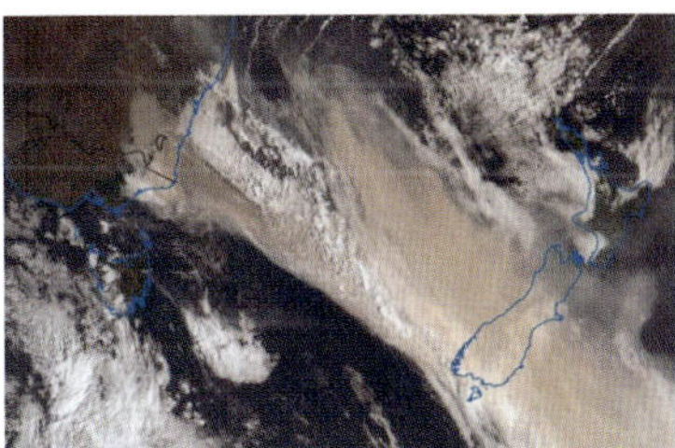

(Fig. 1)

Impact of wildfires in the atmosphere

Australia has relatively good air quality, with annual average $PM_{2.5}$ concentrations around 8 μg/m^3, which are below the World Health Organization guideline of 10 μg/m^3. As with any developed country, there are a number of important sources of air pollutant emissions in Australia, including fossil fuel combustion, specifically motor vehicle derived pollutants, coal-fired power stations, industrial processes, ships and domestic wood heaters in winter.[*38] The ambient air quality in Australia is exceptionally good compared to many other countries, although concentrations of PM and NO_2 can exceed national standards on occasions. These instances are generally related to stable meteorological patterns, and bushfire-hazard-reduction burns in summer, which can cause severe pollution events for a few days in most years. (Fig. 1)

Fig. 1. Smoke from Australian bushfires extending across the Tasman Sea and blanketing New Zealand on January 3, 2020. Image by the NASA Suomi National Polar-orbiting Partnership satellite.

years. The burnt area was three times larger than 2019 fires in the Amazon (906,000 hectares).

These bushfires confirmed researchers' warnings from several years ago about an increase in wildfires resulting from climate change in Australia.[*40] Fire-susceptible vegetation has been promoted by both a decrease in rainfall and an increase in extremely hot temperatures. According to the Australian Bureau of Meteorology, the Southern Downs (QLD) and Northern Tablelands (NSW) experienced record low rainfall from January to August 2019, making large areas of vegetation very dry and flammable. Australia has warmed by more than 1°C since 1910. The warming climate in Australia has been accompanied by heatwaves that have increased in frequency, duration, and maximum temperatures. In 2019, both states entered the bushfire season after a year of hot temperatures and low rainfall, putting many districts under high risk. A similar situation occurred in the 2009 Black Saturday fires in Victoria, when Melbourne reached a record-breaking high temperature (46·4°C) following a long drought.

The bushfires in New South Wales destroyed about 700 homes and untold wildlife, including seriously threatening koala populations due to habitat loss. The fate of many species in the bushfire affected areas remains widely unknown, with ancient ecosystems impacted. Additionally, it has been estimated that major Australian bushfires during 1967–2013 resulted in over 8000 direct human injuries and 433 direct fatalities, costing approximately Australian $4.7 billion. However, this estimate did not consider indirect costs, which mainly result from the adverse health effects of bushfire smoke. By way of comparison, the US Environmental Protection Agency has estimated the indirect effects of air pollution from wildland fires on excess premature deaths and morbidity in the USA during 2008–12 led to health costs of US$513 billion.

Health effects of wildfire smoke have been well documented worldwide, through large studies and hospital admissions data, namely from Australia, the United States and Canada. A recent study estimated that an average of 339,000 people died in 2012 due to wildfire smoke related causes worldwide. Johnston et al. and colleagues also estimated that when climatic events such as El Niño occur, deaths could increase to as high as 532,000.[*41] As our climate changes, there is compelling evidence that the likelihood of extreme weather events, like El Niño, will increase.

The parts of Australia most affected by the bushfires lie on a coastal lowland plain between the Pacific Ocean and elevated sandstone tablelands. The climate for these areas is warm and temperate, and have been described as sub-tropical.[*42] Days in which rainfall events occur are evenly distributed throughout the year, however rainfall volume is maximal in Autumn (March–May).

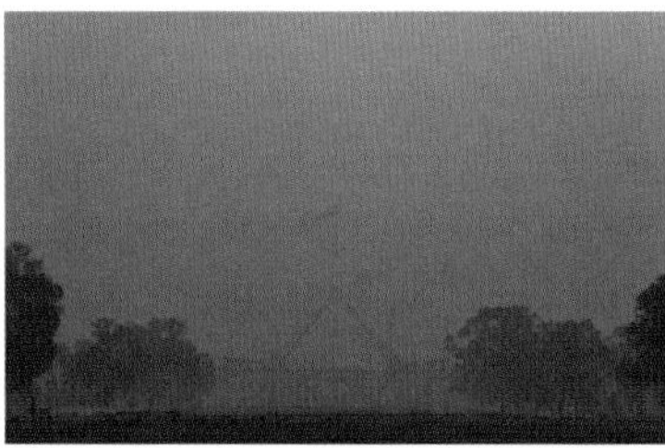

(Fig. 2)

Fig. 2. Australian Parliament House, Canberra, during a bushfire event on January 1, 2020. Photograph by AAP Image/Lukas Coch.

The most hazardous component of bushfire smoke is suspended particulate matter. (Fig. 2) As a result of bushfire smoke, in December 2020 most areas of Sydney recorded, over a twenty-four-hour period, average $PM_{2.5}$ concentrations that exceeded 100 $\mu g/m^3$ (and as high as 500 $\mu g/m^3$), which is four-times higher than the WHO guideline value of 25 $\mu g/m^3$. By comparison, the daily average $PM_{2.5}$ concentration before the bushfire was approximately 20 $\mu g/m^3$.

Furthermore, bushfire smoke has also been associated with increased risks of hospitalisation and emergency department visits due to respiratory diseases such as asthma, chronic obstructive pulmonary disease, and respiratory infections. Increasing evidence also suggests bushfire smoke might increase cardiovascular morbidity, psychological disorders, adverse birth outcomes, and eye irritation. However, our knowledge about the health effects of bushfire smoke is still insufficient. The long-term and lasting effects of bushfire smoke and which subgroups are most vulnerable to its effects remain largely unknown. It has been suggested that PM_{10} generated from bushfires might have different health effects compared with PM_{10} from urban background sources (such as traffic emissions). Therefore, more studies focusing on air pollutants from bushfires are needed.

Unfortunately, there is no current effective way to reduce the effects of bushfire smoke on human health, although wearing facemasks and staying indoors are commonly recommended, and many people consider facemasks the best protection. Yet facemasks might be not effective; sometimes they provide a false sense of security. Their effectiveness depends on their filtration capacity: fine particles can still get through them if their filtration capacity is low. Additionally, an individual's behaviour and characteristics (such as facial hair or the duration and frequency of use) also affect the efficiency of the facemask. Importantly, wearing a facemask can be uncomfortable in very hot weather when bushfires are most frequent. Even if facemasks could protect adults, it is still questionable whether they could protect children, older individuals, pregnant women, and those with chronic diseases, as these groups often cannot tolerate the inconvenience and discomfort of wearing a mask.

Staying indoors might provide some protection against bushfire smoke, but this depends on building quality and ventilation. In general, most residential houses are not equipped with air purifiers or air conditioning systems with high-efficiency filters. Hence, outdoor pollutants can still penetrate the interior. Subsequently, indoor and outdoor concentrations of fine particles are often very similar in many buildings, especially residential ones.

Climate change will continue to exacerbate catastrophic bushfire conditions. It has been estimated that days with a high-to-extreme risk of fire will increase by 15 to 70 per cent by 2050, and by more than 100 per cent by 2100, as compared with 2010. Although some politicians claim that climate action is too expensive, the increasing intensity and frequency of bushfires clearly indicate that the price of climate inaction is even higher. Unfortunately, the Australian Government has not engaged well in climate action over the past decade. Australia is on track to meet less than half of its carbon emission reduction targets, which are to reduce emissions by 26 to 28 per cent relative to 2005 by 2030, and achieve net zero emissions by 2050.

Peter Irga & Fraser Torpy
Understanding the impacts of air pollution on human experience: Two case studies
* **footnotes & references**

*1 P. Kumar, A. Druckman, J. Gallagher, B. Gatersleben, S. Allison, T. S. Eisenman, U. Hoang, S. Hama, A. Tiwari, A. Sharma, K. V. Abhijith, D. Adlakha, A. Mcnabola, T. Astell-Burt, X. Feng, A. C. Skeldon, S. De Lusignan, & L. Morawska, "The Nexus Between Air Pollution, Green Infrastructure and Human Health," *Environment International* 133, (2019): 105181.

*2 Who Regional Office for Europe, *Economic Cost of the Health Impact of Air Pollution in Europe: Clean Air, Health and Wealth* (Copenhagen: WHO Regional Office for Europe, 2015), 66.

*3 World Health Organization, *Global Report on Urban Health: Equitable Healthier Cities for Sustainable Development* (Geneva: WHO, 2016).

*4 K. Kitamori, T. Manders, R. Dellink & A. Tabeau, *OECD Environmental Outlook to 2050: The Consequences of Inaction* (OECD, 2012).

*5 L. Bai, J. Wang, X. Ma & H. Lu, "Air Pollution Forecasts: An Overview," *International Journal of Environmental Research and Public Health* 15 (2018): 780.

*6 F. Reisen, J. C. Powell, M. Dennekamp, F. H. Johnston & A. J. Wheeler, "Is Remaining Indoors an Effective Way of Reducing Exposure to Fine Particulate Matter During Biomass Burning Events?" *Journal of the Air & Waste Management Association* 69, (2019): 611-622.

*7 J. Lelieveld, J.S. Evans, M. Fnais, D. Giannadaki & A. Pozzer, "The Contribution of Outdoor Air Pollution Sources to Premature Mortality on a Global Scale," *Nature* 525, (2015): 367; E. VAN DER WALL, Air Pollution: 6.6 Million Premature Deaths in 2050!" *Netherlands Heart Journal* 23 (2015): 557-558.

*8 V. Jayaram, H. Agrawal, W. A. Welch, J. W. Miller & D. R. Cocker, "Real-Time Gaseous, PM and Ultrafine Particle Emissions from a Modern Marine Engine Operating on Biodiesel," *Environmental Science & Technology*, 45 (2011): 2286-2292.

*9 L. Morawska, G. A. Ayoko, G. N. Bae, G. Buonanno, C. Y. H. Chao, S. Clifford, S. C. Fu, O. Hänninen, C. He, C. Isaxon, M. Mazaheri, T. Salthammer, M. S. Waring & A. Wierzbicka, "Airborne Particles in Indoor Environment of Homes, Schools, Offices and Aged Care Facilities: The Main Routes of Exposure," *Environment International* 108 (2017): 75-83.

*10 H. Yin, C. Liu, L. Zhang, A. Li& Z. Ma, "Measurement and Evaluation of Indoor Air Quality in Naturally Ventilated Residential Buildings," *Indoor and Built Environment* 28, no. 10 (2019): 1307-1323, 1420326X19833118.

*11 Z. H. Shon & K. H. Kim, "Impact of Emission Control Strategy on NO2 in Urban Areas of Korea," *Atmospheric Environment* 45 (2011): 808-812.

*12 E. V. Bräuner, D. G. Karottki, M. Frederiksen, B. Kolarik, M. Spilak, Z. J. Andersen, A. Vibenholt, T. Ellermann, L. Gunnarsen& S. Loft, "Residential Ozone and Lung Function in the Elderly," *Indoor and Built Environment* 25 (2014): 93-105.

*13 M. Hyttinen, P. Pasanen, J. Salo, M. Björkroth, M. Vartiainen & P. Kalliokoski, "Reactions of Ozone on Ventilation Filters," *Indoor and Built Environment*, 12, (2003): 151-158.

*14 N. L. Lam, K. R. Smith, A. Gauthier & M. N. Bates, "Kerosene: A Review of Household Uses and Their Hazards in Low-and Middle-income Countries," *Journal of Toxicology and Environmental Health, Part B* 15 (2012): 396-432.

*15 T. G. Mason, K. P. Chan, C. M. Schooling, S. Sun, A. Yang, Y. Yang, B. Barratt & L. Tian, "Air Quality Changes after Hong Kong Shipping Emission Policy: An Accountability Study," *Chemosphere* 226 (2019): 616-624.

*16 R. M. Hoesly, S. J. Smith, L. Feng, Z. Klimont, G. Janssens-Maenhout, T. Pitkanen, J. J. Seibert, L. Vu, R. J. Andres & R. M. Bolt, "Historical (1750 – 2014) Anthropogenic Emissions of Reactive Gases and Aerosols from the Community Emissions Data System (CEDS)," *Geoscientific Model Development (Online)* (2018): 11.

*17 A. J. Conley, D. M. Westervelt, J. F. Lamarque, A. M. Fiore, D. Shindell, G. Correa, G. Faluvegi & L. W. Horowitz, "Multimodel Surface Temperature Responses to Removal of U.S. Sulfur Dioxide Emissions," *Journal of Geophysical Research: Atmospheres* 123 (2018): 2773-2796.

*18 K. Zhong, F. Yang & Y. Kang, "Indoor and Outdoor Relationships of CO Concentrations in Natural Ventilating Rooms in Summer, Shanghai," *Building and Environment* 62, (2013): 69-76.

*19 M. Fazlzadeh, R. Rostami, S. Hazrati & A. Rastgu, "Concentrations of Carbon Monoxide in Indoor and Outdoor Air of Ghalyun Cafes," *Atmospheric Pollution Research* 6 (2015): 550-555.

*20 P. M. Mannucci & M. Franchini, "Health Effects of Ambient Air Pollution in Developing Countries," *International Journal of Environmental Research and Public Health* 14 (2017): 1048.

*21 D. E. Bowler, L. M. Buyung-Ali, T. M. Knight & A. S. Pullin, "A Systematic Review of Evidence for the Added Benefits to Health of Exposure to Natural Environments," *BMC Public Health* 10 (2010): 456; B. J. LEE, B. KIM & K. LEE, "Air Pollution Exposure and Cardiovascular Disease," *Toxicological Research* 30 (2014): 71-75; C. WANG, Y. TU, Z. YU & R. LU, "PM2. 5 and Cardiovascular Diseases in the Elderly: An Overview," *International Journal of Environmental Research and Public Health* 12 (2015): 8187-8197.

*22 L. T. Molina, G. Li, M. A. Zavala & W. Lei, "Megacities Air Pollution Lessons Learned Relevant to Asia," *AGUFM* (2019): A54B-01.

*23 N. Goyal, M. Karra & D. Canning, "Early-life Exposure to Ambient Fine Particulate Air Pollution and Infant Mortality: Pooled Evidence from 43 Low-and Middle-income Countries," *International Journal of Epidemiology* 48 (2019): 1125-1141.

*24 B. Zheng, Q. Zhang, J. Borken-Kleefeld, H. Huo, D. Guan, Z. Klimont, G. P. Peters & K. He, "How Will Greenhouse Gas Emissions from Motor Vehicles be Constrained in China Around 2030?" *Applied Energy* 156 (2015): 230-240.

*25 S. Wang, Q. Li, C. Fang & C. Zhou, "The Relationship Between Economic Growth, Energy Consumption, and CO2 Emissions: Empirical Evidence from China," *Science of the Total Environment* 542 (2016): 360-371.

*26 B. Zhang, T. Yang, B. Chen & X. Sun, "China's Regional CH4 Emissions: Characteristics, Interregional Transfer and Mitigation Policies," *Applied Energy*, 184 (2016): 1184-1195.

*27 M. Zhang, T. Lv, Y. Zhao & J. Pan, "Effectiveness of Clean Development Policies on Coal-fired Power Generation: An Empirical Study in China," *Environmental Science and Pollution Research* 27, no. 13 (2020): 14654-14667.

*28 J. Li, Y. Zhang, Y. Tian, W. Cheng, J. Yang, D. Xu, Y. Wang, K. Xie & A. Y. Ku, "Reduction of Carbon Emissions from China's Coal-fired Power Industry: Insights from the Province-level Data," *Journal of Cleaner Production* 242 (2020): 118518.

*29 S. Wang, C. Zhou, Z. Wang, K. Feng & K. Hubacek, "The Characteristics and Drivers of Fine Particulate Matter (PM2. 5) Distribution in China," *Journal of Cleaner Production* 142 (2017): 1800-1809.

*30 J. Chai, M. Du, T. Liang, X. C. Sun, J. Yu & Z. G. Zhang, "Coal Consumption in China: How to Bend Down the Curve?" *Energy Economics* 80 (2019): 38-47.

*31 S. Chen & D. E. Bloom, "The Macroeconomic Burden of Noncommunicable Diseases Associated with Air Pollution in China," *PLOS one* 14, no. 4 (2019).

*32 S. Sun, G. Zhao, T. Wang, J. Jin, P. Wang, Y. Lin, H. Li, Q. Ying & H. Mao, "Past and Future Trends of Vehicle Emissions in Tianjin, China, from 2000 to 2030," *Atmospheric Environment* 209 (2019): 182-191.

*33 D. Meng, X. Zhicun, L. Wu & Y. Yang, "Predict the Particulate Matter Concentrations in 128 Cities of China," *Air Quality, Atmosphere & Health* 13 (2020): 399-407.

*34 F. Duan, K. He, Y. Ma, F. Yang, X. Yu, S. Cadle, T. Chan & P. Mulawa, "Concentration and Chemical Characteristics of PM2. 5 in Beijing, China: 2001–2002," *Science of the Total Environment* 355 (2006): 264-275.

*35 J. Cao, H. Xu, Q. Xu, B. Chen & H. Kan, "Fine Particulate Matter Constituents and Cardiopulmonary Mortality in a Heavily Polluted Chinese City," *Environmental Health Perspectives* 120 (2012) 373-378.

*36 B. Tilt, "China's Air Pollution Crisis: Science and Policy Perspectives," *Environmental Science & Policy* 92 (2019): 275-280.

*37 Q. Wang, J. Wang, J. Zhou, J. Ban, T. Li, "Estimation of PM2· 5-associated Disease Burden in China in 2020 and 2030 Using Population and Air Quality Scenarios: A Modelling Study," *The Lancet Planetary Health* 3 (2019): 71-80.

*38 R. A. Broome, J. Powell, M. E. Cope & G. G. Morgan, "The Mortality Effect of PM2.5 Sources in the Greater Metropolitan Region of Sydney, Australia," *Environment International* 137 (2020): 105429.

*39 M. Hibberd, M. Keywood, P. Selleck, D. Cohen, E. Stelcer, Y. Scorgie & L. Chang, *Lower Hunter Particle Characterisation Study, Final Report* (Sydney: NSW Environment Protection Authority, 2016).

*40 S. J. Prichard, S. M. O'neill, P. Eagle, A. G. Andreu, B. Drye, J. Dubowy, S. Urbanski & T. M. Strand, "Wildland Fire Emission Factors in North America: Synthesis of Existing Data, Measurement Needs and Management Applications," *International Journal of Wildland Fire* 29 (2020): 132-147.

*41 F. H. Johnston, S. B. Henderson, Y. Chen, J. T. Randerson, M. Marlier, R. S. Defries, P. Kinney, D. M. Bowman & M. Brauer, "Estimated Global Mortality Attributable to Smoke from Landscape Fires," *Environmental Health Perspectives* 120 (2012): 695-701.

*42 P. Stewart, *Changing Fire Regimes in Tropical and Subtropical Australia*, PhD, (PhD diss., the University of Queensland, 2017).

Sharbendu De
An Elegy for Ecology

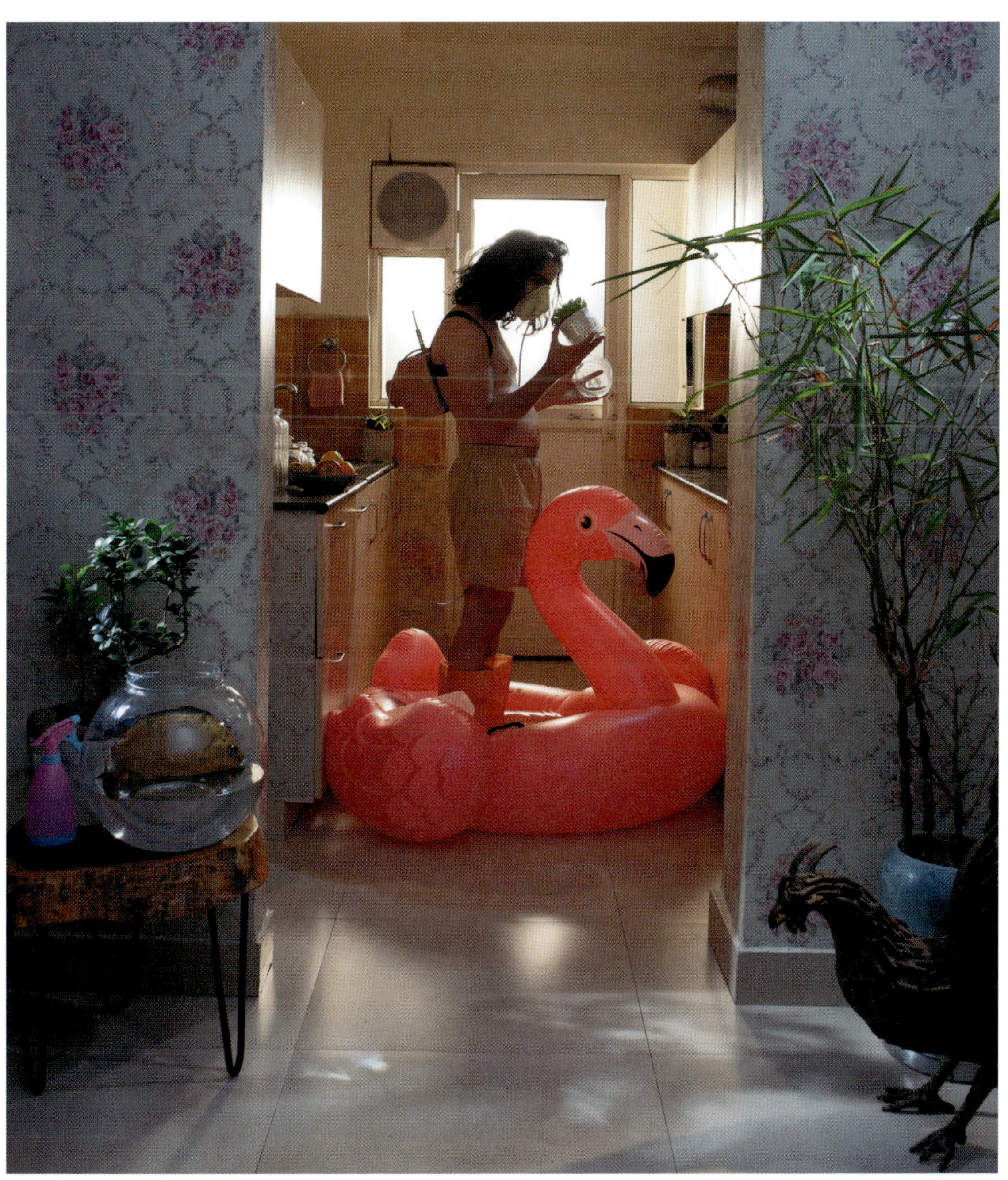

Another Day Blazing, An Elegy for Ecology, 2021

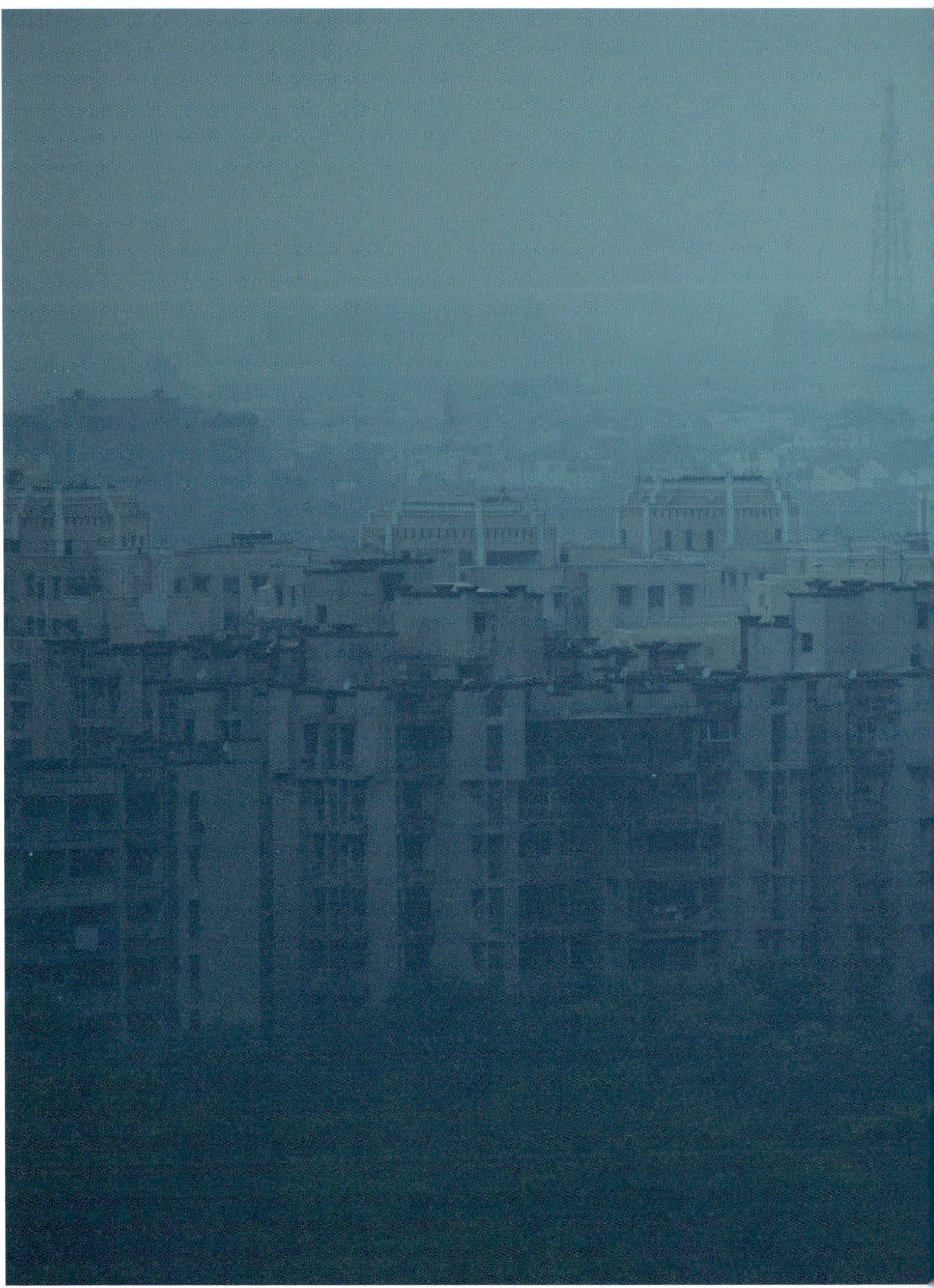

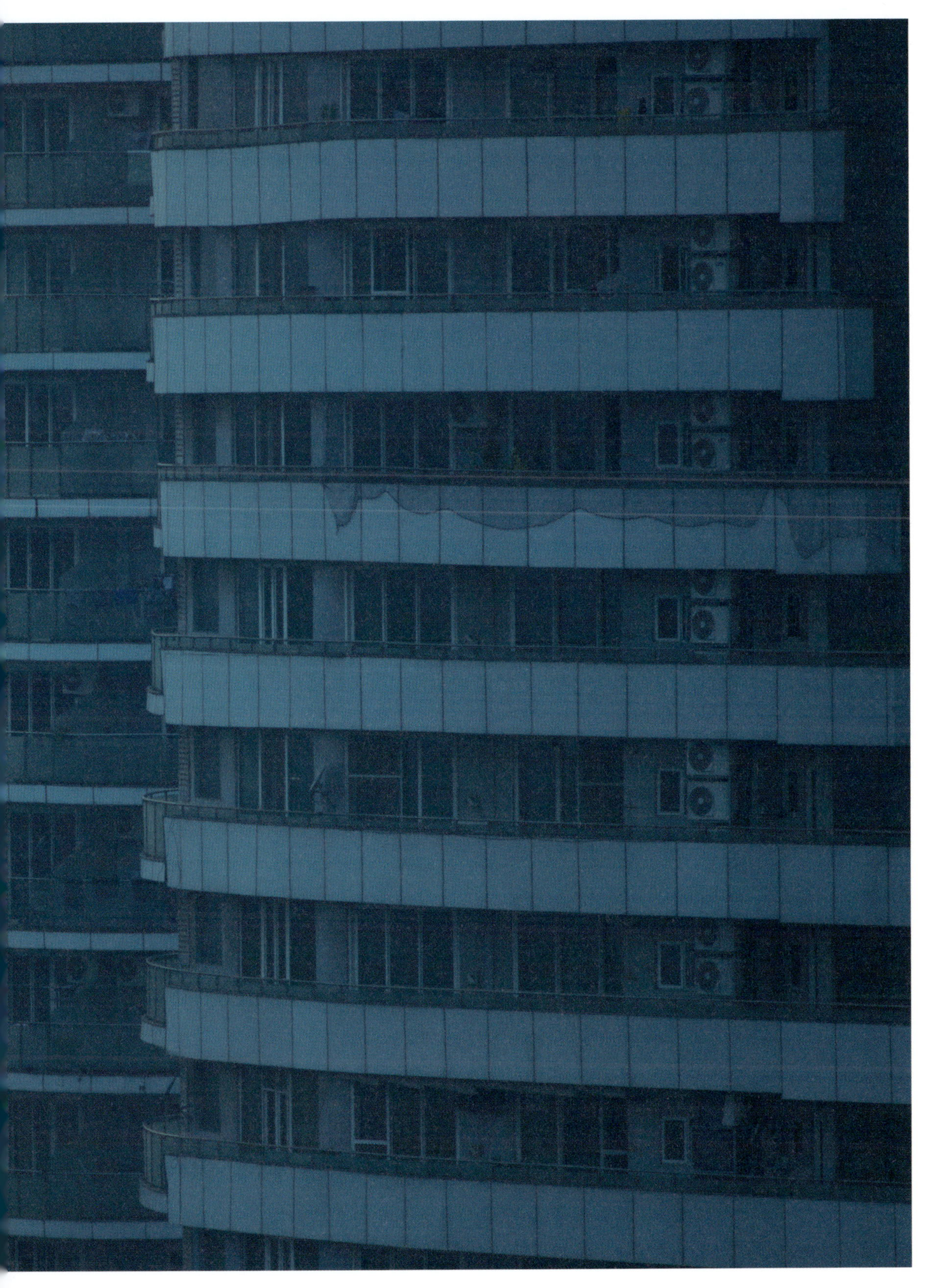

The Great Derangement (after Ghosh), An Elegy for Ecology, 2019

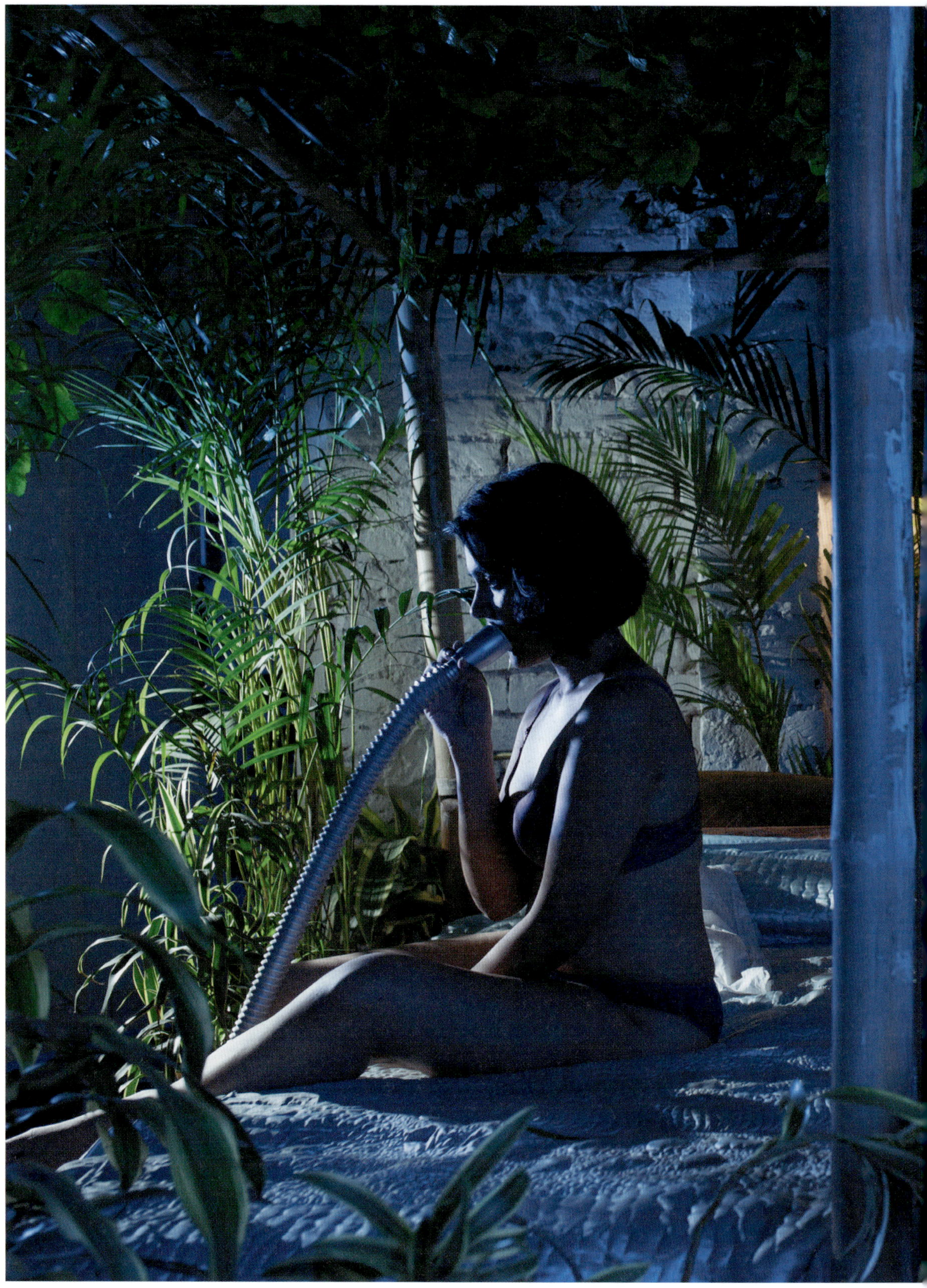

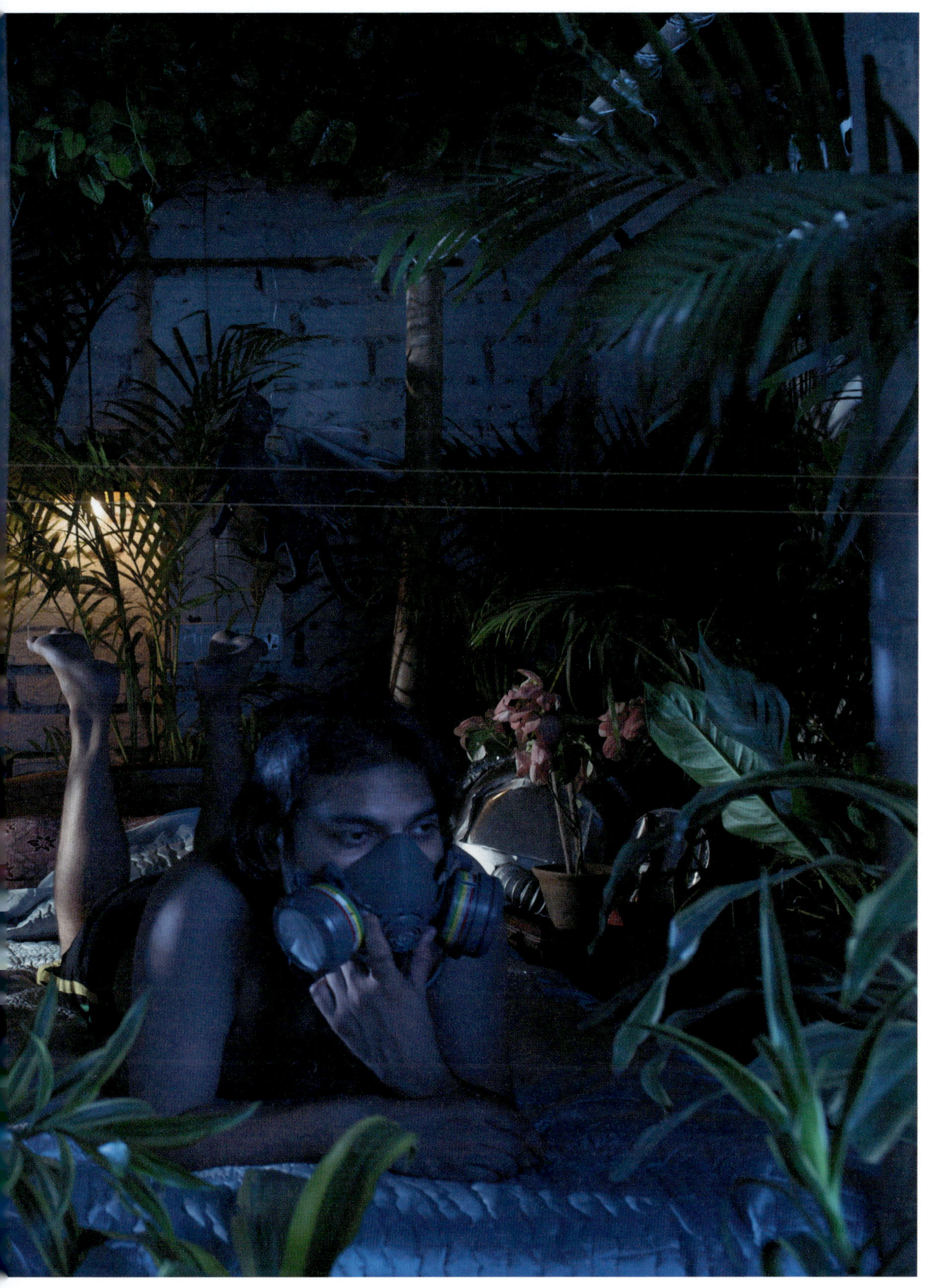

Family, An Elegy for Ecology, 2016

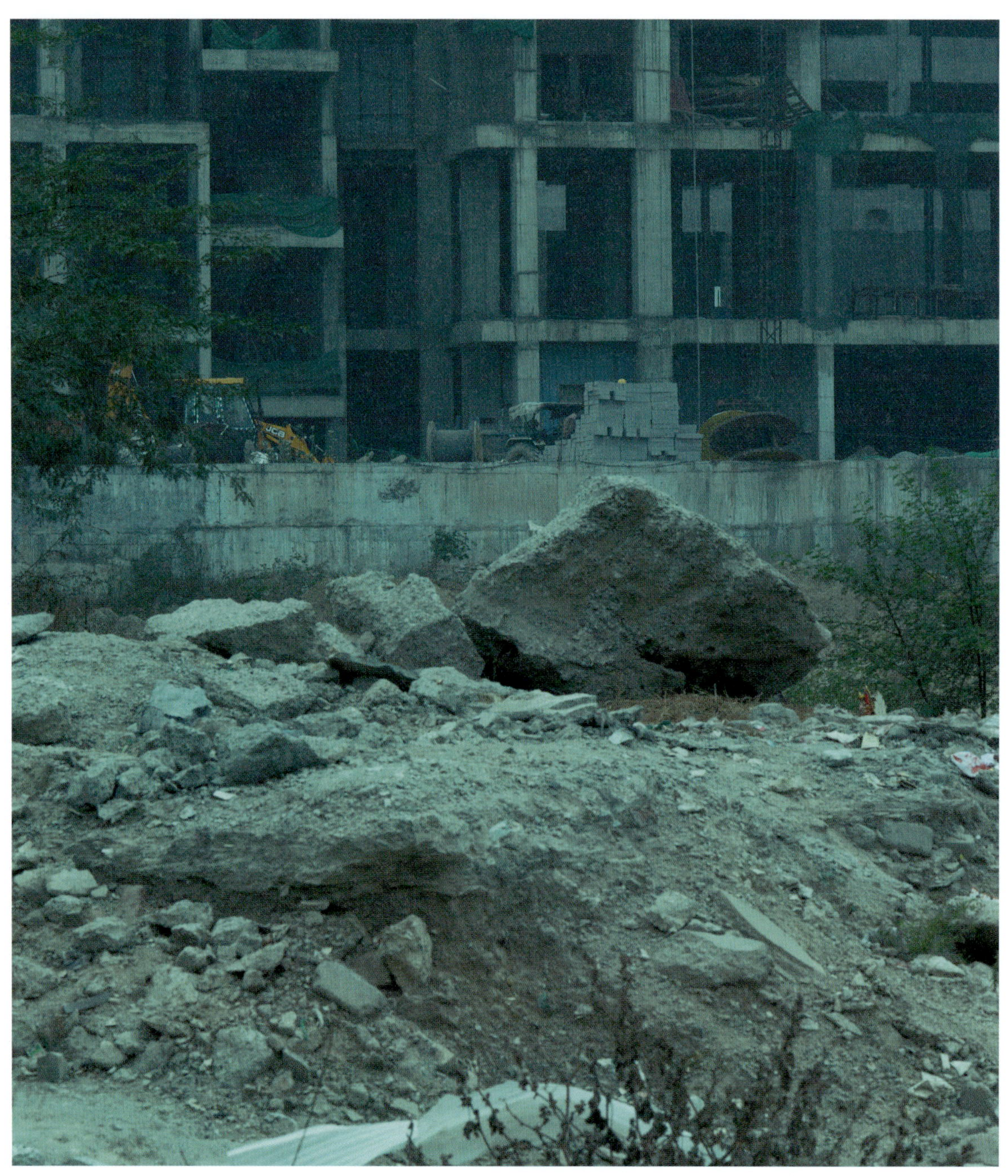

Noida NCR-III, An Elegy for Ecology, 2020

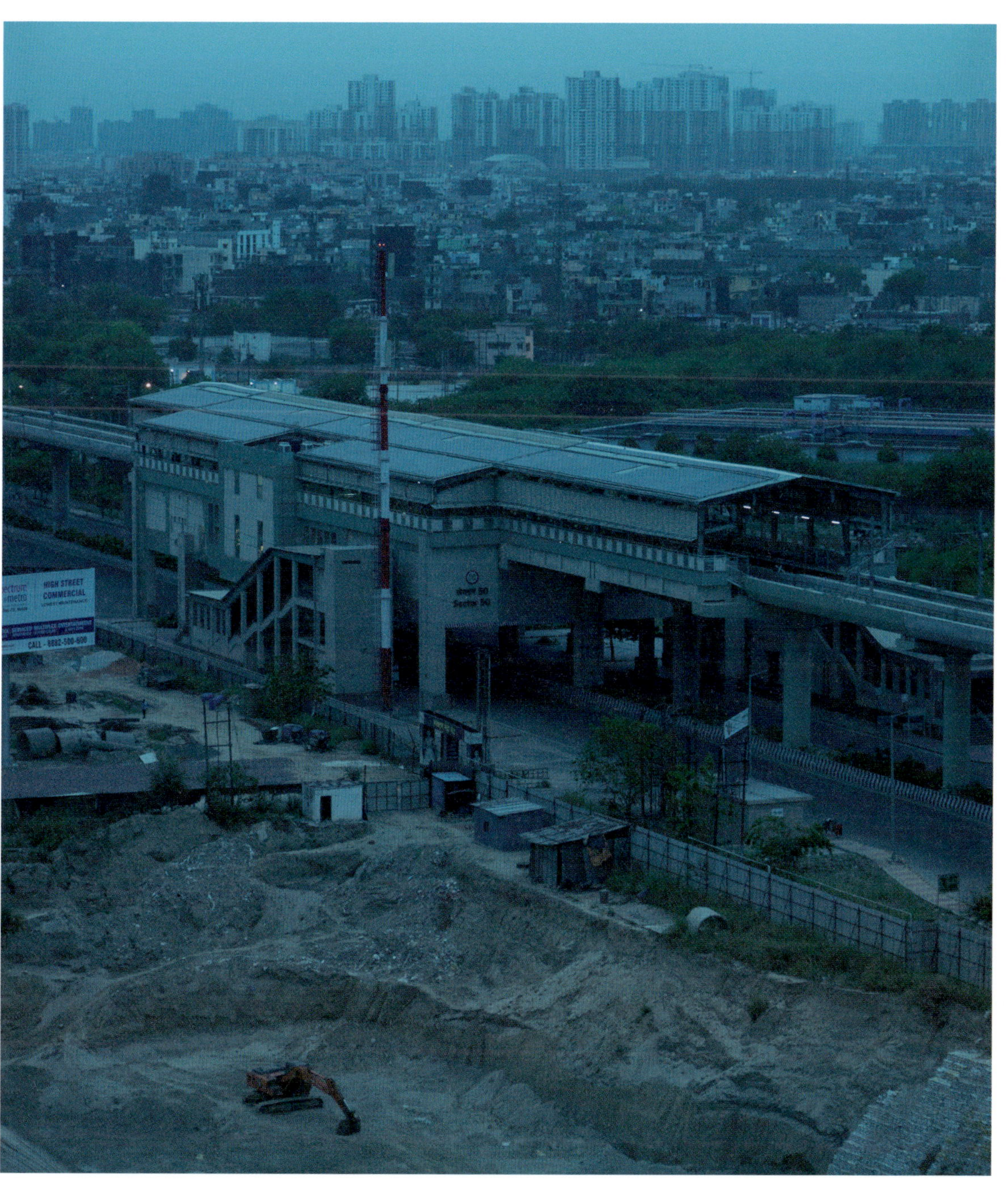

Civilisation, An Elegy for Ecology, 2020

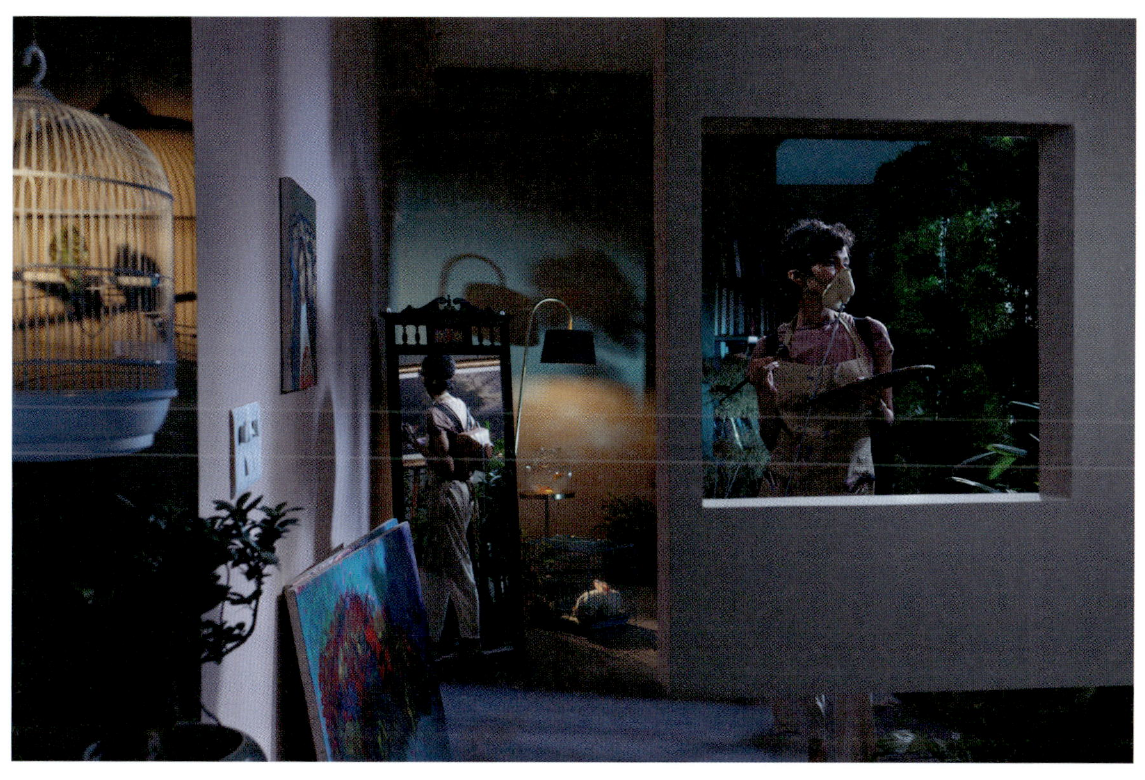

Penned Cohabitants, An Elegy for Ecology, 2021

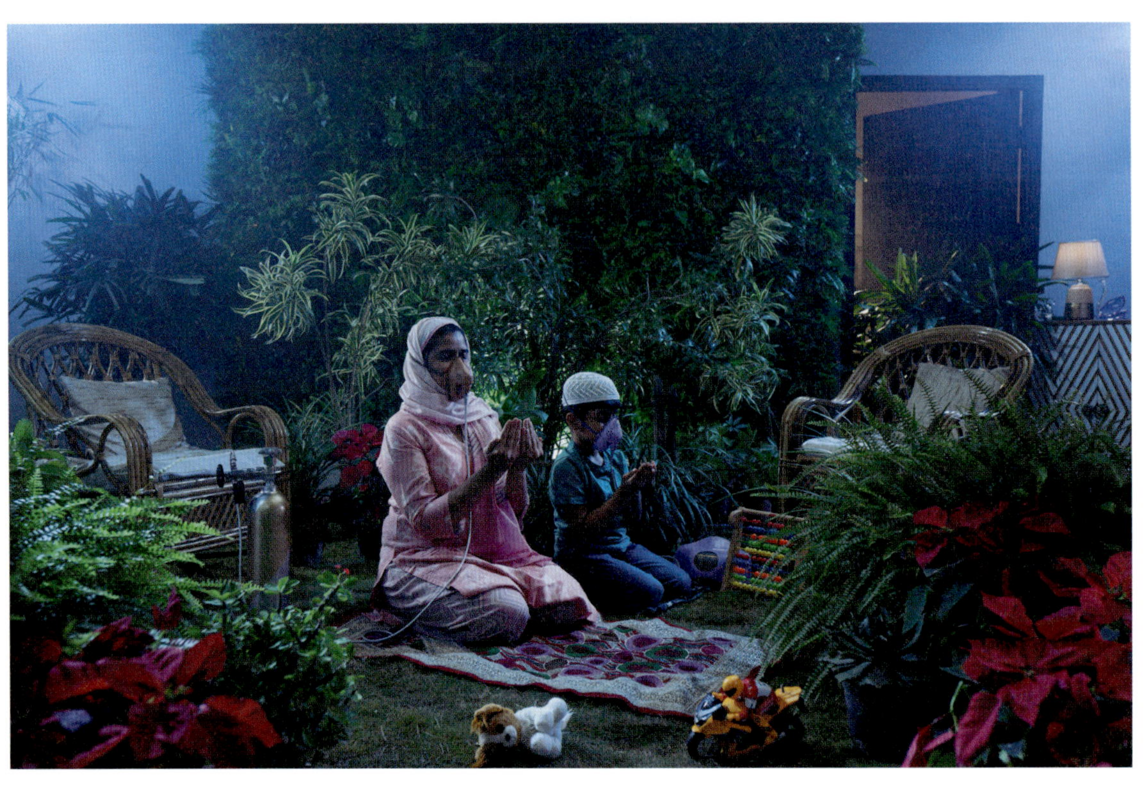

Untitled, An Elegy for Ecology, 2021

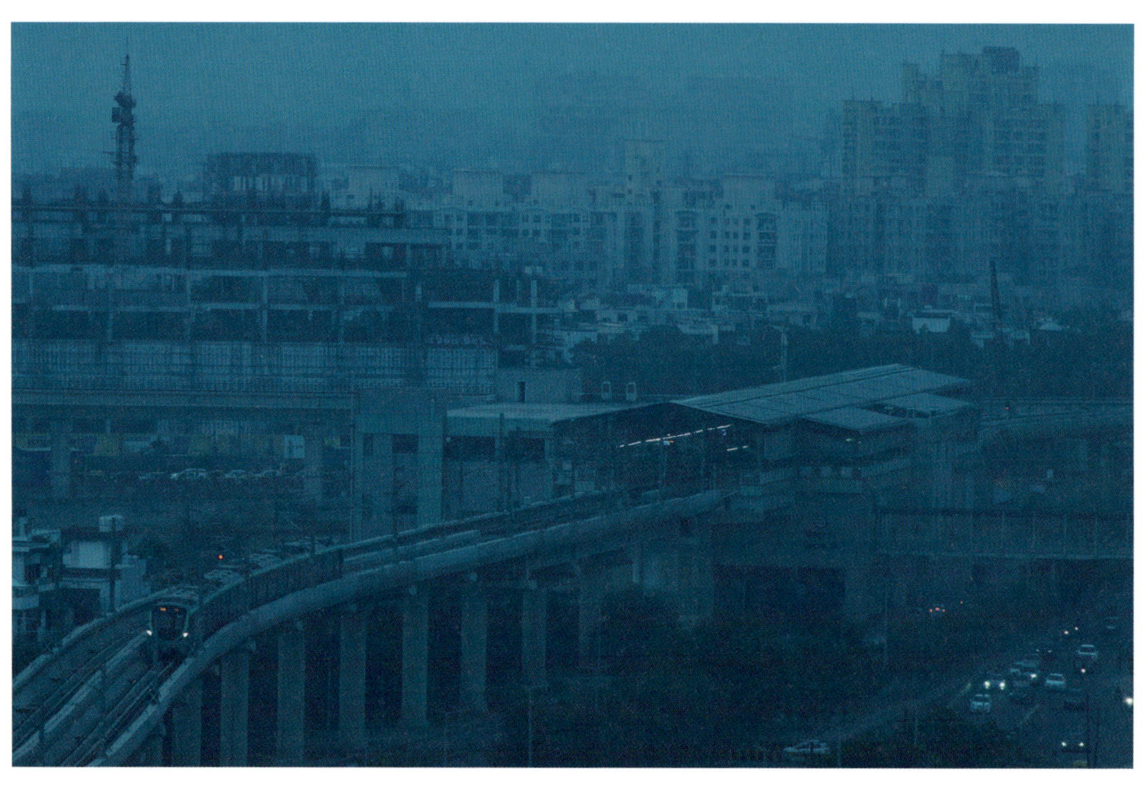

This is Not Hubris, An Elegy for Ecology, 2019

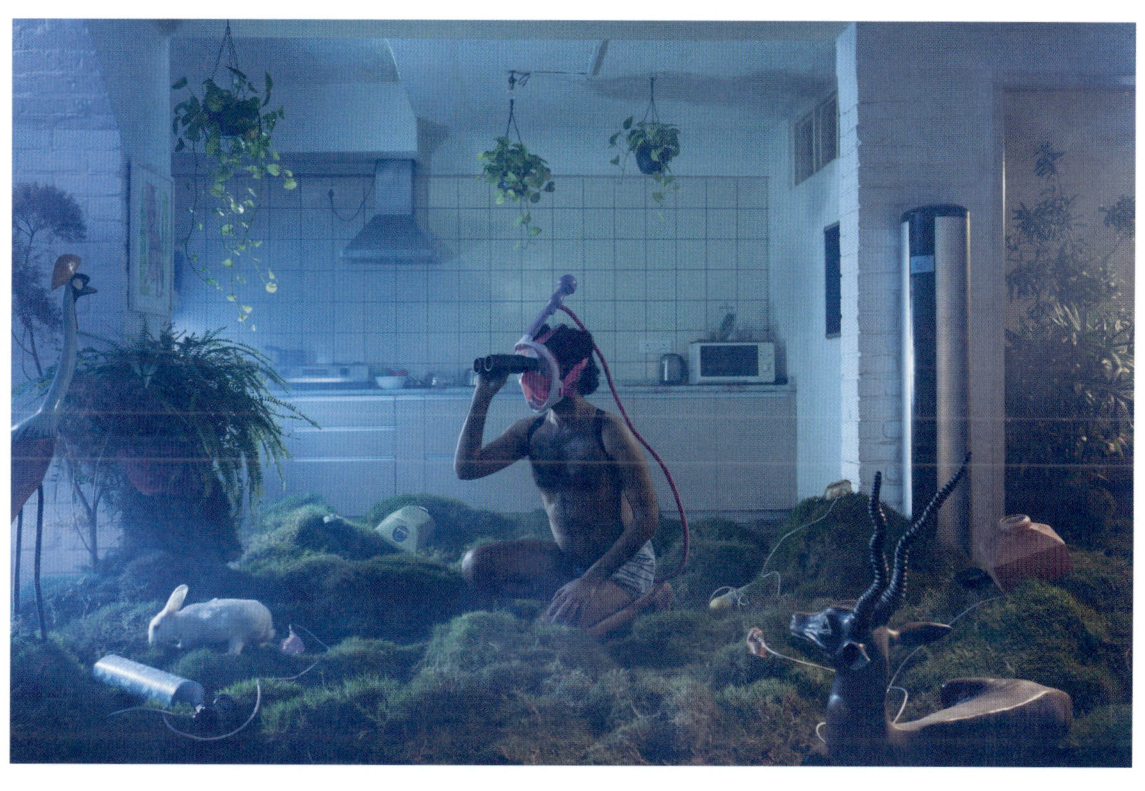

Dzukou Valley, An Elegy for Ecology, 2021

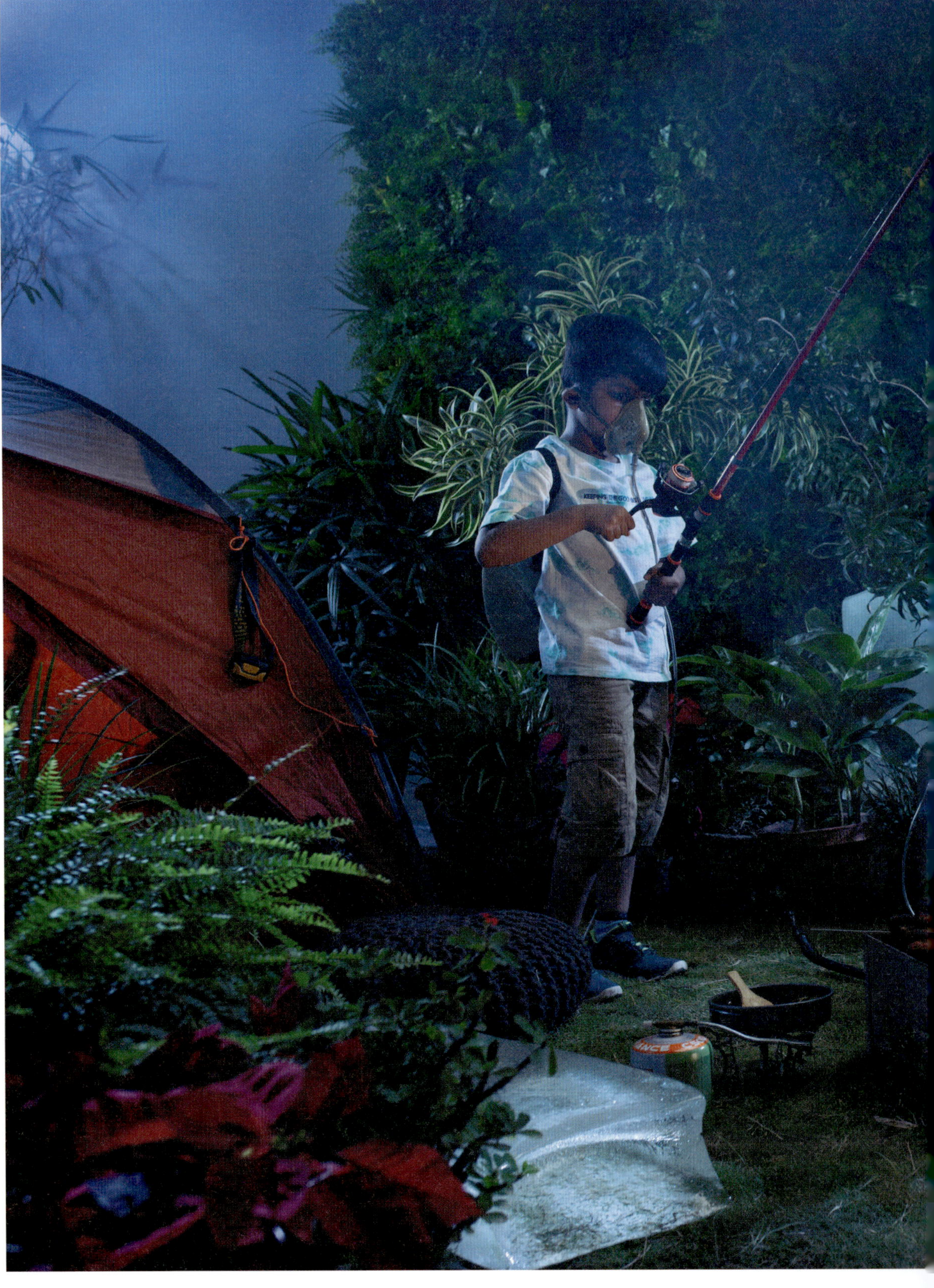

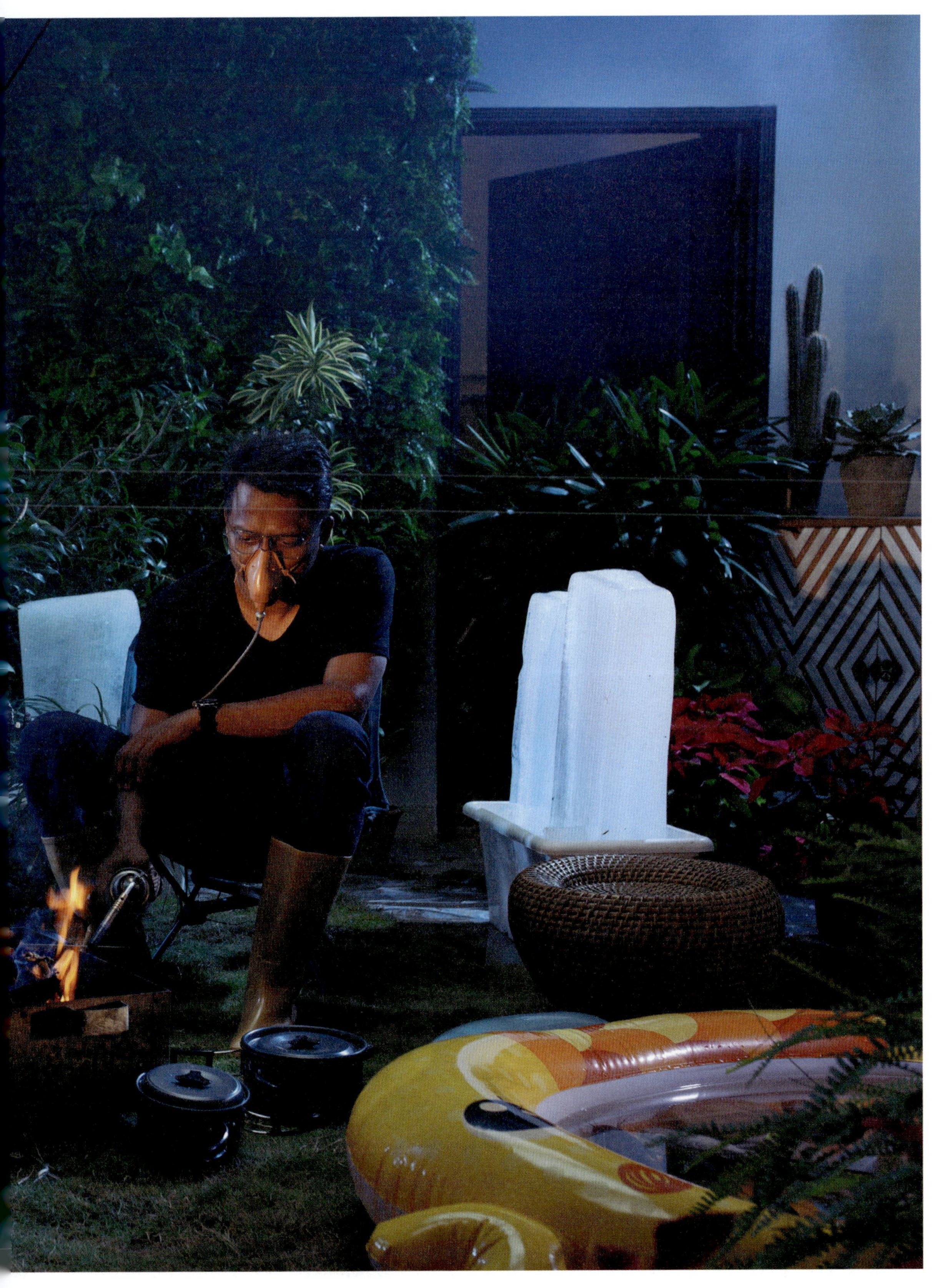

Placebo, An Elegy for Ecology, 2021

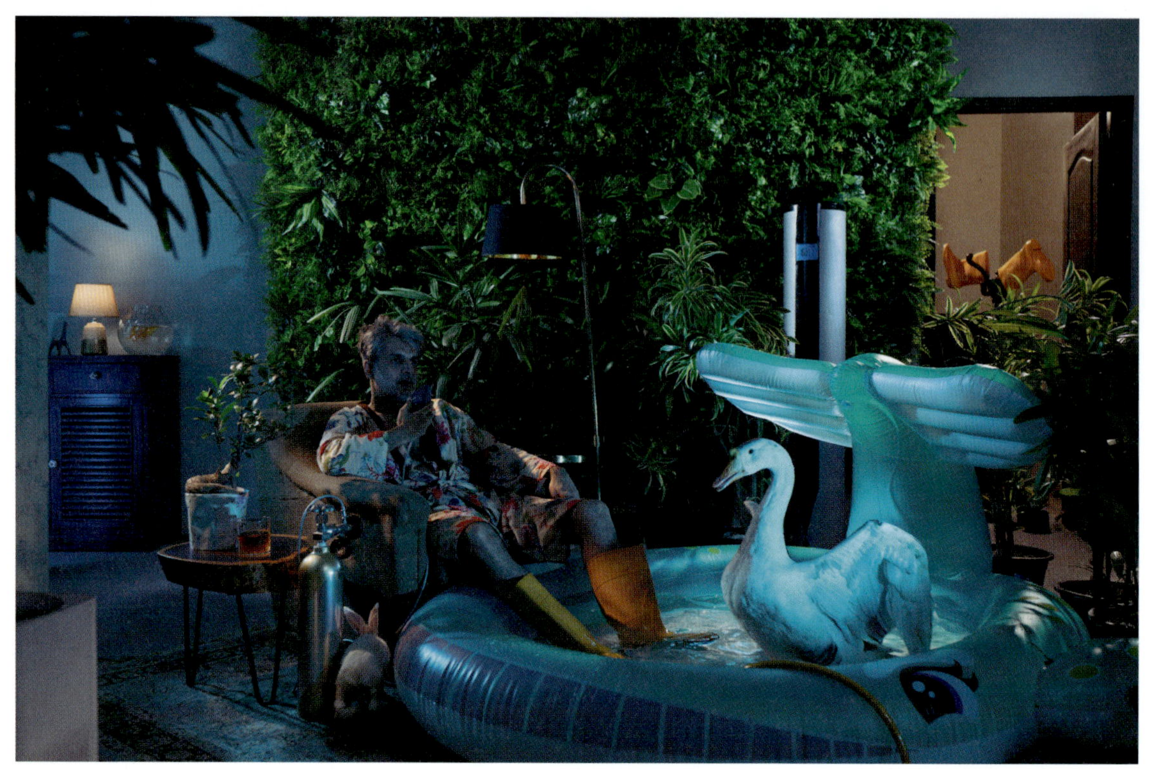

Lonely Man, An Elegy for Ecology, 2021

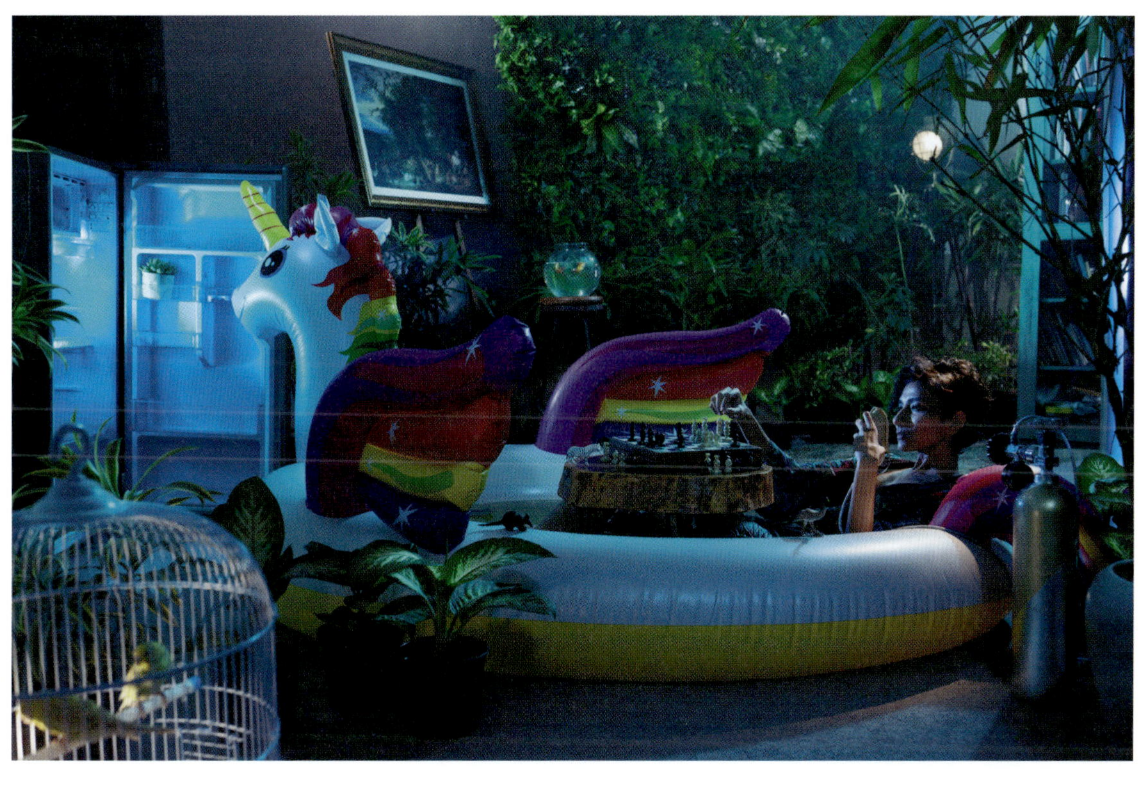

The Temptation in the Garden of Eden (After Jan Brueghel the Elder), An Elegy for Ecology, 2021

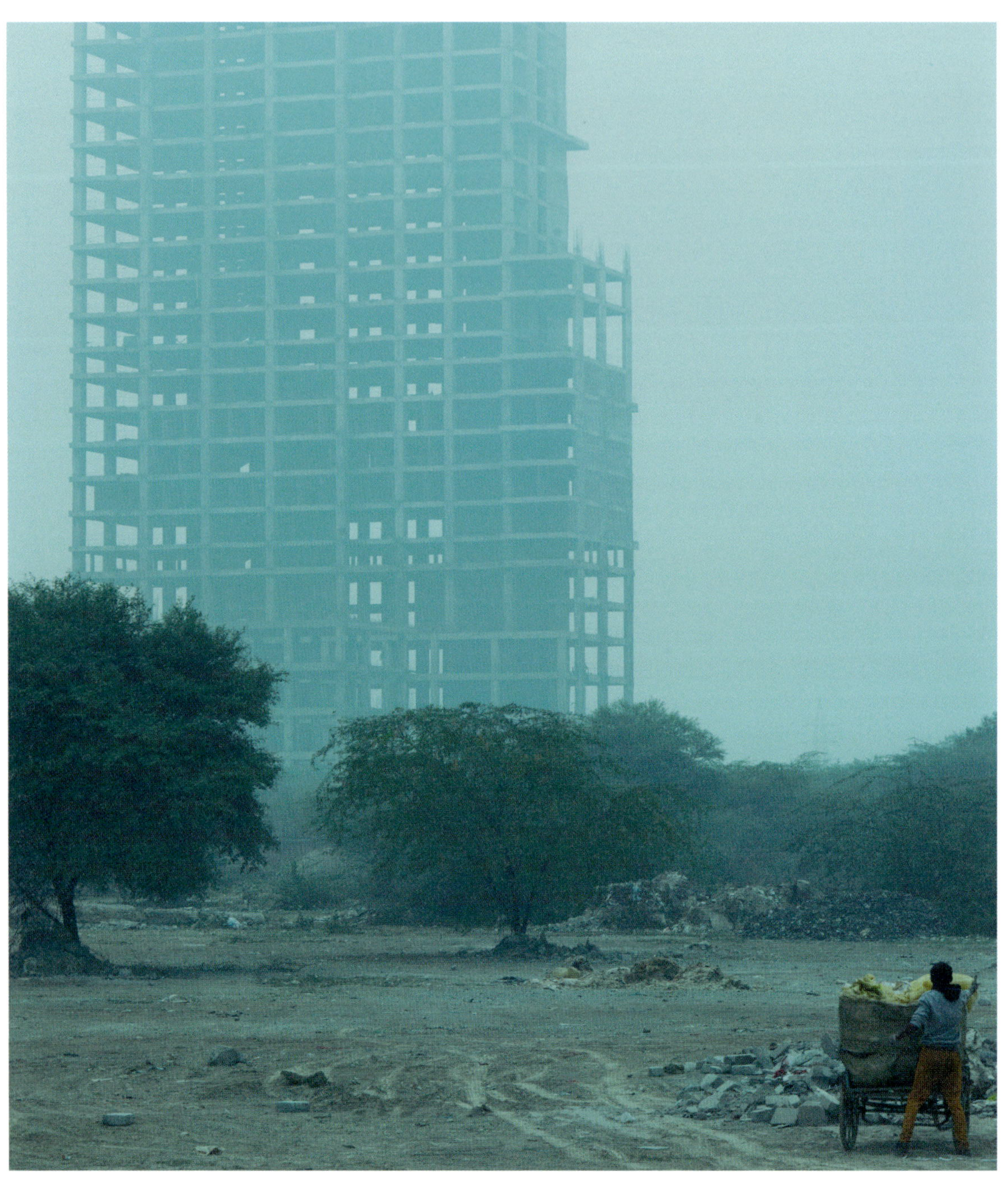

Noida-NCR-IV, An Elegy for Ecology, 2020

An Elegy for Ecology is made possible through generous support from PhotoSouthAsia, an initiative of the MurthyNAYAK Foundation, and KHOJ International Artists' Association under their project titled 'Does the Blue Sky Lie? Testimonies of Air's Toxicities'. Several artworks were produced as part of a commission by the National Taiwan Museum of Fine Arts.

Record of proceedings, 'Supreme Court of India

156

Severe problem being faced by the citizens in Delhi and adjoining areas due to acute air pollution

ITEM NO.302 COURT NO.1 SECTION XVII

S U P R E M E C O U R T O F I N D I A
RECORD OF PROCEEDINGS

SUO MOTU WRIT PETITION (CIVIL) No.4/2019

RE: SEVERE PROBLEM BEING FACED BY THE CITIZENS IN DELHI AND ADJOINING AREAS DUE TO ACUTE AIR POLLUTION

Date : 13-11-2019 This petition was called on for hearing today.

CORAM :
HON'BLE THE CHIEF JUSTICE
HON'BLE MR. JUSTICE S.A. BOBDE

For Petitioner(s) By Courts Motion

For Respondent(s) Mr. Tushar Mehta, SG
158 Mr. Rajat Nair, Adv.
Mr. Kanu Agrawal, Adv.
Mr. B.V. Balaram Das, Adv.

UPON hearing the counsel the Court made the following

O R D E R

This *suo motu* writ petition has been registered to deal with the issues pertaining to pollution in National Capital Region (NCR) and the whole of northern India, particularly during the winter months.

We have thought it appropriate to register the *suo motu* writ petition as, in our considered view, little constructive efforts have been made by the government and other stake holders to find a solution to the problem. From what has transpired in similar matters taken up by this Court on the earlier occasions, apart from apportioning blame and liabilities for the near catastrophic environment that engulfs the whole of northern India and particularly the NCR and Delhi in the winter months. Nothing concrete has

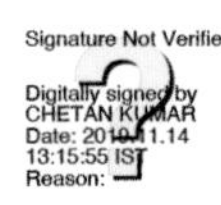

Severe problem being faced by the citizens in Delhi and adjoining areas due to acute air pollution

emerged. We have also thought it appropriate to register this *suo motu* action in the interest of the vast majority of the population in northern India, who are deprived of access to the Court or to ventilate their grievances in this regard.

To a pointed query made by the Court, Shri Tushar Mehta, learned Solicitor General of India, who is present in the Court, has stated that the Government of India is in seisin of the matter and has, in fact, made some head progress. One particular instance that Shri Mehta has mentioned is the availability of technology to provide a viable solution to the problem in Japan. In this regard, Shri Mehta, learned Solicitor General has informed the Court that he has interacted with one Mr. Vishawanth R. Joshi, who is a Bachelor of Engineering and is presently doing research work in the Kyushu University, Fukuoka, Japan. Shri Joshi is
159 **familiar with the problems of pollution and is presently engaged in the development of appropriate technology to deal with the problem.**

Shri Mehta, learned Solicitor General has assured the Court that the appropriate authority, at the highest level, will take up the matter and would interact with Shri Joshi and others and explore the feasibility of the technology that is stated to be available. Thereafter, Shri Mehta, learned Solicitor General would inform the Court of the developments with the utmost expedition.

We direct that the aforesaid course of action be adopted and expedited and the outcome thereof be laid before the Court on 3rd December, 2019. Office to list the case accordingly.

(Chetan Kumar)	**(Anand Prakash)**
A.R.-cum-P.S.	**Court Master**

Enoch Cheng
The polyester kissed my lips

I.

'Sir, you've forgotten your mask'. My building's security guard reminded me in the lobby, pointing to his face. Being machines, the guards themselves didn't wear them.

'Oh sorry'. I felt embarrassed.

'Don't worry, sir.'

He offered me a white surgical mask. I put it on. As I turned around, I saw a blue light from under his beret reflect in the glass door. It was to disinfect the machines from head to toe after direct contact with human beings.

Earlier on today, when I came out of my house without a mask, the cool air inside the elevator brushed my face. For a moment, there was a sense of ease. It made me think of the old days. If it were the old days, we might have been sending our fellow clients to Mars by now. The original plan was to execute 'Plan B': find a second home, and solutions for the earth. The effect of climate change was worse than anything that had been predicted. Forest fires, melting ice, flooding, strong wind, contagious diseases. If we could just go somewhere untouched, we might be able to work out how to undo all this damage to the earth. The original plan had been further developed since the Great Pandemic started ten years ago, which, we had accepted, was not going to end anytime soon. Going to Mars would be an opportunity to start from scratch. We could not wait for a real international cooperation to come anymore. Each country had too much on their plates to see beyond their borders. Like climate change, it had been impossible for all the countries to propose a global plan to pull us out of this Great Pandemic.

A universal corporation would be more pragmatic. A few visionaries had cooperated and invested in a Kickstarter plan for the universal interest of the human race. Those who had enrolled in our program crowdfunded the first stage of the Mars project. Together as a community, we yearned for the possibility of leaving 10 years of misery behind. We knew that we could let go of the past and build something better. Despite the delays to the ultimate journey to the new planet, some people even boosted their funds. There was consensus that the pandemic was a great time for us to try new things out for the future. New reports and articles were being published in films, podcasts, and on our internal social media every hour. Everyone in the program was connected by the imagination of a new world, a new reality.

My job was to contribute to this program by testing the details of the future experience with my senses. The benefit for me, as one of the recruited members, was not only a free ticket to live on Mars one day, but the fact that I could already taste the future. And we could lay out the possible options for our patrons' lives tomorrow.

II.

Another machine guard opened the doors for me. Every day, he would wait with me outside the building for my car to arrive. The corners of his dry red lips lifted in an automatic smile. I remembered not liking it at first. The friendliness was fake. But having not seen human faces for some time, I began to appreciate the conviviality. I smiled back. He wouldn't see it through my mask, but at least I wasn't indifferent. The camera in his eyes could certainly recognize my facial expression and his program could see that I was a safe, non-offensive being.

My jaw got stiff from the smile. Sighing into the mask, I smelled the minty toothpaste from the morning mixed with the odour of my breath. It was also warm. I supposed everyone had their unique breath odour. The last time I had smelled someone else's was from a kiss some years ago. It was infused with sugary red wine. The music of the club around us was loud, but I could still hear the passion of our kiss. We were not out of practice and we kissed as if there were no tomorrow.

The machine guard waited with me, and looked at me intently. I quickly switched my gaze to my phone to check on the whereabouts of my car.

'It will be here in exactly 1 minute and 20 seconds. Don't you worry, sir. You were just early today.'

His eyes appeared even more earnest. I decided to look ahead, as if my car were about to emerge from around the corner.

Kissing seemed strange these days. At first, there had been underground parties for those with proof of vaccination and booster shots that promoted unmasking, kissing, and all the grey areas. One day, the virus mutated, and the parties instantly became hot spots for diseases, and were shut down. People had to stay home for a long time. The numbers infected and the death toll skyrocketed every day; hospitals were overloaded; medical workers were exhausted, infected—many died. Months later, the situation got better for a while. We went out, we met other people, we kissed. But then, another mutation, another explosion of numbers, and another lockdown. The first series of viruses settled down after three years. Six months later, a new virus emerged. Everyone blamed the country that did not report the first new case. But now we have gotten used to something new every 9-18 months. The new normal was no longer shocking, just as the novelties of a decade ago—huge fires in Australia, or the melting of icebergs in Antarctica—were normalised. After several rounds of lockdowns, in the fourth year, even the air we were breathing was suspected to be a risk. And a lot of infected patients got sent to the quarantine camp. Those who recovered and were released were reported to have signs of depression. They would not talk for weeks at a time. Some avoided strangers, or even involuntarily cried in public.

Like many people, I had even ordered a chemical respirator online. By the time it was delivered to my house six weeks later, they told us the air was safe. We just needed to double up the masks to filter the smaller virus particles. And not exchange saliva. It was also highly advisable to spend as much time alone as possible.

But not everyone could live alone. Not everyone preferred to be alone. Around the fifth year, some people couldn't take it anymore. They suggested breaking the laws of social distancing, and gathering together as the 'unmasked'. So, they unmasked and even kissed in front of the camera on social media as an action of resistance and togetherness. The video went viral. Different kissing zones started to spread like wild fire and became transmitting hot spots. I watched these red bubbles growing on the map on TV. I didn't go out, and my company sent me work at home.

People died, but people continued kissing. Some governments tried to intervene. They tear-gassed people. The images of the people kissing in tears among the smoke (hashtagged #epic) encouraged more to join in order to share the collective 'epic' experience. Some governments did not do much. Perhaps they believed in the democracy of people taking charge, or they were waiting to see what other countries would do. Or they were just ready to let go of the people.

One kissing crowd from an island covered the façade of their parliament with a gigantic mask of white canvas. It was embroidered with two huge black letters: 'xx'. There were lootings, riots, curfews. In ten days, the XX crowd won. Their government stepped down. Some media called their XX action an independence referendum. The former leaders and the troops took the military planes home. We watched on the news as hundreds of people hoping to leave rushed to the airport, only to watch the last plane take off. A new government was formed. They immediately closed the border, and stopped most connections with the rest of the world. The number of infections dropped. Slowly, the news stopped covering them—there were more newsworthy and more disastrous crises to report. They were like a mythical tribe that disappeared from our attention.

While the small unmasking and kissing protests took place in our country, there was a week of curfew. Every night after 8pm, helicopters whirred in the sky until 2am. This extended to 6am when the new country, XX, was first established. There was speculation that we might follow the same path, just as the fall of the Berlin Wall in the last century had triggered many other international collapses. But we were only a small island country. No one knew what was the next step if our country fell. We had closed our border once in history, and it took several decades to open up again. Meanwhile, our quarantine camps were full, there were still no new vaccines and our immunity was not developed. And we loved our freedom despite our imperfect government. As soon as XX cut itself off from the rest of the world, our government began to insist that we protect the front-line workers by keeping masks on. Celebrities on social media and TV were singing about their appreciation for the front-line workers.

It seemed to be the most rational and empathetic thing to do. And we did it. Mask on, and no kissing. Kissing felt disruptive, uncivil. We needed a sense of unity. Every day at 7pm, we would go outside to the balcony, or position ourselves by the windows, with our sounding tools (pots, bowls, and spatulas) to cheer the essential workers.

Three months later, our city opened up again. Some people started to go back to work. Schools went back to in-person learning. The cheers ceased. The essential workforce groups began to demand a raise, one after the other: the food delivery motorcyclists, grocery counter persons, sewage and street cleaners, waste collectors, security guards, day-care staff, teachers, nurses, doctors. The unions said they didn't want cheers, but an acknowledgement of one's contribution through a fair amount of income. Those who were willing to do the dirty or maintenance jobs were the first to settle, followed by the high-skilled professionals. Then the rest had to, one way or the other, wait for their annual contract to expire before they could formerly negotiate their terms.

A few weeks later, I came home to a masked human security guard in the lobby, spraying some sanitizer onto the face of another person wearing a beret but not a mask. This person had a face with red lips. He looked at me and blinked slowly. The masked human guard turned his head, greeted me with a nod and said, 'This is our new guard.'

I was aware from the stiff smile that the new guard was a machine. Our company had reported this technological invention a while ago. I just didn't realize that it would be coming to our building so soon.

'What about you?' I asked the human guard, who I had seen almost every day since I moved in.

'I'll be their manager up there', he said, indicating the surveillance camera.

Since that day, I saw him once more. There was a power cut, so he stood in while the machines were unplugged.

'How has your work been up there?' I asked him.

'Where?'

I pointed to the surveillance camera.

'No, they didn't put me up there. I am only on when the machines need a break.'

'Do you like it?'

'Well, not everyone gets to have a job these days. Even the guard of my building got laid off.'

I tried to lighten up the conversation before entering the elevator.

'So, I guess I'd see you around some time.'

But I never saw him again.

By then there were machines everywhere. Anyone not wearing a mask would be a machine. We called them machine helpers. They were not all that scary. So far, none of them had demonstrated any intention to take over our world. And since many people had died, and more people now chose to work from home, surveys had shown that it would more beneficial for the mental health of the citizens to 'populate' the city and preserve a level of visible interaction, rather than having an empty ghost town.

Before their introduction into the human world, the machines would have their face checked by the Design Bureau. Their design would have to meet the new Laws of Uncanniness, as a sign of distinction. That is, they would be unmasked and reveal their facial features. Besides stiff smiles, they sometimes had huge nostrils that didn't breathe, mouths without teeth, lips that could not be tightly sealed, and chins that did not move. Each year, the bio-skins of new machines improved enormously. They kept looking more like humans, whereas it was becoming weirder to see a human being.

Many times, when a new human acquaintance removed their mask, I'd feel surprised. Their actual nose might be bigger than my imagination, or their lips too pale. And when they saw my face, their smiles were usually taut for half a second before another larger smile was forced to cover up. After that, no one arranged a second date. Some people began going on dates with the machine helpers. But removing the masks was still a ritual that added a special layer to the process of human encounters.

III.

The electric car arranged by my company finally arrived.

> 'It was exactly 1 minute and 20 seconds', the machine guard reminded me.

The car door lifted like a wing. The bob-haired driver came out of the car and put their hand above my head to prevent any accident. Their eyes were sparkling today.

> They told me, 'Sir, we'll be at the centre in 4 minutes and 33 seconds.'

We travelled along a long highway. The traffic has always been smooth, thanks to the coordination among machines themselves. Never had it taken more than 4 minutes and 33 seconds for us to reach the other end of the city, a port that was deserted since the first year of the pandemic.

When I arrived at the Mars Testing Centre, I went to the front desk to check in. My other bob-haired machine colleague behind the desk told me that our company had just launched a new design feature for their pupils.

> 'They shine like diamonds', they said. 'Made of the new crystal.'

I knew from our company video report that this 'new crystal' was a recycled material from other 'retired' machine helpers produced in XX. XX, despite removing itself from the public eye, had financially begun to sustain itself with its best geographic advantage: the ocean. As an island country, they became the international electronic waste disposal area for other countries that could afford to pay.

> 'Windows of souls', my colleague continued, blinking their diamonded-eyes, which were also a camera.

They looked straight into my eyes. Our faces were so close that I noticed the skin around their non-breathing single nostril was dotted with a few blackheads. My pupils got scanned, temperature checked and identity verified. I stepped back and turned to head up to my room. The fringes of their bob-hair emitted the blue disinfecting light through corridor.

Inside the elevator, through the mask, I smelled Silphium. I had sampled it in my room two weeks ago.

> My feedback was: 'It smells too much like celery, but I'd prefer for it to smell like cooked choy sum, so it would feel more homey.'

I knew that Silphium was supposed to smell like celery. In fact, the machine experts had had all the factual data available about this extinct plant. Based on my intelligence, they had created a 20-minute documentary for me to watch with the programmed-voice of the narrator from the Blue Planet series. I had picked up this nature program during the second lockdown. It became popular once more at that time because there had been a warning about the long freezing weather. The narrator's wise voice and the image of animals running around my 75-inch plasma TV screen (which I also bought during the second lockdown) created a soothing ambience for dinner in my warm home. Now that I thought about it, the bob-haired, diamond-eyed driver this morning actually sounded like the Blue Planet narrator. Of course, by now, they sometimes knew more about me than myself.

Sometimes. Our company also prided itself for taking what was outside the 'sometimes' seriously. A thousand people were recruited based on gender, age, race, sexual orientation, religion, language background and many other categories. We'd come here every day to contribute all our senses and select the best samples of our time for everyone who had crowdfunded for the future of infinite unknowns. People who had signed up to go to Mars would not return. The mission was to ensure that the future was built to cater for all for us and keep us in check. I opened the door to my room. It looked exactly like my living room. The 75-inch TV took up almost the whole grey wall. In front of it was a brown wooden oval coffee table on top of a green fluffy faux rug. When I first moved into my new home provided by the company, everything had been arranged for me. Apart from the TV that I later replaced, I quite liked all the furniture and utensils, and didn't bother to change anything. Besides, I'd thought we'd be in Mars soon.

The wind blowing the yellow striped polyester curtain across the large window at the end of this room was exactly as it was at home. I had input a lot of data to fine-tune this effect: the wind during the late summer, approaching the fall. This seasonal moment was rather short. I tried my best to dig into memory and find the fresh cool breeze of the opening days after the first lockdown. It turned out that what mattered was not only the temperature, but also the humidity and vibration of the air. The light of the sun had to come in at the right angle. After multiple attempts over the course of three months, the machine experts finally scaled it down to the last crucial factor based on all my data.

There was a smell that they had to mix with crustose lichens. I'd had never put my nose close to a lichen in my life. They gave me many samples to smell for three days. After every three samples, I would have to rest by lying on the white faux-leather sofa, listening to classical music for 15 minutes, and then smelling some coffee beans in order to regain the sharpness of my nose. I didn't know how many times I'd tried, but the final trial hit the mark. I asked them what lichens smelled like. Fish, they said. But I didn't smell fish, I said. They told me that the amount of lichens they put inside was so low that human beings would not be able to detect them. When you lose a smell on earth, you wouldn't notice its absence. But when you were extracting it in a laboratory environment, your brain would recognise that something was missing.

They showed me a five-minute documentary about lichens tailored for me. While watching, I was offered some snacks: three slices of black sourdough bread, buttered with creamy hummus, each topped with a sliced of pickle. As I was eating, I suddenly lost my sense of smell. But I did taste the sourness and nuttiness of the bread, mixed with the sesame oil from the hummus, and the sweet-and-sourness of the pickle. I was worried and told the doctor that I even tasted meat.

The machine doctor opened their thin smile that showed the plain white teeth and said, 'That's just the chemical effect that the mixture of food was doing to your brain. It is not a symptom.'

A sigh of relief for me.

'But your loss of smell is', the doctor confirmed.

They sent me home for seven days. I had a fever for the first two, and I had to sleep most of the time. They didn't give me any work. They delivered food for me every day. They sent me testing kits twice each day, followed by a tele-health session on my 75-inch TV with a machine doctor. I felt frustrated and asked them how I could get infected.

'I basically just went from home and work each day without seeing other people.'

'We have all your data. You have been in a low risk environment. Almost impossible to catch the virus', said the machine voice of the Blue Planet narrator.

'So how then? I don't want to go to the camp!' I protested.

'Maybe the air. We have reported the data to the Global Health Centre and will let their supercomputer analyse it.'

The following day, they told me the report was the same.

'Maybe the air. Don't worry, you are safe with us.'

Then, based on my testing result, they started giving me physical exercise on TV to work along to. It was to train my lungs, so that they could fight against the respiratory virus. By the fourth day, when they brought me the turmeric saffron rice, my smell came back. I was overjoyed—like a sniffing dog. They suggested that I stayed home for a few more days just to be safe. I asked if I could train my body to be fit. I didn't want to be infected again. They programmed some full-body yoga routines for me to work on, and said that it was better to train the mind too. Within minutes while I was still eating the yellow rice, they sent in a yoga mat, and a bottle of lube. For the rest of the week, I felt healthy and strong.

The final test this morning was negative. So, I was ready to go back to work.

> 'Sir, you forgot your mask', my security guard in the beret had reminded me before I left my building.

I didn't forget—I just hadn't remembered. I got used to not wearing it over the past seven days of quarantine. How could I forget?

Or maybe I could.

IV.

Now in this room that looked exactly like my living room, I excitedly opened the box of today's experiment. The TV was on. My bob-haired colleague appeared.

> 'Hello again', their diamonded-eyes blinked. 'The task today is simple. But the instruction is a bit complicated.'

I looked at the beige mask inside the box. They explained to me that this mask was made of viscose. It was a silk replacement, made of plastic bottles, something they could produce more easily on Mars.

> 'As you put on the mask', said the Blue Planet narrator, 'please first lie down on your sofa.'

That's not complicated, I thought.

> They continued, 'Then remove the mask on your face, and exhale all the air in one go. Gently hold your breath at the top, and put on this new mask.'

> 'Sure, I can absolutely do that.'

> 'We could also send in someone to help.'
> 'That won't be necessary.'

I gave them a smile of assurance behind the mask.

> 'We trust you can, just make sure you are doing it with the breathing movement.'

Later, after this experiment, they would explain to me that the inhalation was important for the faux silk to wrap tightly around my face. The tiny respiratory droplets of the virus would then bounce away instead of going in.

> I jumped in, 'But why do we still need the mask in the future? I assume there would be no virus in Mars.'

> 'The viruses should be much more in control. We'll have the data about the patterns of how humans tend to behave, and non-humans evolve in a controlled environment. But we still need to have *all* the data collected and analysed. It will still take some time to complete a new world to its fullest scale. Before that, most humans will remain inside our land.'

I knew by 'inside our land' that they meant the infinitely vast confinement they were building on Mars to maintain the safety of human race. I saw the pictures of the numerous gardens and outdoor spaces, as drawn up in all the master plans publicised in our reports.

> 'Perfect, but…'

> My colleague interrupted, 'Besides, many humans prefer the mask as a fashion item.'

The movement of the yellow striped curtain in the wind caught my attention. I felt the late summer breeze blowing heavier in the room. I had been excited that we would bring this airflow to Mars, something that I had selected from the past to keep for future generations, as a sense scientist. The collaboration between the human mind and the machine had perfected the sun, which now came in at the right angle.

The warm orange lighting brought me back to the moment. I was still lying on the sofa for the experiment.

V.

In this room that looked exactly like my living room, I closed my eyes and lay on the white faux sofa, testing the new mask. I pinched the ear-loops of my mask, a practice that I'd mastered at the beginning of the Great Pandemic, so as to avoid touching the virus collected on the mask's surface.

I removed my mask, and slowly exhaled all the air inside me. I held my breath. My hand searched for the new mask on the faux leather of the sofa. This sofa would be cleaner than the one at home. Three days ago, when they brought me the turmeric saffron rice, I dropped some of it on the sofa. By the time I noticed it, the rice was already dry. That night I felt so tired. My body demanded that I lie down. And when I surrendered, my spine pulled my back downward and the muscles around it melted. I was looking at the yellow stain below the dried rice which gradually blurred in my vision. I fell into a long deep sleep. I had many dreams but I remembered none. My watch recorded a high number from my rapid eye movement.

From the surface of this non-stained sofa, my fingers fetched the silky mask. I ringed the loops around the ears, inhaled. The mask instantly enveloped my lower face. The last bit of air got filtered into my mouth. The viscose fabric kissed my lips.

Then there was music playing. New classical music, written based on the algorithm and my previous selections.

My eyelids got heavy. I dreamed of a long kiss from a faceless person with tongues. It was in the world before the Great Pandemic, or maybe after. No one wore a mask. There were no machine helpers. Only people. And then, we were all in a quarantine camp, waiting for a dinner that never came. My heart was beating so fast. I told myself that it was a dream.

I woke up, and the whole experiment was finished. I had a dialogue with my machine colleague on TV about why we would still need to wear masks on Mars in the future.

At last, the machine colleague who sounded like documentary narrator asked me, 'What was your question, sir?'
'What question?'

'Sorry sir, I interrupted you. I told you that humans prefer the mask as a fashion item. But before that you were just saying "Perfect, but ..."'

My colleague replayed the last line for me—'Perfect, but ...' I heard my own voice.

I watched the orange sunlight warming the floor. The yellow striped curtain was dancing.

'You said that you could send in someone to help me with wearing this new silk ... viscose mask. Who would it be?'

'No, sir. It's poly-viscose, made of recycled plastic bottles. 95 per cent polyester, 5 per cent viscose. Anyway, sir, should you need help, we can play you a documentary that we know you would enjoy.'

The sunlight was moving very slowly, but it was certainly moving across the wooden floor. We had programmed this movement. The light shone onto an area that was spotless. Every time when the late afternoon sun came into my living room at home, the light beam would cast the dust in the air, where it would hover.

During the first lockdown, I was laid off as a tourist holiday booking agent. I was depressed, staying in bed at my old studio flat, watching the dust, but with no desire to clean the floor. Dust became fluffs on the windowsill. A few weeks later, I found a nightshift job packing meat. Three days after, the factory was shut down. It hadn't provided personal protective equipment to the workers, and two of them died. Later in the week, I went back to get my pay cheque for the three days of work. The boxed rotten meat was repugnant, penetrating the thick scarf I was wearing to cover my nose. I couldn't pay rent for so long that I almost got kicked out. At the very last minute, I saw this job posting on Facebook for sense-testers, who were now known as sense scientists. The company even provided housing. When I got my first month's salary, I bought a machine vacuum that rolled around the floor. But later during the day, the dust would come back. The vacuum never got tired of cleaning the floor in the new flat.
It produced a soft humming sound as it worked. But one day, it broke down without warning. Our company offered me a new one, which could both vacuum and disinfect the floor with UV light at the same time. It broke down in nine months. I wrote a report to the company and got a new one which included floor mopping. And recently I had a new one that had a silence button.

The dust should be gathering at home at this very moment.

'But was that your question when you said 'Perfect, but…?"' My colleague sounded sincere.

I harked back to my memory, 'You mentioned that it would still take some time to build a new world.'

'That's correct, sir.'

I stared at my bob-haired colleague and their non-breathing nose, and sparkling eyes on TV. The silky mask caressed my lips as I articulated each word.

'But how long will it take?'

Samaneh Moafi
The Cloud and the Roundabout

The year 2019 saw an increase of social uprisings across the globe. While chants of ‘el violador eres tú’ shook Santiago’s Plaza de la Dignidad, the words “ كلن يعني كلن” erupted in Beirut’ s Martyr Square. From Chile to Lebanon, from Iraq and Iran to Hong Kong, people’s movements sought to overthrow authoritarian regimes and reclaim public space. The occupations were sustained week after week and month after month. Slowly, the residential neighbourhoods that hosted these occupations began to suffer acute manifestations of police brutality. Distrusting the police, residents used their smartphones to document the acts of violence and post them on social media as evidence, in the hope that this

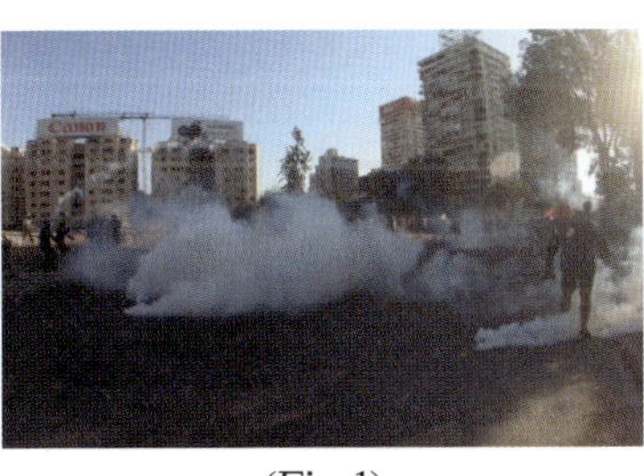

(Fig. 1)

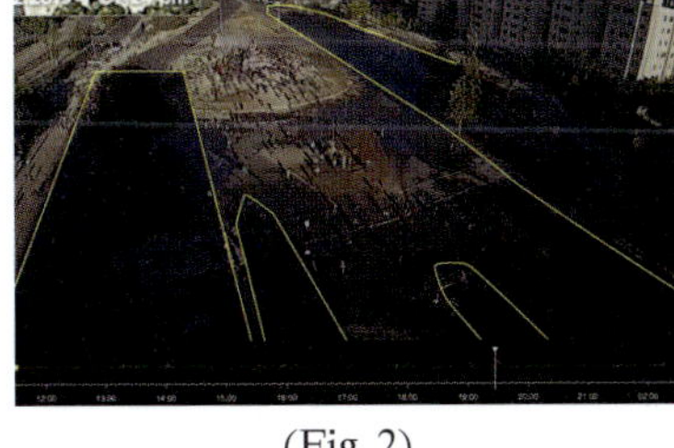

(Fig. 2)

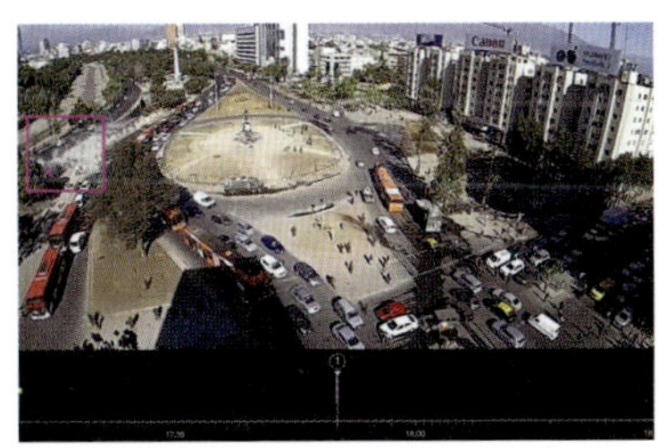

(Fig. 3)

would hold them to account. Weapons of riot control that are evidenced in these images and videos varied across the globe, but common to them all was the signature white cloud, known as tear gas or CS gas.

Launched by projectiles or armoured vehicles, clouds of tear gas remain visible for a short period of time before they dissipate in the pixels of the videos. But as the testimonies of videographers suggest, they continue to affect the bodies whose air they occupy long after they disappear from vision. According to the American Lung Association, tear gas causes chest tightness, coughing, a choking sensation, wheezing, shortness of breath, a burning sensation in the eyes, mouth and nose, blurred vision and

Fig. 1. Chile takes Place of Dignity, Courtesy of Black Soul (YouTube video archive), 20 Dec 2019.

Fig. 2. Confirming the shadows. Still from *Teargas in Plaza de la Dignidad.* Courtesy of Forensic Architecture.

Fig. 3. Analysis of Galeria Cima footage: First tear-gas cloud on 20 Dec 2019. Still from *Teargas in Plaza de la Dignidad.* Courtesy of Forensic Architecture.

difficulty swallowing, effectively rendering those who inhale it as unable to function. The association notes that ‘while tear gas is typically perceived as causing mostly short-term health impacts, there is evidence of permanent disability in some cases.’[*1]

The history of the weaponization of toxic clouds can be traced back to the turn of the twentieth century when the strategy was not so much to target the enemy’s body, but their environment.[*2] The case of the 1915 Battle of Ypres serves as one of the earliest such examples: German soldiers released thousands of chlorine gas cylinders along their trench lines to clear the border of French and British troops. In his analysis of this terror, Peter Sloterdijk states that ‘the breather, by continuing his elementary habitus, i.e. the necessity to breathe, becomes at once a victim and an unwilling accomplice in his own annihilation’.[*3] With the end of WWI, the 1925 Geneva Protocol prohibited the use of asphyxiating clouds in warfare. Later in 1993, the United Nation tightened the legal framework of toxic clouds with a new convention, but also introduced an exception for their use for the domestic purpose of riot control.

With the 1993 convention, the frontiers of environmental wars shifted to the streets and roundabouts of our cities and even closer to our living rooms. Around the time of the uprising in Hong Kong, Forensic Architecture, the research group that I’m part of, examined a case where the police had thrown a canister into a home forcing a domestic worker to run barefoot, in distress, for her life. On the margins of a *gilets jaunes* protest in Marseille, we helped investigate the case of the 80-year-old Zineb Radouane who was fatally wounded by a tear gas grenade as she stood by the window of her fourth-floor apartment. In the aftermath of the Black Lives Matter protests in Portland, we are studying cases where clouds of tear gas have repeatedly filled the homes of elderly residents. In these cases, war is no longer a practice of egregious violence between militaries of state enemies, but a deliberate act waged by the riot police against civilians, the elderly and children, women and men.

CS manufacturers often provide detailed specifications for their products, but they fail to offer a reliable account of how they might behave in urban environments. Their product comes in a powdery solid form. When deployed, the pressurized powder is mixed into a liquid formulation that is then released into the air as droplets. The speed and the direction of the wind, the temperature and even humidity would influence the behaviour of such droplets. While medical reports have evidenced their brutal impact, toxic clouds are yet to be prohibited. As with other environmental forms of violence, new sets of investigative methods are necessary to explain the way they might affect the health of their inhalers in residential neighbourhoods.

In February 2020, I led a team at Forensic Architecture that took up the challenge of investigating teargas on environmental grounds.[*4] A Chilean medical-activist group, *no+lacrimógenas*, had contacted us through our collaborators Angeles Donoso and Cesar Barros, to look into the Carabineros use of CS in residential neighbourhoods of Santiago. Together, we decided to shape an investigation around the archive of a YouTube video channel. The archive held uninterrupted daily live streamings from a camera installed on the building of Galleria Cima near Plaza de la Dignidad. The camera was pointed at the roundabout, an urban-architectural space that was one of the centres of protests. The archive's earliest record is shortly after the rise in public transport fares on 18 October 2019. As such, it held a rigorous documentation of the rise of the people's movement, the largest of its kind for a generation.

The archive of Galleria Cima exhibited a relation between protests and urban forms that resonated with the 'Roundabout Revolutions' of Tunisia, Egypt, Bahrain, Oman, Yemen, Libya and Syria in 2010, which I had previously studied together with the director of Forensic Architecture, Eyal Weizman.[*5] The space of the roundabout pulled the Chilean working class, indigenous groups, students and feminist advocacy groups together, and it was from this space their voice was streamed live in every home across the globe. Another architectural simulacrum of these uprisings was the cloud of teargas. If the roundabout acted as a vortex, pulling people in, the cloud pushed them out. In effect, the cloud and the roundabout were two opposing forms of commons.

To examine the scale of the use of tear gas in Plaza de la Dignidad, we focused on one day, 20 December 2019. Our aim was to evaluate the severity of health risks that residents had been exposed to. On this day, hundreds of tear gas canisters were deployed against protesters in an egregious display of disregard for public health by Chilean authorities. First, we developed a 3D model of the roundabout. We reconstructed the camera's cone of vision and confirmed its time code using shadows. Then, we developed an automated method of video analysis for detecting the extent of each tear gas cloud and marking the approximate location

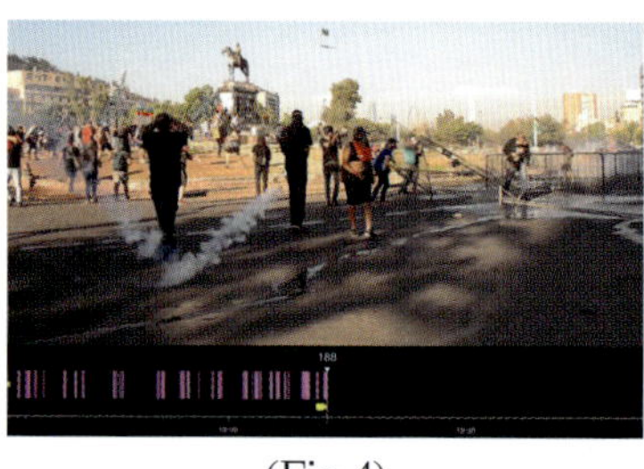

(Fig. 4)

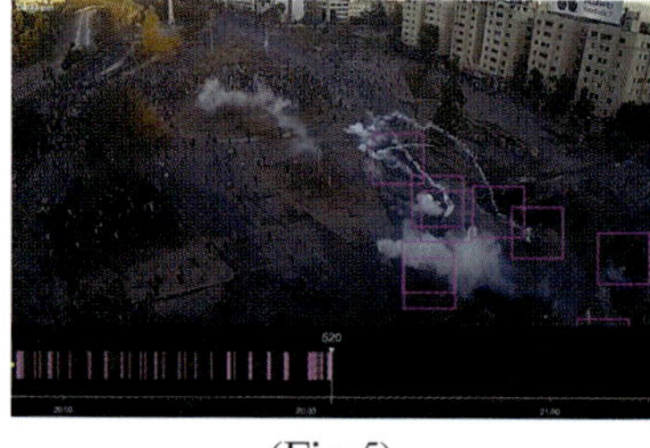

(Fig. 5)

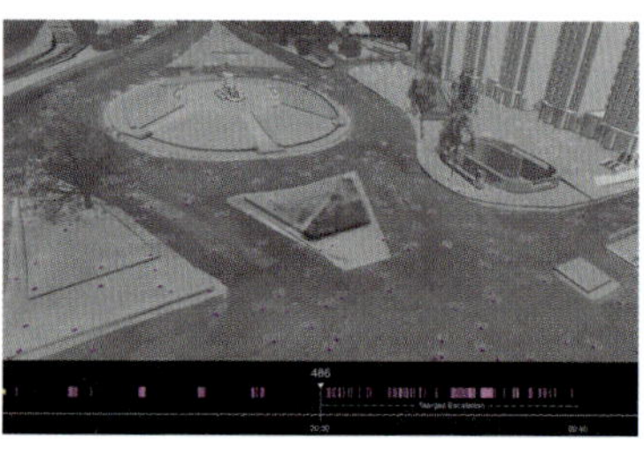

(Fig. 6)

Fig. 4. Analysis of footage by Marucela Ramirez (AFI Woman): Removing the barricades on 20 Dec 2019. Still from *Teargas in Plaza de la Dignidad.* Courtesy of Forensic Architecture.

Fig. 5. The automated system helps identify the exact time and location of visible CS clouds. Still from *Teargas in Plaza de la Dignidad.* Courtesy of Forensic Architecture.

Fig. 6. Teargas clouds mapped in 3D model of Plaza de la Dignidad. Still from *Teargas in Plaza de la Dignidad.* Courtesy of Forensic Architecture.

of its source, the canister. We located a total of 596 tear-gas clouds in our 3D model.

For the past three years, we have been working with the Imperial College London to develop a method for mapping the shape and concentrations of toxic clouds using open source data. Our method involves mathematical simulations of the fluid dynamics of toxic clouds in digital laboratory conditions, taking into account meteorological data such as temperature and wind. With the locations of tear gas canisters accurately mapped within our 3D model of Plaza de la Dignidad, we are able to map the architecture of tear-gas clouds. The wind carried the CS particles from southwest to northeast across the roundabout, ultimately depositing them on the ground and onto the Mapocho river. The surrounding buildings generated irregular turbulences that carried airborne toxins into the surrounding neighbourhoods. We showed that the contours of the clouds that accumulated in the air and were deposited on the ground extended well beyond the perimeter of the roundabout.

Our simulation also allowed us to measure saturation of toxicity at any point in the space of our 3D model. Chilean Police's Manual for Crowd Control states that exposure to tear gas should be limited to 0.4 milligrams per cubic meter, and concentrations above the 2-milligram threshold constitute a serious danger. Our model showed that this threshold was surpassed at a sample point for a total duration of one hundred and eighty-five seconds, between 8:30 and 8:40pm. In other words, the concentration of tear gas in Plaza de la Dignidad had reached toxicity levels 40 times the allowed limit, risking the lives of not only the protesters, but also residents of the surrounding neighbourhoods.

Breathing, Achille Mbembe foregrounded, is beyond a purely biological act. It is that which we hold in common; that which is 'unquantifiable' and 'cannot be appropriated'.*6 If the turn of the twentieth century was characterised by environmental wars where the target was the air of the inhaler, the turn of the twenty-first century might be an opening for the breathless, to claim what Mbembe articulated as the 'universal right to breathe'. Today, we hear residents of Santiago are opening a case against the Carabinero for the destruction of the flora and fauna in their neighbourhoods caused by tear-gas use.*7 This is a beginning. The ban on the use of tear gas is a universal right, and our benchmark investigative method on the architecture of the cloud offers reliable evidence in its support.

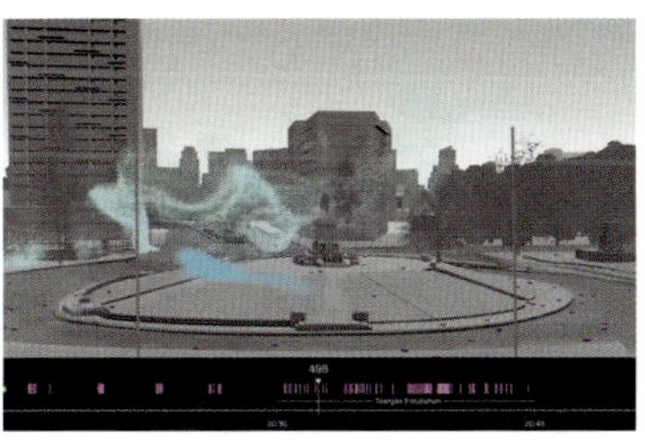

(Fig. 7)

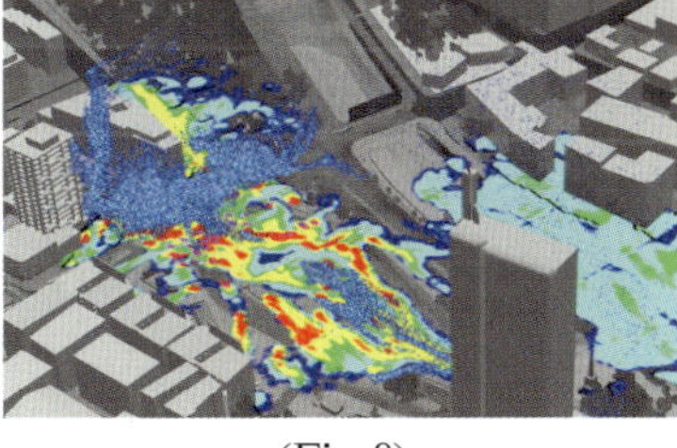

(Fig. 8)

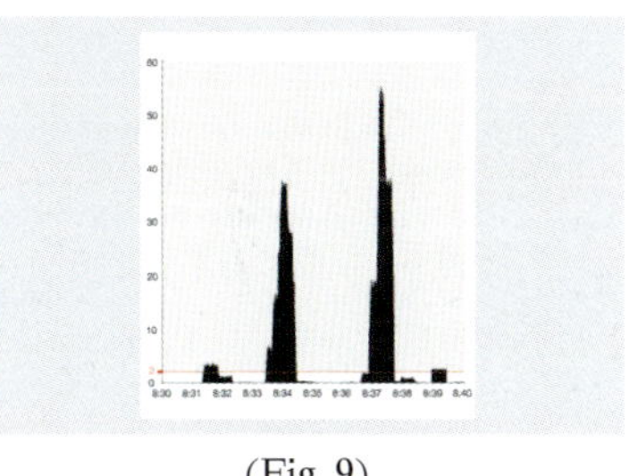

(Fig. 9)

Note: An earlier edit of this article was published in 2021. Moafi, Samaneh, 'The Cloud and the Roundabout,' ARQ 107 (2021): 22-29.

Fig. 7. Mathematical fluid dynamic simulation of teargas in air. Still from *Teargas in Plaza de la Dignidad.* Courtesy of Forensic Architecture.

Fig. 8. Toxic CS particles are carried with the wind and eventually deposed on the ground. Still from *Teargas in Plaza de la Dignidad.* Courtesy of Forensic Architecture.

Fig. 9. Concentration of CS per cubic meter at a sample point in Plaza de la Dignidad between 8:30 and 8:40pm. Courtesy of Forensic Architecture.

*1 “Toxic air Pollutants: Teargas,” American Lung Association, last modified June 6, 2020, https://www.lung.org/clean-air/outdoors/what-makes-air-unhealthy/toxic-air-pollutants/tear-gas.

*2 Peter Sloterdijk, *Terror from Air* (Los Angeles: Semiotext(e), 2009), 14.

*3 Peter Sloterdijk, *Terror from Air* (Los Angeles: Semiotext(e), 2009), 22.

*4 My team in Forensic Architecture included Martyna Marciniak, Robert Trafford, Mark Nieto and Tamara Z. Jamil, and greatly benefited from supervision of Eyal Weizman.

*5 Eyal Wiezman, *The Roundabout Revolutions* (Berlin: Sternberg Press, 2015).

*6 Achille Mbembe, “The Universal Right to Breath,” *Critical Inquiry* 47, no. S2 (Winter 2021). The article is re-published in this publication.

*7 Ortiz, J. Riffo, F. Velásquez, “Vecinos de Plaza Dignidad Acusan Desprotección de Tribunales por Uso Indiscriminado de Lacrimógenas,” *Interferencia*, January 10, 2021, https://interferencia.cl/articulos/vecinos-de-plaza-dignidad-acusan-desproteccion-de-tribunales-por-uso-indiscriminado-de.

Sumayya Vally
Folded skies

When it is clear, the Joburg sky moves gracefully and soundlessly through shades of all the colours you have never known, as the sun drops behind the horizon line at the end of a day. It looks idyllic. You want to touch it, hold it, never let it go, breathe in all of the magnificence.

The amount of pollution, dust and chemical particles in Joburg's air, produced by its legacy of mining, creates a colour scape of refracted light and inorganic pigments that can be considered visually beautiful.

– Sumayya Vally, *Counterspace*

24/07, 17:50, -26.2233 / 27.9975

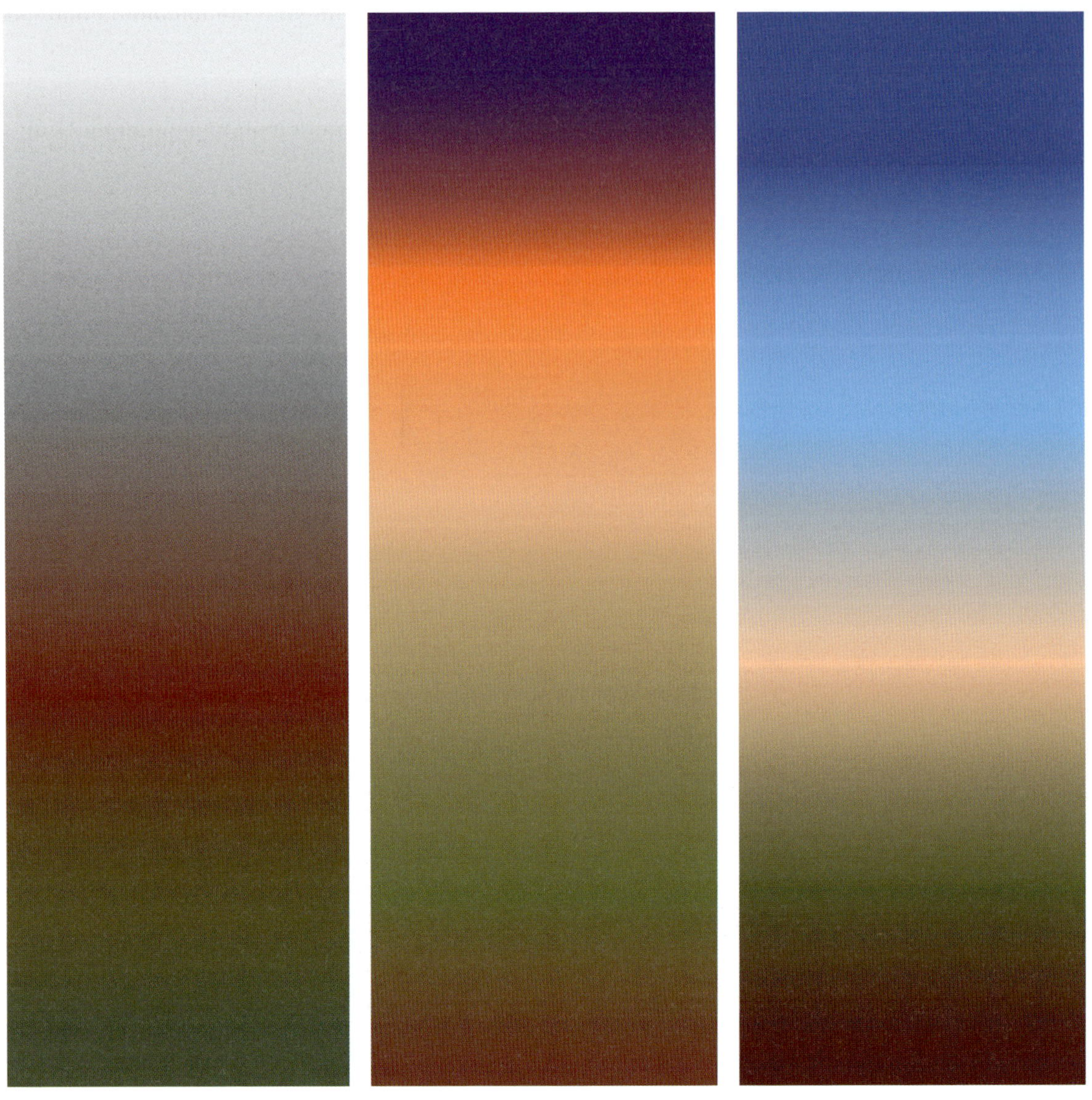

07/07, 12:30, -26.1919 / 27.9469   24/07, 17:30, -26.1919 / 27.9469   07/12, 16:30, -26.1919 / 27.9469

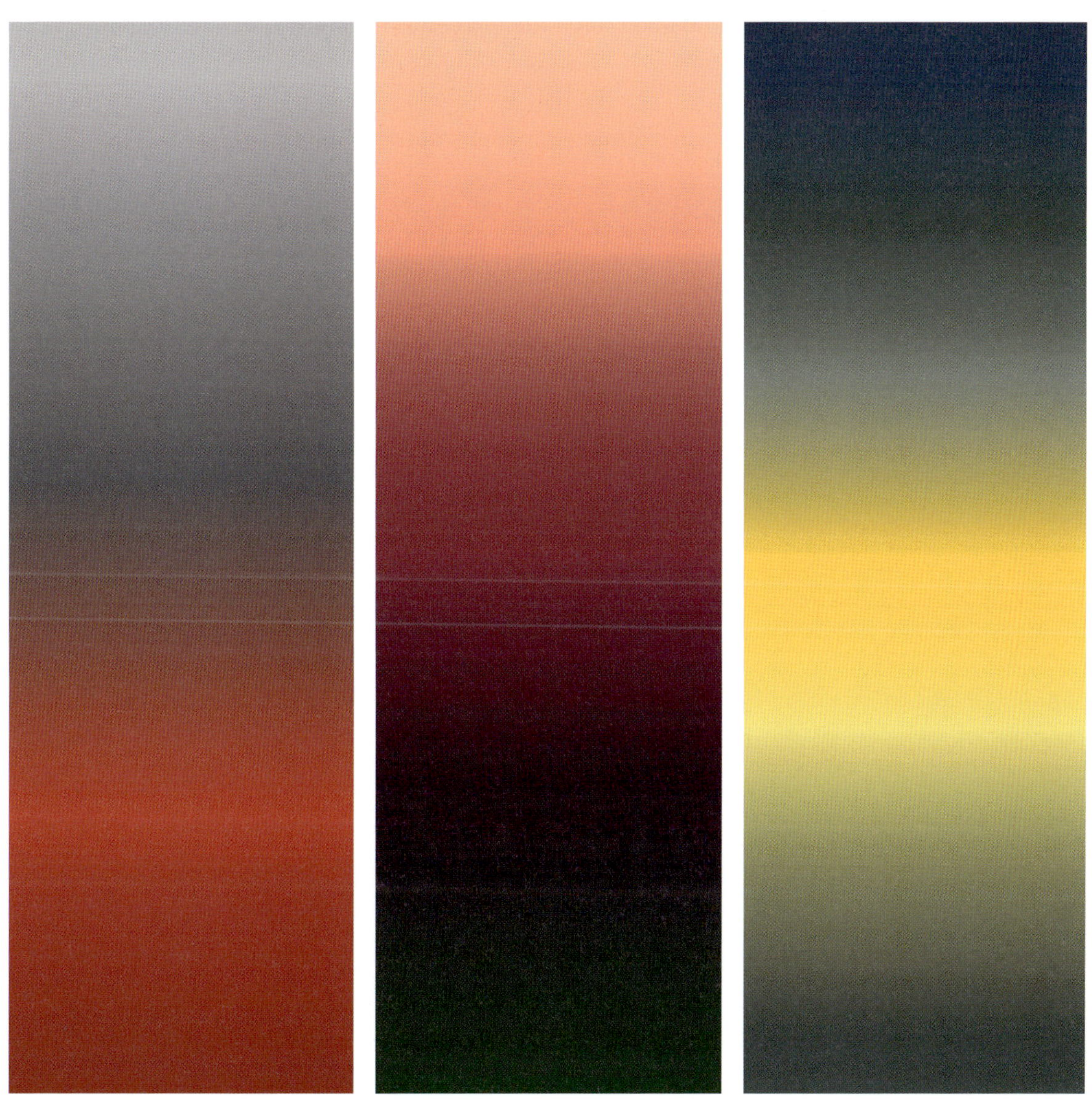

27/03, 13:30, -26.2218 / 28.0569   04/10, 17:00, -26.3464 / 28.3164   04/06, 6:00, -26.1939 / 28.1898

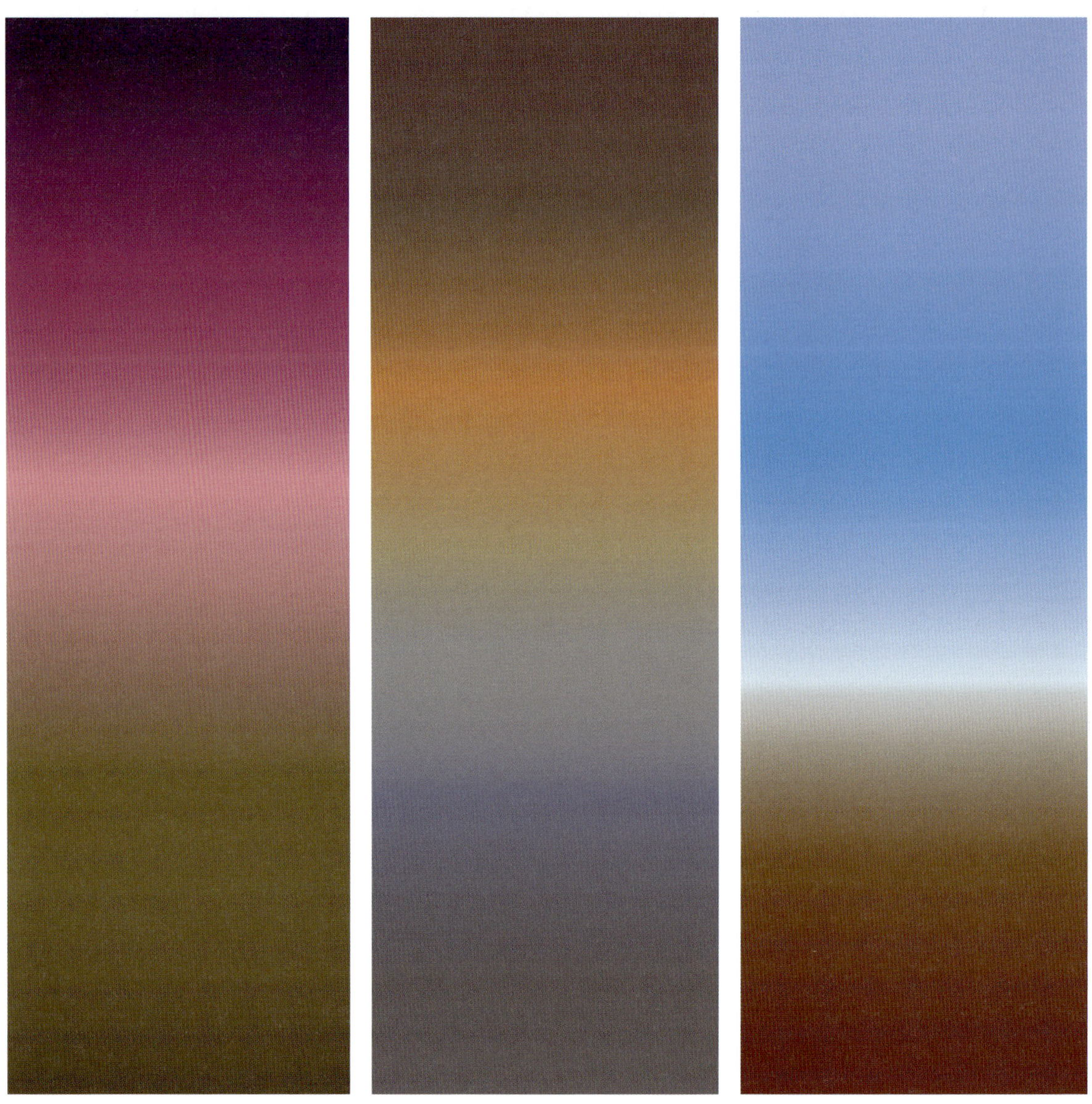

25/10, 15:45, -26.2225 / 27.9593 28/12, 17:00, -26.2218 / 28.0569 20/12, 14:00, -26.2236 / 27.9795

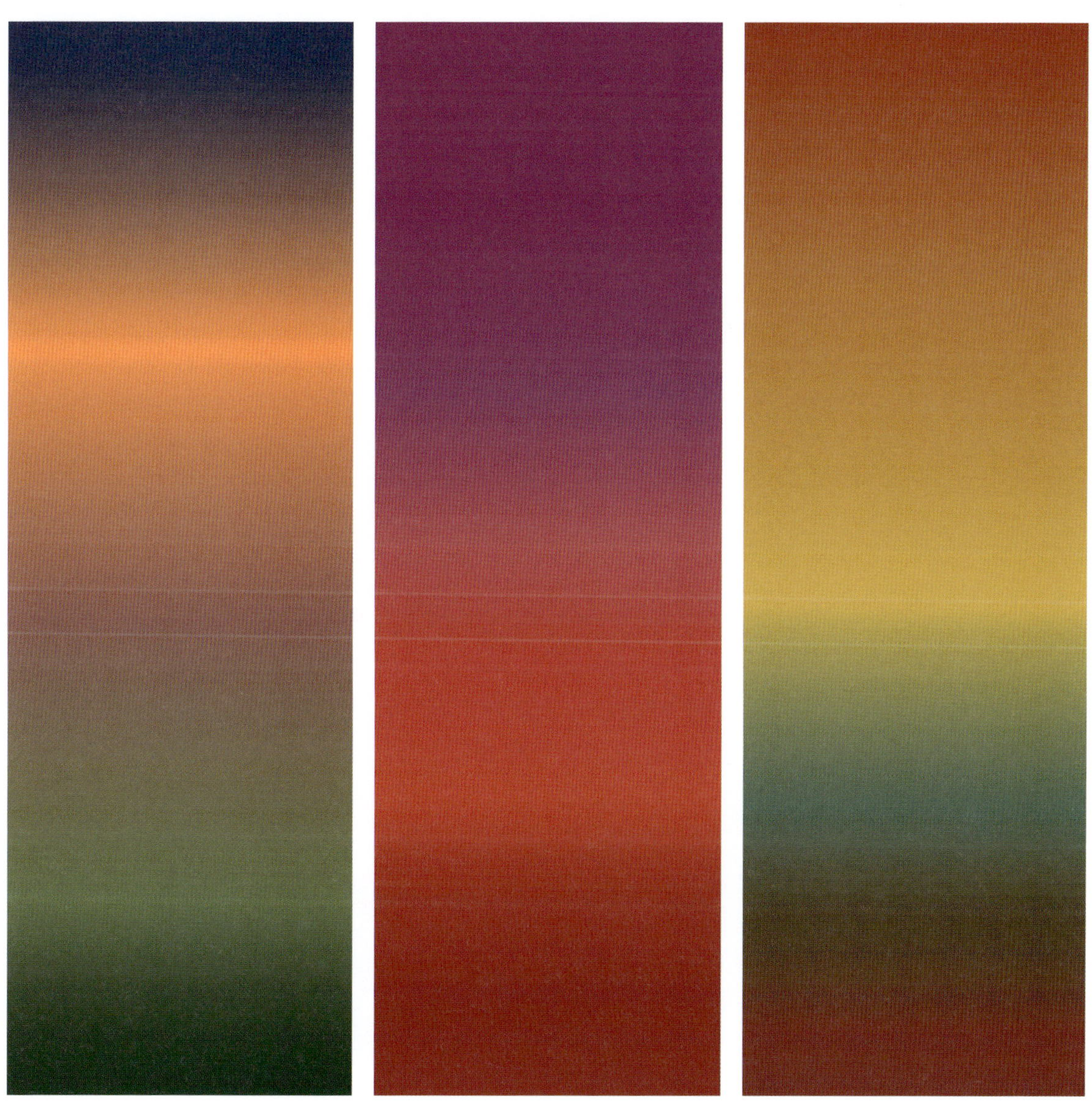

01/01, 19:00, -26.3464 / 28.3164   28/12, 17:00, -26.2218 / 28.0569   11/11, 19:00, -26.2278 / 28.0129

18/07, 12:30, -26.2202 / 27.9578

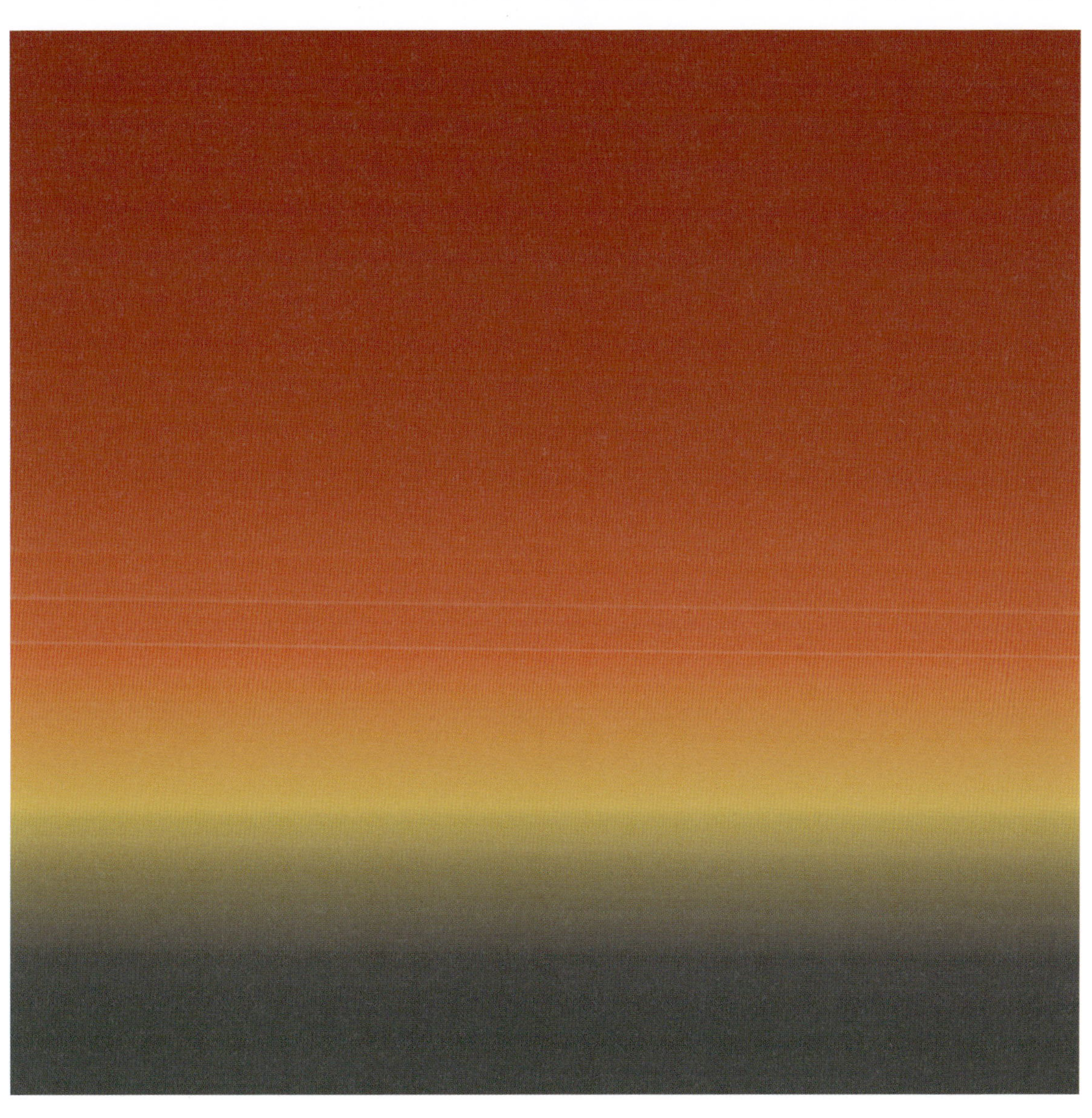

16/04, 17:30, -26.1939 / 28.1897

08/11, 15:30, -26.3464 / 28.3164

06/12, 19:00, -26.2229 / 28.0613

29/10, 16:30, -26.2254 / 28.0023

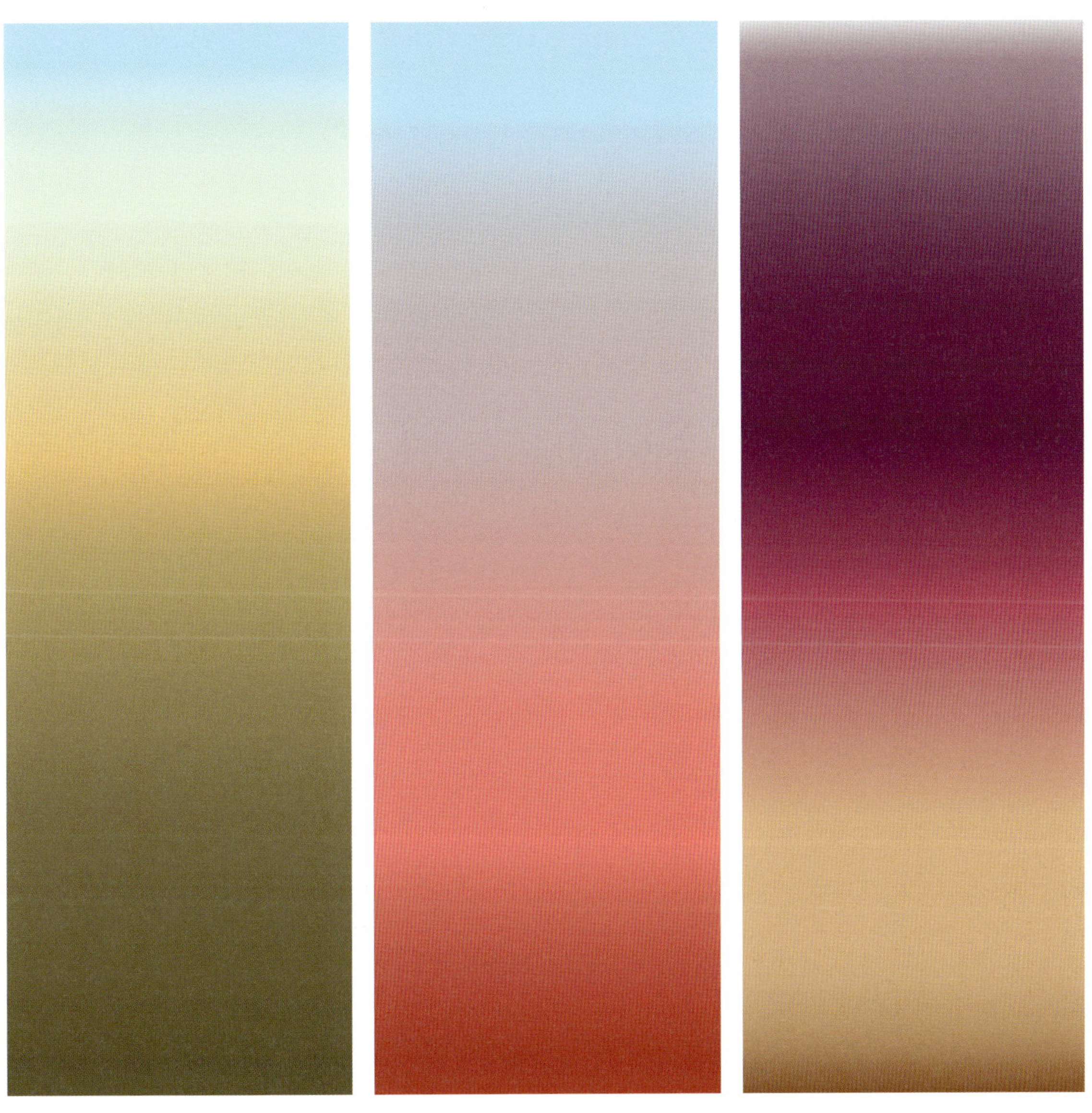

06/03, 09:00, -26.2127 / 27.9323 06/12, 07:00, -26.2218 / 28.0569 22/12, 18:45, -26.2272 / 27.9961

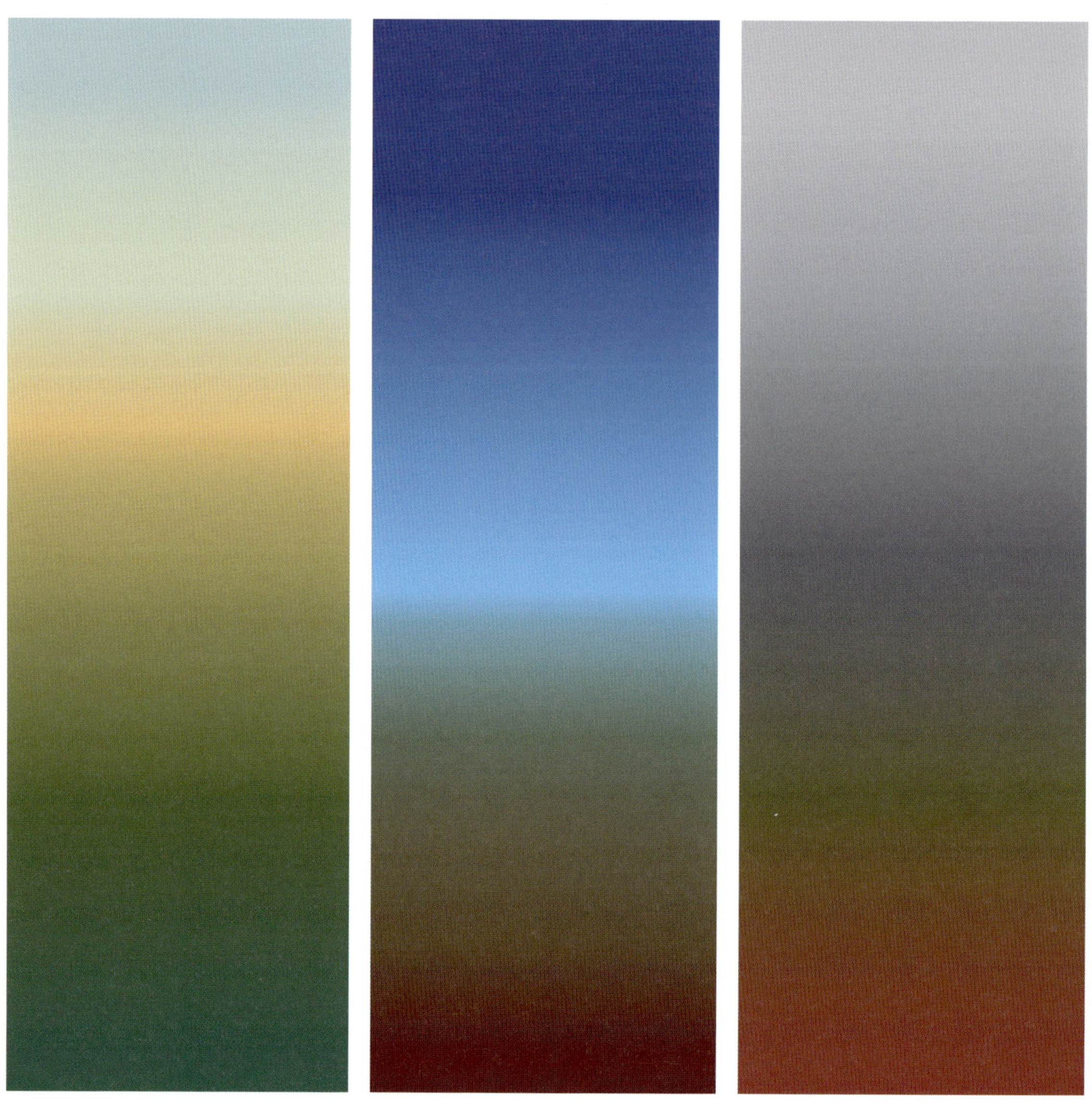

12/04, 6:30, -26.3464 / 28.3164 10/03, 14:30, -26.2278 / 28.0129 31/10, 14:00, -26.2263 / 28.0339

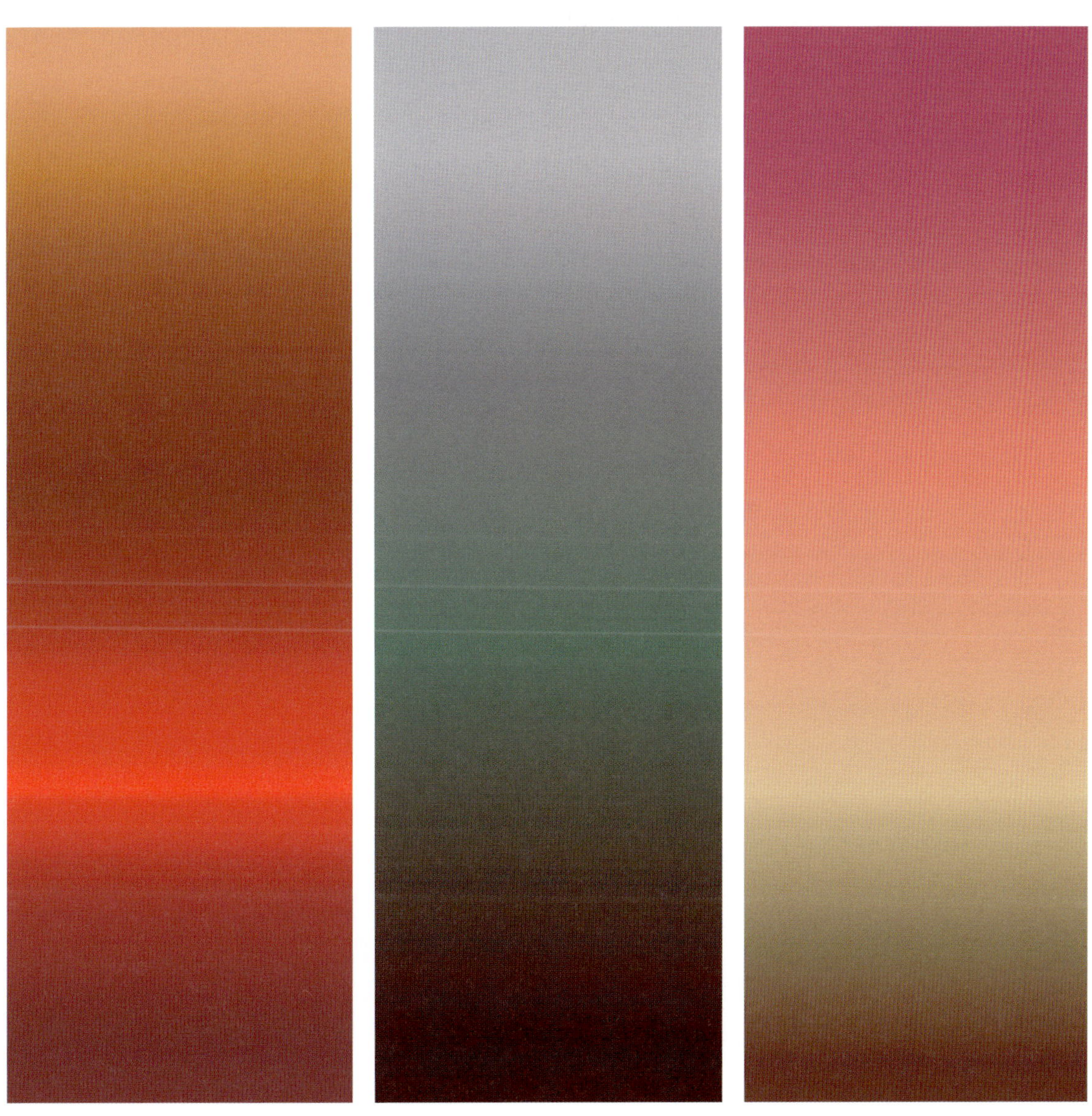

04/04, 16:00, -26.2218 / 28.0569   25/05, 14:30, -26.2278 / 28.0129   06/03, 19:20, -26.2229 / 28.0613

22/12, 6:00, -26.2282 / 28.0130

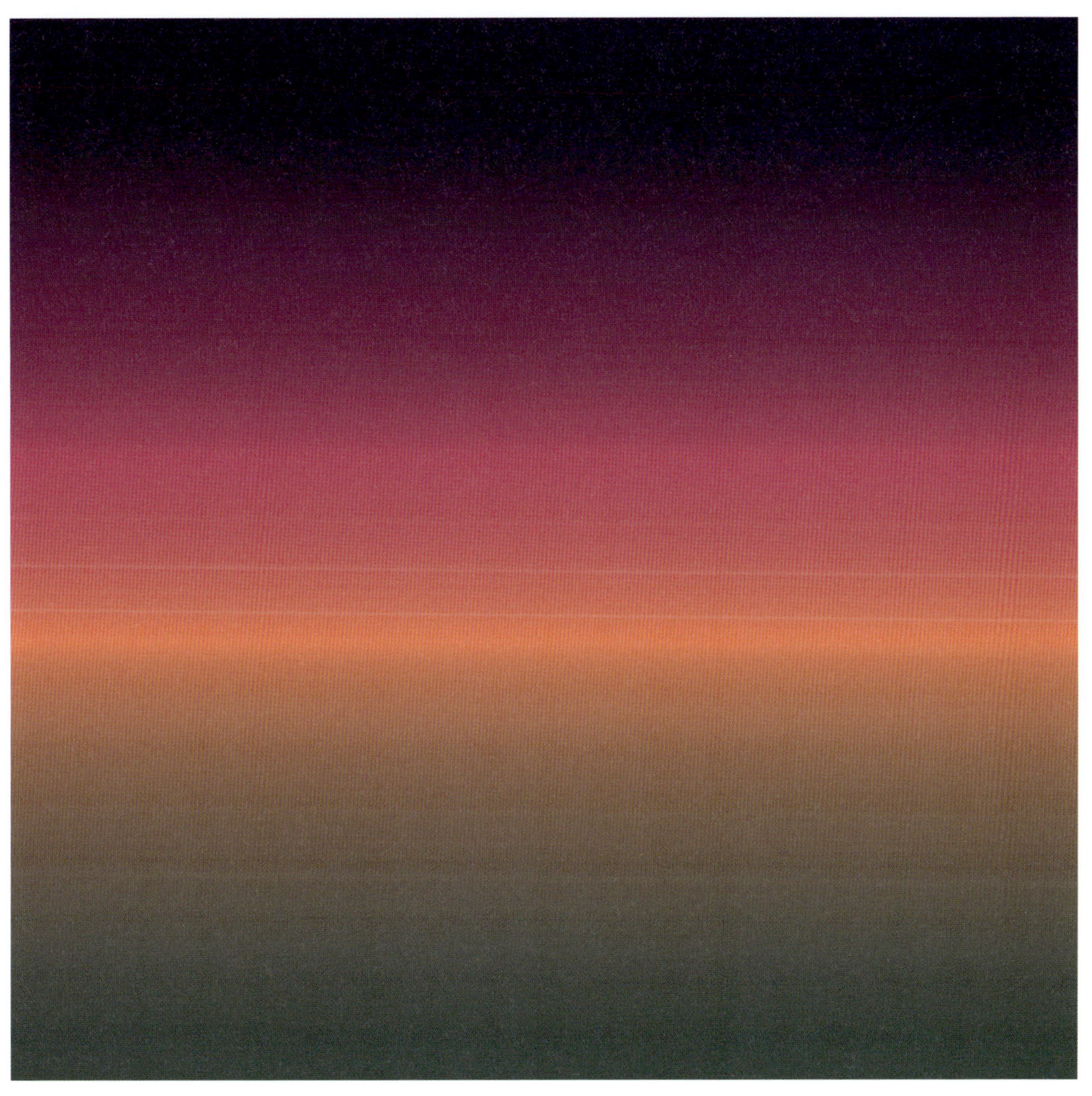

09/12, 19:00, -26.1939 / 28.1897

192

Matteo Dal Vera

Hybrid Aerial Creatures (Documented)

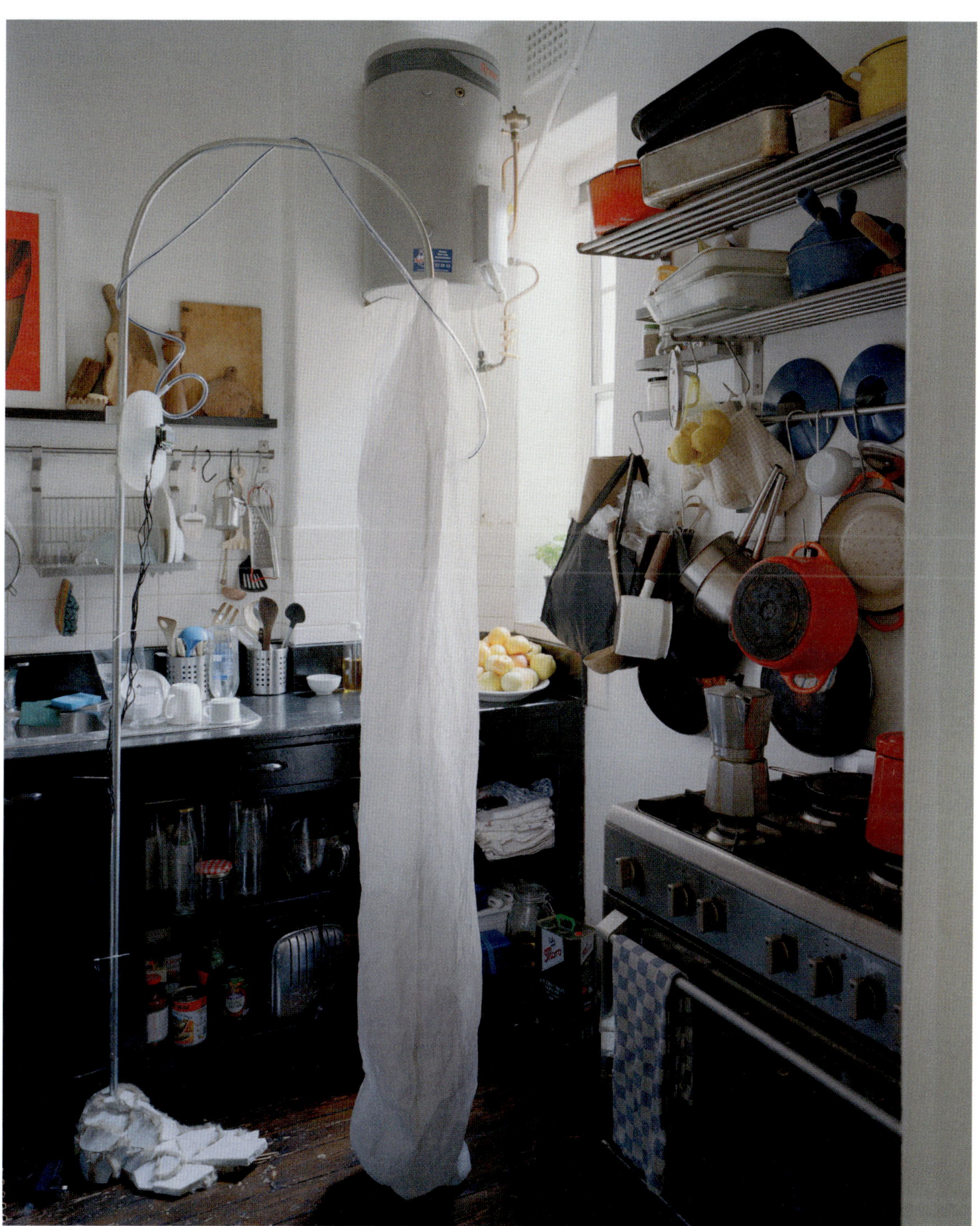

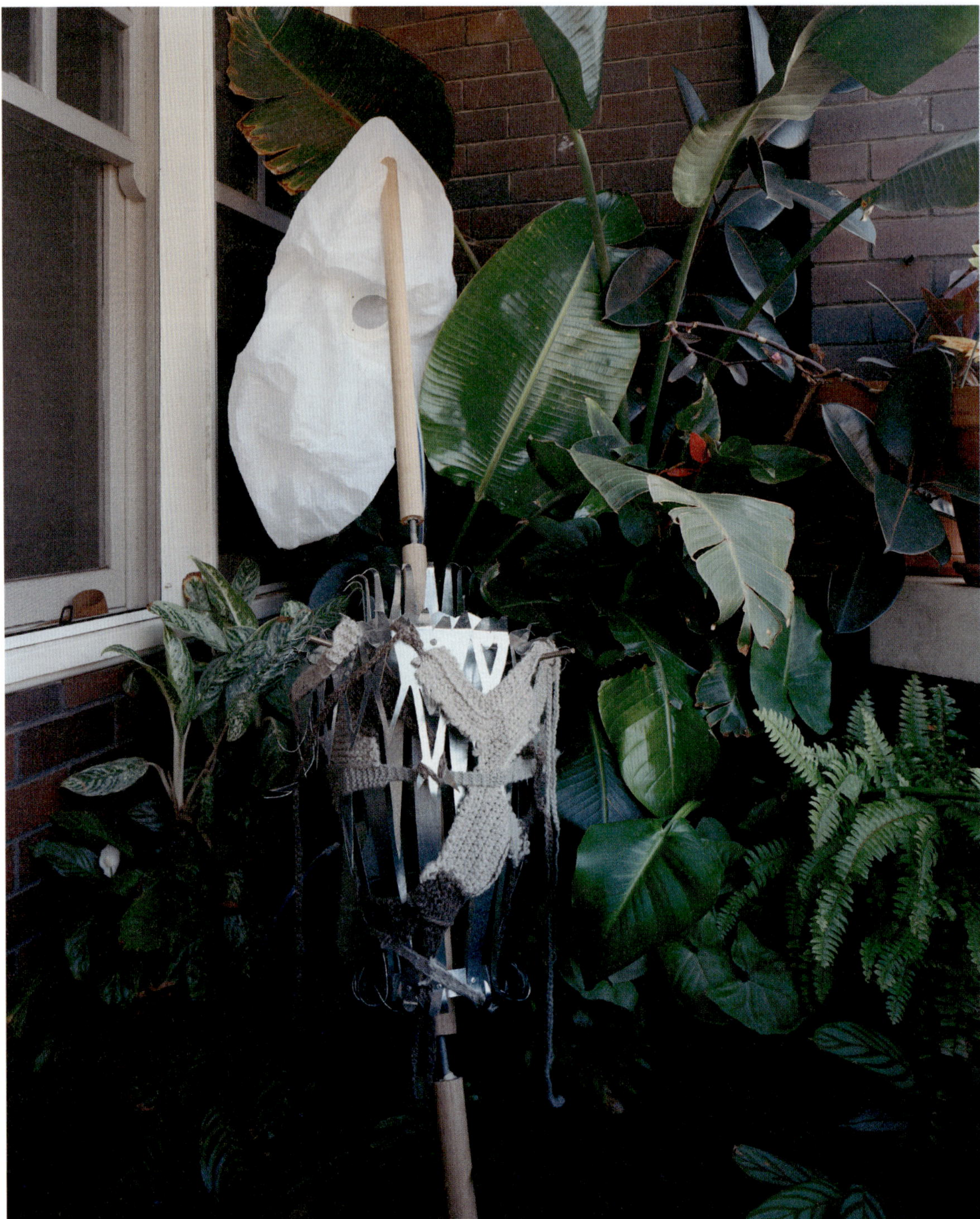

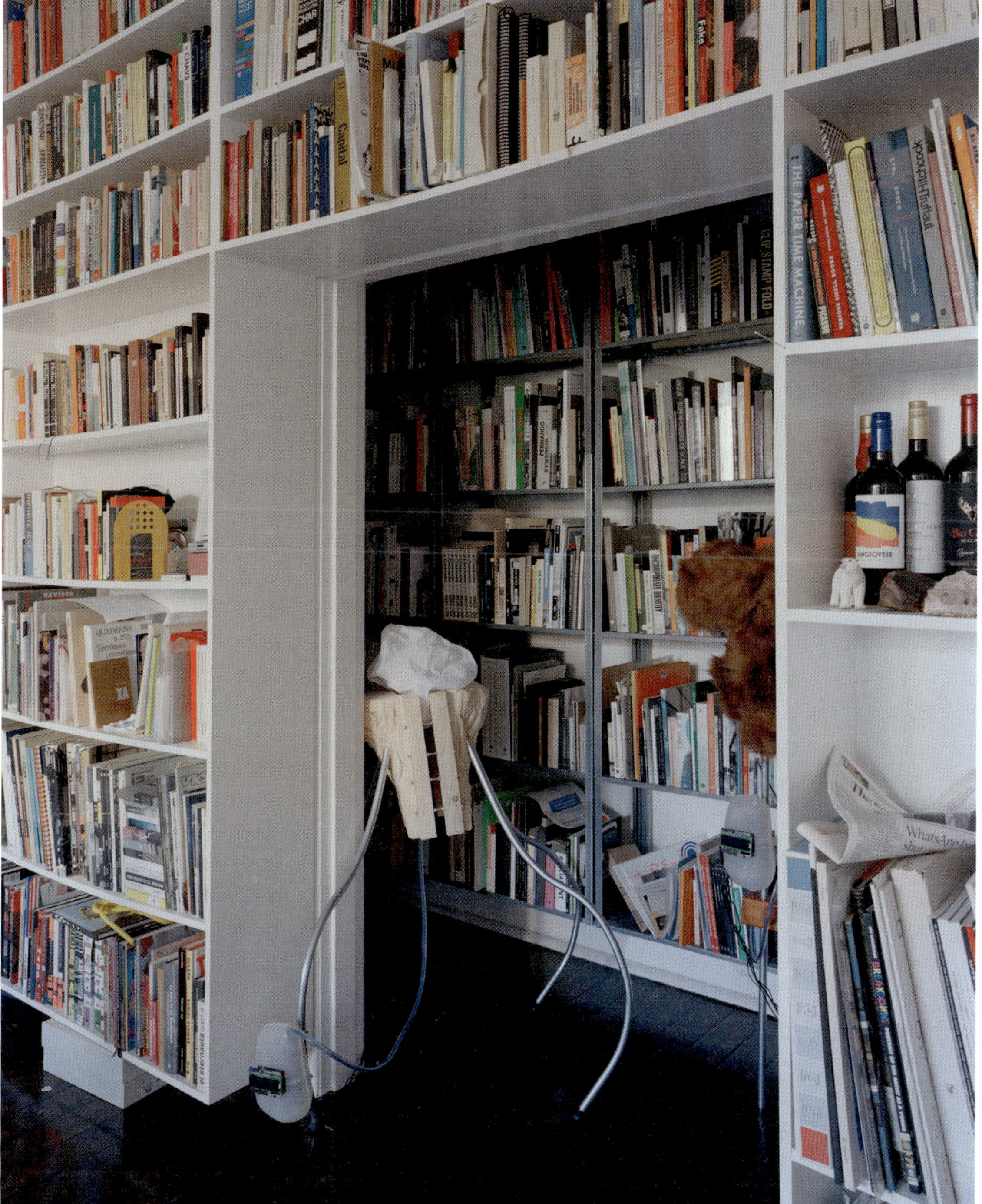
THE PAPER TIME MACHINE
CLIP STAMP FOLD
Hitchcock Truffaut
Capital
QUADERNS
n. 272
SANGIOVESE
WhatsApp

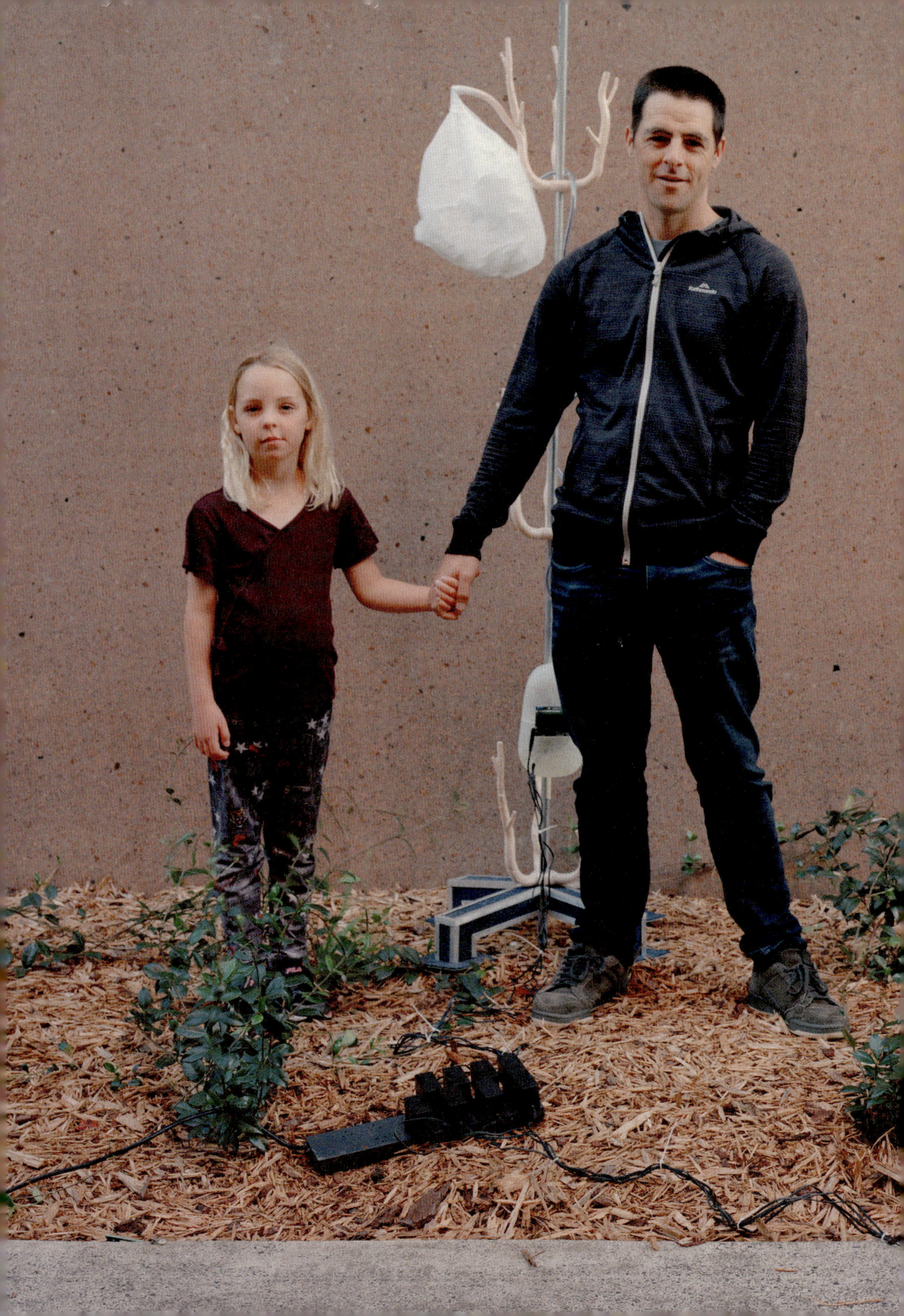

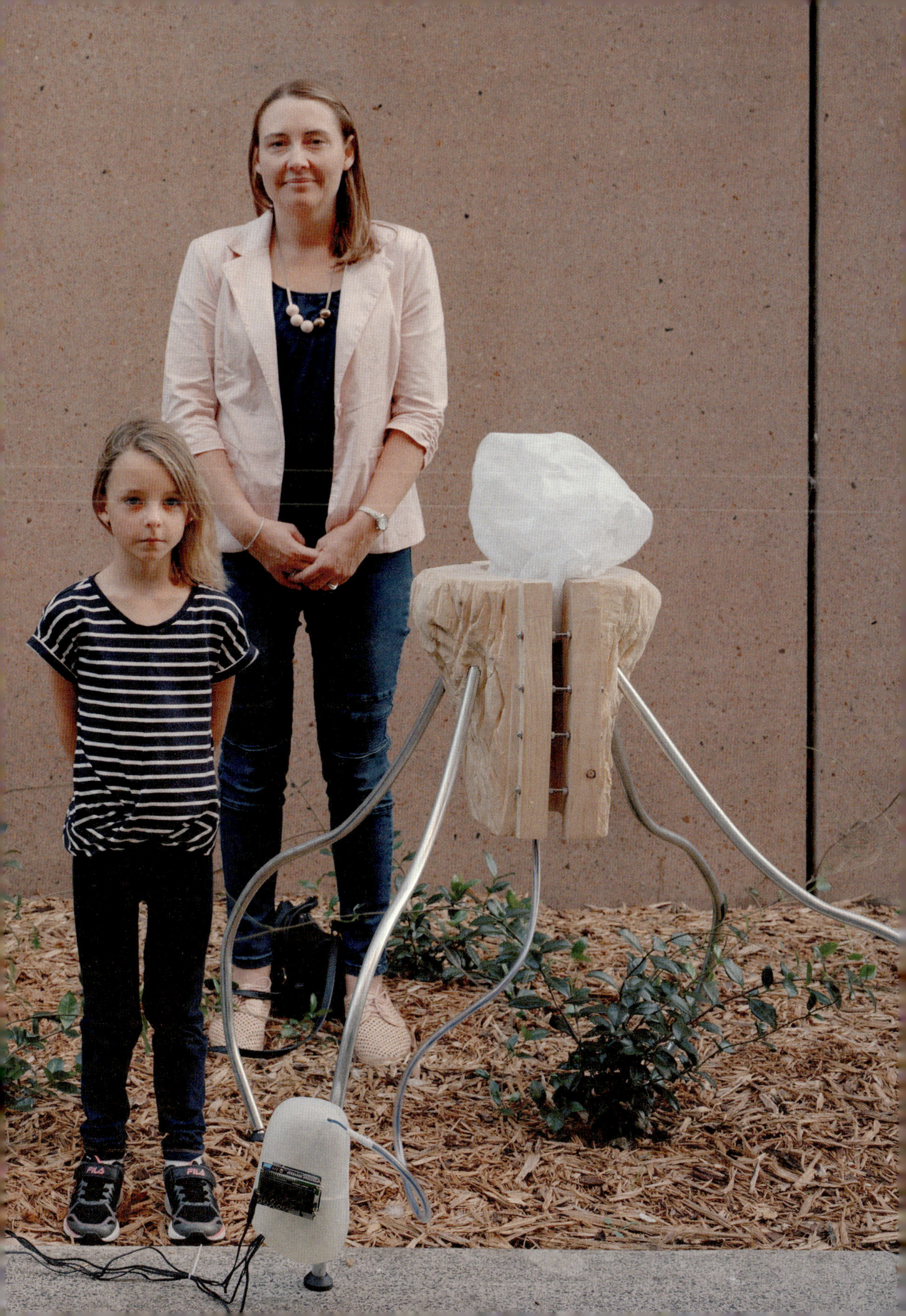
FILA
FILA

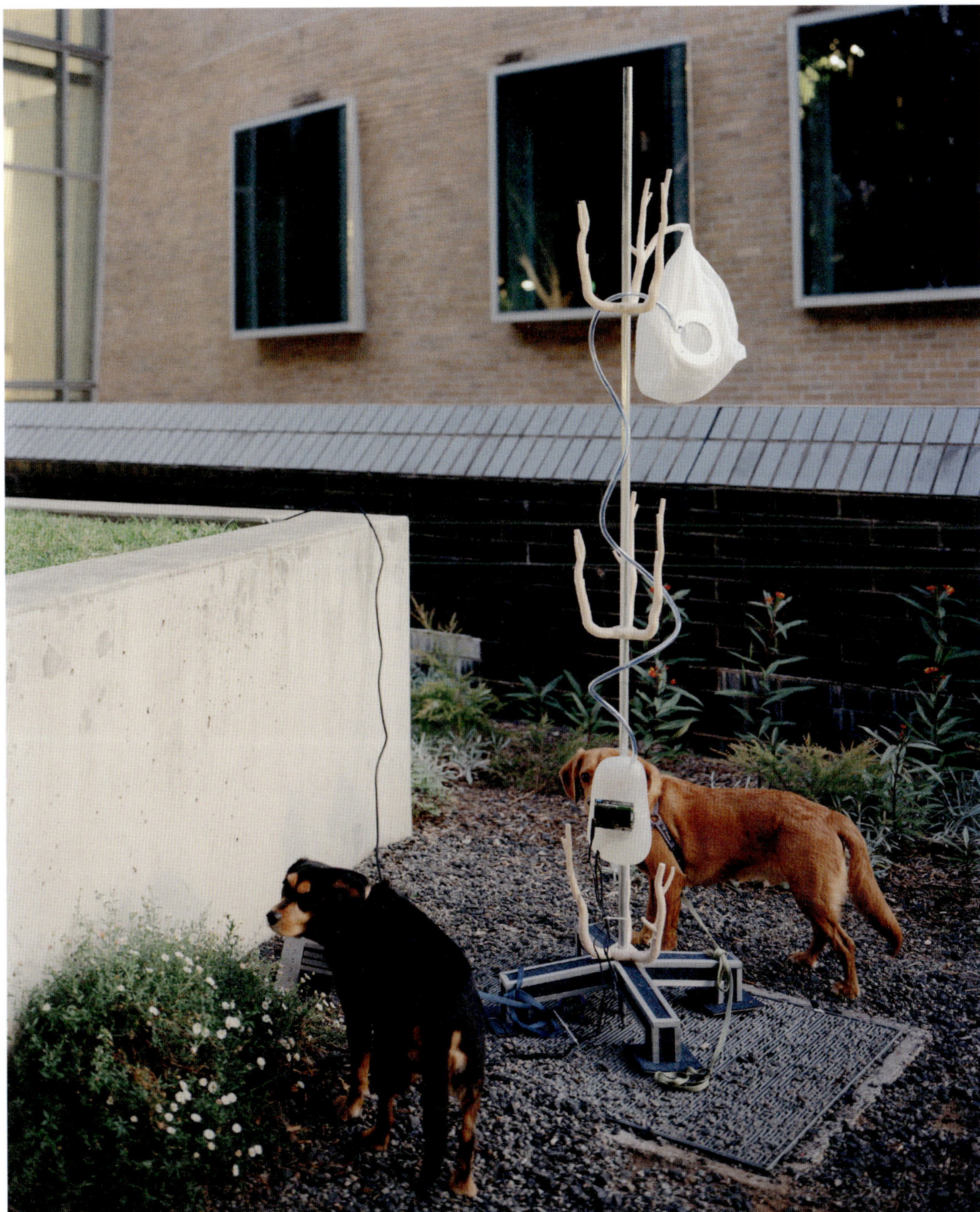

200

Achille Mbembe
The Universal Right to Breathe[*]

[*] translated by Carolyn Shread

13 April 2020

Already some people are talking about post-COVID-19.*[1] And why should they not? Even if, for most of us, especially those in parts of the world where health care systems have been devastated by years of organized neglect, the worst is yet to come. With no hospital beds, no respirators, no mass testing, no masks nor disinfectants nor arrangements for placing those who are infected in quarantine, unfortunately, many will not pass through the eye of the needle.

1.

It is one thing to worry about the death of others in a distant land and quite another to suddenly become aware of one's own putrescence, to be forced to live intimately with one's own death, contemplating it as a real possibility. Such is, for many, the terror triggered by confinement: having to finally answer for one's own life, to one's own name. We must answer here and now for our life on Earth *with others* (including viruses) and our shared fate. Such is the injunction this pathogenic period addresses to humankind. It is pathogenic but also the catabolic period *par excellence,* with the decomposition of bodies, the sorting and expulsion of all sorts of human waste—the "great separation" and great confinement caused by the stunning spread of the virus—and along with it, the widespread digitisation of the world.

Try as we might to rid ourselves of it, in the end everything brings us back to the body. We tried to graft it onto other media, to turn it into an object body, a machine body, a digital body, an ontophanic body. It returns to us now as a horrifying, giant mandible, a vehicle for contamination, a vector for pollen, spores, and mould. Knowing that we do not face this ordeal alone, that many will not escape it, is vain comfort. For we have never learned to live with all living species, have never really worried about the damage we as humans wreak on the lungs of the Earth and on its body. Thus, we have never learned how to die. With the advent of the New World and, several centuries later, the appearance of the 'industrialized races,' we essentially chose to delegate our death to others, to make a great sacrificial repast of existence itself via a kind of ontological vicariate.

Soon, it will no longer be possible to delegate one's death to others. It will no longer be possible for that person to die in our place. Not only will we be condemned to assume our own demise, unmediated, but farewells will be few and far between. The hour of autophagy is upon us and, with it, the death of community, as there is no community worthy of its name in which saying one's last farewell, that is, remembering the living at the moment of death, becomes impossible. Community—or rather the in—common—is not based solely on the possibility of saying goodbye, that is, of having a unique encounter with others and honouring this meeting time and again. The in-common is based also on the possibility of sharing unconditionally, each time drawing from it something absolutely intrinsic, a thing uncountable, incalculable, priceless.

2.

There is no doubt that the skies are closing in. Caught in the strangle hold of injustice and inequality, much of humanity is threatened by a great chokehold as the sense that our world is in a state of reprieve spreads far and wide. If, in these circumstances, a day after comes, it cannot come at the expense of some, always the same ones, as in the Ancienne Économie—the economy that preceded this revolution. It must necessarily be a day for all the inhabitants of Earth, without distinction as to species, race, sex, citizenship, religion, or other differentiating markers. In other words, a day after will come but only with a giant rupture, the result of radical imagination.

Papering over the cracks simply won't do. Deep in the heart of this crater, literally everything must be reinvented, starting with the social. Once working, shopping, keeping up with the news and keeping in touch, nurturing and preserving connections, talking to one another and sharing, drinking together, worshipping and organizing funerals begin to take place solely across the interface of screens, it is time to acknowledge that on all sides we are surrounded by rings of fire. To a great extent, the digital is the new gaping hole exploding Earth. Simultaneously a trench, a tunnel, a moonscape, it is the bunker where men and women are all invited to hide away, in isolation.

They say that through the digital, the body of flesh and bones, the physical and mortal body, will be freed of its weight and inertia. At the end of this transfiguration, it will eventually be able to move through the looking glass, cut away from biological corruption and restituted to a synthetic universe of flux. But this is an illusion, for just as there is no humanity without bodies, likewise, humanity will never know freedom alone, outside of society and community, and never can freedom come at the expense of the biosphere.

3.

We must start afresh. To survive, we must return to all living things—including the biosphere—the space and energy they need. In its dank underbelly, modernity has been an interminable war on life. And it is far from over. One of the primary modes of this war, leading straight to the impoverishment of the world and to the desiccation of entire swathes of the planet, is the subjection to the digital.

In the aftermath of this calamity there is a danger that rather than offering sanctuary to all living species, sadly the world will enter a new period of tension and brutality.[*2] In terms of geopolitics, the logic of power and might will continue to dominate. For lack of a common infrastructure, a vicious partitioning of the globe will intensify, and the dividing lines will become even more entrenched. Many states will seek to fortify their borders in the hope of protecting themselves from the outside. They will also seek to conceal the constitutive violence that they continue to habitually direct at the most vulnerable. Life behind screens and in gated communities will become the norm.

In Africa especially, but in many places in the Global South, energy-intensive extraction, agricultural expansion, predatory sales of land, and destruction of forests will continue unabated. The powering and cooling of computer chips and supercomputers depends on it. The purveying and supplying of the resources and energy necessary for the global computing infrastructure will require further restrictions on human mobility. Keeping the world at a distance will become the norm so as to keep risks of all kinds on the outside. But because it does not address our ecological precariousness, this catabolic vision of the world, inspired by theories of immunisation and contagion, does little to break out of the planetary impasse in which we find ourselves.

4.

All these wars on life begin by taking away breath. Likewise, as it impedes breathing and blocks the resuscitation of human bodies and tissues, COVID-19 shares this same tendency. After all, what is the purpose of breathing if not the absorption of oxygen and release of carbon dioxide in a dynamic exchange between blood and tissues? But at the rate that life on Earth is going, and given what remains of the wealth of the planet, how far away are we really from the time when there will be more carbon dioxide than oxygen to breathe?

Before this virus, humanity was already threatened with suffocation. If war there must be, it cannot so much be against a specific virus as against everything that condemns the majority of humankind to a premature cessation of breathing, everything that fundamentally attacks the respiratory tract, everything that, in the long reign of capitalism, has constrained entire segments of the world population, entire races, to a difficult, panting breath and life of oppression. To come through this constriction would mean that we conceive of breathing beyond its purely biological aspect, and instead as that which we hold in common, that which, by definition, eludes all calculation. By which I mean the universal right to breathe.

As that which is both ungrounded and our common ground, the universal right to breath is unquantifiable and cannot be appropriated. From a universal perspective, not only is it the right of every member of humankind, but of all life. It must therefore be understood as a fundamental right to existence. Consequently, it cannot be confiscated and thereby eludes all sovereignty, symbolizing the sovereign principle par excellence. Moreover, it is an originary right to living on Earth, a right that belongs to the universal community of earthly inhabitants, human and other.[*3]

Coda

The case has been pressed already a thousand times. We recite the charges eyes shut. Whether it is the destruction of the biosphere, the takeover of minds by technoscience, the criminalizing of resistance, repeated attacks on reason, generalized cretinisation, or the rise of determinisms (genetic, neuronal, biological, environmental), the dangers faced by humanity are increasingly existential.

Of all these dangers, the greatest is that all forms of life will be rendered impossible. Between those who dream of uploading our conscience to machines and those who are sure that the next mutation of our species lies in freeing ourselves from our biological husk, there's little difference. The eugenicist temptation has not dissipated. Far from it, in fact, since it is at the root of recent advances in science and technology.

At this juncture, this sudden arrest arrives, an interruption not of history but of something that still eludes our grasp.

Since it was imposed upon us, this cessation derives not from our will.

In many respects, it is simultaneously unforeseen and unpredictable. Yet what we need is a voluntary cessation, a conscious and fully consensual interruption. Without which there will be no tomorrow. Without which nothing will exist but an endless series of unforeseen events.

If, indeed, COVID-19 is the spectacular expression of the planetary impasse in which humanity finds itself today, then it is a matter of no less than reconstructing a habitable earth to give all of us the breath of life. We must reclaim the lungs of our world with a view to forging new ground. Humankind and biosphere are one. Alone, humanity has no future. Are we capable of rediscovering that each of us belongs to the same species, that we have an indivisible bond with all life? Perhaps that is the question—the very last— before we draw our last dying breath.

Notes

This text originally appeared in Achille Mbembe, "The Universal Right to Breathe," trans. Carolyn Shread, in "Posts from the Pandemic," ed. Hank Scotch, special issue, *Critical Inquiry* 47, S2 (Winter 2021): S58–S62, https://www.journals.uchicago.edu/toc/ci/2021/47/S2.

Translator Note

Is translation still permissible in COVID-19? We know that its reach is across borders, that it comingles in a way that is rapidly disappearing into a seemingly distant past, that it transfers and transforms. Now, under the regime of social distancing, where I show my care for you by stepping away, what is it to translate? For there's no reading more intimate than a translation—a bodily intimacy that adopts the rhythm of the lungs, the pulse of the heart, the coursing of the blood through the text to the point that we ask, whose breath is it anyway?

I know that this text kept me alive —merci, Achille Mbembe. That it came out of the blue, bringing a breath of fresh air—thank you, Hank Scotch. And that I'll pass it on to you, readers of Critical Inquiry and now of this book, hoping that it frees up the atmosphere. Because we need to breathe together. And there is no solitary breath.

Achille Mbembe
The Universal Right to Breathe
* **footnotes & references**

---

*1 A version of this post appears in French; see Achille Mbembe, "Le droit universel à la respiration," *AOC*, 4 June 2020, aoc.media/opinion/2020/04/05/le-droit-universel-a-la-respiration/.

*2 Building on the terms origins as a mid-twentieth century architectural movement, I have defined "brutalism" as a contemporary process whereby "power is henceforth constituted, expressed, reconfigured, acts and reproduces itself as a geomorphic force." How so? Through processes that include "fracturing and fissuring," "emptying vessels," "drilling," and "expelling organic matter," in a word, by what I term "depletion" (Mbembe, Achille. *Brutalisme* [Paris: La Découverte, 2020], pp. 9, 10, 11).

*3 See Sarah Vanuxem, *La propriété de la Terre* (Paris: Wildproject, 2018), and Marin Schaffner, *Un sol commun. Lutter, habiter, penser* (Paris: Wildproject, 2019).

Dr Ricarda Bigolin is a practice-based researcher, educator and designer, as well as an Associate Professor and the Associate Dean of Fashion and Textiles Design at RMIT University, Melbourne, Australia. Her research explores the social, cultural, ethical and political context of fashion production and consumption. She interrogates fashion languages across multiple mediums as a means of exploring the broader influence and everyday impact of fashion.

Enoch Cheng is an artist whose practice spans moving image, installation, curation, dance, events, theatre, writing, fashion, and performance. His works explore recurrent themes of place, travel, cross-cultural history, fiction, memory, time, migration and extinction. He was a recipient of the Asian Cultural Council Fellowship (2020); an artist-in-residence at the American Museum of Natural History, New York (2020); a Laureate, Institut Francais, Paris (2018); and artist-fellow at Akademie Schloss Solitude, Stuttgart (2017–2018).

Matthew Connors's photographs have been exhibited in museums and galleries worldwide. He has received an ICP Infinity Award, two MacDowell Colony Fellowships, a Headlands Center for the Arts Residency, and the Lightwork Artist-in-Residence Fellowship. He earned a BA in English Literature from the University of Chicago and an MFA in Photography from Yale University. He is a Professor at the Massachusetts College of Art & Design.

Dean Cross was born and raised on Ngunnawal/Ngambri Country and is a Worimi man through his paternal bloodline. He is a paratactical artist interested in collisions of materials, ideas and histories. He is motivated by the understanding that his practice sits within a continuum of the oldest living culture on Earth—and enacts First Nations sovereignty through expanded contemporary art methodologies. He hopes to traverse the poetic and the political in a nuanced choreography of form and ideas. Dean has exhibited widely across the Australian continent and beyond, and his work is held by major institutions including The Art Gallery of South Australia and the National Gallery of Victoria. Dean is represented by Yavuz Gallery Sydney & Singapore.

Matteo Dal Vera is a photographer based in Sydney, Australia. He received a BA for Design in Photography from UTS (University of Technology Sydney) in 2019 and recently completed honours research at UTS (2020). Dal Vera has previously been a William and Winifred Bowness Photography Prize finalist (MGA, 2020), and his collaborative project *The Bridge* (2018–2019) was awarded student photobook winner at the Australian & New Zealand Photobook Awards (2019).

Juan Elvira is a PhD architect, author, and professor at Escuela Técnica Superior de Arquitectura de Madrid, and invited lecturer at various international universities. He has recently published the book *Ghost Architecture*, a primer on spatial eroticism and architecture as a form of atmospheric enchantment. He is co-director of Murado & Elvira Arquitectura, a practice that has been nominated for the EU Mies Award and a Norwegian National Architecture Prize finalist, and has exhibited at the Biennale di Venezia.

Guillermo Fernández-Abascal is an architect, a Practice Fellow at the University of Sydney, and founding partner of the offices GFA and GFA2. Based in Sydney, Australia, and Santander, Spain, his recent work destabilises the dichotomy between research and buildings, and includes diagrams, stories, exhibitions, films, prototypes, housing, and public buildings across the globe. His recent projects include the books *Learning to Live Together: Cars, Humans, and Kerbs in Solidarity; Regional Bureaucracy; Better Together: 33 Documents of Contemporary Australian Architecture and Their Associated Short Stories*, and the Enaire Foundation building in Santander, the Murrin Bridge Preschool and Community Hub, and the masterplan for the Machine Khana in Kabul, Afghanistan.

Hélène Frichot is Professor of Architecture and Philosophy, and the Director of the Bachelor of Design, Faculty of Architecture, Building and Planning, University of Melbourne, Australia. Her recent publications include *Creative Ecologies: Theorizing the Practice of Architecture* (Bloomsbury 2018) and *Dirty Theory: Troubling Architecture (AADR 2019). She edited Writing Architectures: Ficto-Critical Approaches* (Bloomsbury 2020) with Naomi Stead, and *Architectural Affects After Deleuze and Guattari* (Routledge 2021) with Marco Jobst.

Umi Graham is a Japanese-Australian graduate architect and co-founder of Mori—an independent space for architecture in Sydney. She is interested in cultural spaces as ephemeral choreographies of objects and people. Her research concerns the value of these indeterminate, open and intangible spaces to the discipline of architecture. She is constantly searching for other ways of practising architecture and has found herself in publication, fashion and art worlds.

Urtzi Grau is an architect, academic, Senior Lecturer in the School of Architecture at UTS and founding partner of the offices GFA and Fake Industries. His research explores the role of architecture in responding to critical challenges impacting the Indo-Pacific region, including climate justice, immigration, land rights and extractive economics. His recent projects include the library of Lorenteggio in Milan, the Murrin Bridge Preschool and Community Hub and the masterplan for Machine Khana in Kabul.

Achille Mbembe is Research Professor in History and Politics at the Wits Institute for Social and Economy Research, University of the Witwatersrand, Johannesburg. He is author of *Brutalisme*, *Critique of Black Reason* and co-editor of *Johannesburg: The Elusive*

Metropolis among other books. Along with Felwine Starr, he is the co-founder of *Ateliers de la pensée* in Dakar.

Hamish McIntosh is a photographer based in Sydney, Australia. His interest in urbanism and the built environment has led to collaborations with architects and designers, along with contributions to publications both local and international. He is a co-author of *Regional Bureaucracy* (Perimeter Books, 2022). Hamish received his Bachelor of Design in Photography (Hons) from the University of Technology Sydney in 2020.

Dr Peter McNeil is the Distinguished Professor of Design History at the University of Technology Sydney and was awarded a distinguished professorship at Aalto University Helsinki, Finland. An award-winning author, he is a Fellow of the Australian Academy of the Humanities. He writes and lectures internationally in areas of art and design, including fashion, textiles, interiors and queer studies, and has published monographs including *Luxury: A Rich History;* and *Pretty Gentlemen.*

Dr Samaneh Moafi is Forensic Architecture (FA)'s Senior Researcher. She is based at Goldsmiths University of London where she provides conceptual oversight across FA projects and oversees the Centre for Contemporary Nature (CCN) in particular, where new investigative techniques are developed for environmental violence. She earned her PhD from the Architectural Association (AA) School of Architecture with a dissertation on the contemporary history of state-initiated mass housing in Iran and the class identities and gender roles it informed.

Lidia Morawska is a physicist, Distinguished Professor at the Queensland University of Technology in Brisbane, Australia, and a Vice-Chancellor Fellow, Global Centre for Clean Air Research, University of Surrey, UK. She conducts research on air quality and its impact on human health and the environment. An author of over nine hundred publications, Lidia is a member of the Australian Academy of Science and a recipient of numerous scientific awards.

Ellie Skinner is a co-editor of Paradise Journal, casual tutor, and masters student based in Sydney. Since 2020, she works at Supercontext Architecture Studio and is slowly realising how to build things.

Harrison Stockdale is a graduate architect working in Sydney.

Dr Fraser Torpy is the Director of the UTS Plants and Environmental Quality Research Group, University of Technology Sydney. Since 2000, the group has delivered high-impact research across diverse disciplines, focussing on urban sustainability and resilience, green infrastructure, air pollution control, environmental engineering and phytoremediation. He has published over 65 research papers, and his research is supported by nationally competitive Category 1 research grants including from the Australian Research Council.

Sumayya Vally is the Principal Architect at Counterspace, a Johannesburg/London-based architecture and research studio. Sumayya's design, research and pedagogical practice is searching for expression of hybrid identities and contested territories. Her work is often forensic, and draws on the aural, performance, the supernatural, the wayward and the overlooked as generative places of history and work. A TIME100 Next List honouree and designer of the 20th Serpentine Pavilion (2020/2021), Vally is the youngest architect to be commissioned for the internationally renowned architecture programme. She has recently worked on initiating and developing Support Structures for Support Structures, a new fellowship programme launched at the Serpentine, an initiative which supports and networks artists working at the intersections of arts and ecology, arts and social justice and arts and the archive. Vally is currently serving as the Pelli Distinguished Visiting Lecturer at the Illinois School of Architecture.

La Escuela Nunca y los Otros Futuros began operating in January 2020, in Santiago de Chile, as an experimental, Latin-American, para-institutional, non-bureaucratic, collective and independent school. It is approached from a deeply affective and non-hierarchical position, seeking to investigate other forms of learning and living together, exploring the critical powers of spatial practices as a weapon to question neoliberal progress, both culturally and symbolically.

copy nature office aims to think about the value of things, specifically how an archetype, a type of nature, or a singular thing is considered more valuable than any other thing. copy nature office hopes to act micro-politically and 'make things', without succumbing to pragmatism in an unavoidable market context.

Colophon

APE#206

Folk Costumes, Indo-Pacific Air
Guillermo Fernandez-Abascal
Urtzi Grau

ISBN 9789493146921
www.artpapereditions.org
First edition of 700 copies
June 2022

Contributions: Ricarda Bigolin, Enoch Cheng, Dean Cross, Matthew Connors, Matteo Dal Vera, Sharbendu De, Juan Elvira, Hélène Frichot, Achille Mbembe, Hamish McIntosh, Peter McNeil, Samaneh Moafi, Lidia Morawska, Ellie Skinner, Harrison Stockdale, Fraser Torpy, Sumayya Vally/Counterspace, Ed Cook (copy nature office) and Umi Graham, and La Escuela Nunca y los Otros Futuros

Design: Lien Van Leemput for 6'56" (www.6m56s.com)
Translation: Carolyn Shread for *The Universal Right to Breathe*
Printed and bound in Tallinn.

We acknowledge the Gadigal people of the Eora Nation, upon whose ancestral lands the writing of this publication took place. We pay our respects to the Elders both past and present, acknowledging them as the traditional custodians of knowledge for this land. They have never ceded sovereignty, and remain strong in their enduring connection to land and culture.

This book has been supported by a Strategic Grant from the Alastair Swayn Foundation.

This publication has been conceived with the support and cooperation of the University of Sydney and the University of Technology Sydney. We are grateful to the Dean of the University of Sydney's School of Architecture, Design and Planning, Professor Robyn Dowling, the Associate Dean of Research, Professor Donald McNeill, and the Head of Architecture, Associate Professor Lee Stickells. We also wish to thank the Dean Elizabeth Mossop, and the Head of School, Professor Deborah Ascher Barnstone, from the Faculty of Design Architecture and Building at the University of Technology Sydney for supporting our research.

We want to further extend our appreciation to Hashim Sarkis, Roi Salgueiro Barrio, Gabriel Kozlowski, and Ala Tannir who gave us the opportunity to publicly present our work, to Accion Cultural Española for the support to do so, and to Ella Saddington, Oigåll Projects, Timothy Moore and the National Gallery of Victoria for helping to bring the installation back to Australia.

We would particularly like to thank Ricarda Bigolin, Enoch Cheng, Ed Cook, Dean Cross, Elisa Commanay, Matthew Connors, Matteo Dal Vera, Sharbendu De, Juan Elvira, Hélène Frichot, Umi Graham Achille Mbembe, Hamish McIntosh, Peter McNeil, Samaneh Moafi, Lidia Morawska, Harrison Stockdale, Fraser Torpy, Carolyn Shread, Ellie Skinner, Sumayya Vally, copy nature office, and La Escuela Nunca y los Otros Futuros for their contributions to this publication and the whole project. Thanks to Emma Johnson for her close reading and editing, to Carolyn Shread for her generosity in sharing the translation of *The Universal Right to Breathe*, and to Francisco Díaz for their insightful comments on a previous iteration of our essay, originally published in *ARQ 107*. Thanks to Lien Van Leemput and APE for their impeccable design and for leading the production of the publication you now hold in your hands.

A special thanks to Chloe Grau, Christina Deluchi and Louisa King. Without their love, these pages would simply not exist.